RITA RESTORICK was born in Market Drayton, Shropshire, in 1948. She married John in 1967 and had two sons, Mark (born 1970) and Stephen – the subject of this book (born 1973 and died February 1997). Rita lived in Libya with her husband when he served in the RAF during the time that Colonel Gaddafi seized power. She worked for Peterborough City Council as a secretary until Stephen's death. She received the Champion of Courage Award with Lisa Potts ar of the Year Lunch 1997.

Stephen in his number one dress uniform as best man
at his friend Robin's wedding, 25 February 1995

Death of a soldier

A mother's search for peace in Northern Ireland

RITA RESTORICK

THE
BLACKSTAFF
PRESS

BELFAST

An extract from *An Irish Voice – the quest for peace* by
Gerry Adams is reprinted by permission of
Roberts Reinhart; Vera Brittain's 'Perhaps' is reprinted
by permission of Mark Bostridge and Rebecca Williams,
her literary executors; and an extract from
Pig in the middle: the army in Northern Ireland 1969–84
by Desmond Hamill is reprinted by
permission of Methuen.

First published in 2000 by
The Blackstaff Press Limited
Blackstaff House, Wildflower Way, Apollo Road
Belfast BT12 6TA, Northern Ireland

Typeset by Techniset Typesetters, Newton-le-Willows, Merseyside

Printed in Ireland by ColourBooks Limited

A CIP catalogue record for this book
is available from the British Library

ISBN 0-85640-670-8

This book is dedicated to the memory of all the victims in this conflict named Stephen, to the politicians who are trying to bring peace to that troubled land; and to the Corrymeela community and similar groups who have worked tirelessly over the years for that peace.

ACKNOWLEDGEMENTS

Many thanks to the Blackstaff Press for restoring my faith in publishers after rejection of my manuscript by the large ones, also to Michael Bilton for his advice and encouragement and for insisting that I had to write the book myself for it to have impact. Special thanks go to my husband John for allowing me the time and space to do what I needed after Stephen's death and for understanding why writing this book was so important to me. My thanks also to the Compassionate Friends, a nationwide support group for bereaved families, through which John, Mark and I were helped on this hard road of grieving by the kindness and example of other bereaved parents. Finally, a special thank you to all the people in Northern Ireland and the Republic who through their cards and letters showed us that Stephen's death had touched them deeply and that they wanted an end to the conflict.

CONTENTS

Stephen was killed by a sniper's bullet on 12 February 1997
as he manned a checkpoint in south Armagh.
This photograph was developed from a film found in
his camera at the time of his death.

PROLOGUE

I T WAS MONDAY, 24 FEBRUARY 1997, Stephen's twenty-fourth
birthday, and all our family and his friends were with us. But we
weren't celebrating his birthday. We were at Peterborough crematorium attending his funeral. There on the dais was his coffin draped
with the Union Jack. Stephen was the last British soldier killed in
Northern Ireland before the peace settlement, a victim of the IRA's attempts to bring about a united Ireland by force of arms. He was shot by
an IRA sniper at a vehicle checkpoint in Bessbrook, County Armagh,
close to the border with the Republic of Ireland. In an instant that bullet
had shattered our lives. Nothing would ever be the same again for us
and our wider family.

This book is about Stephen's life and death and my attempt to survive the nightmare that every mother dreads. It follows my efforts to
channel my grief in a positive way, to make Stephen's death and my
grief a focal point of what so many mothers had suffered in Northern
Ireland and Great Britain as a result of IRA and loyalist violence. Instead
of allowing myself to be overtaken by bitterness at people who, as I
saw it at the time, had to a greater or lesser extent caused my son's
death, I wanted to reach out to them, to say that I was just the latest
of many mothers who had suffered the loss of a son. When Stephen
was killed we hoped his death would be the last, but it was a futile
hope and many more killings followed. Stephen was, however, the

1

only soldier killed in Northern Ireland in 1997.

I was driven to do what I could to move the 'peace process' forward. On 9 February 1996, just one year before Stephen's death, the IRA cease-fire that had come into effect on 1 September 1994 had ended with the bombing of the Canary Wharf office complex in London's docklands. A huge opportunity had been allowed to slip away during that cease-fire. The people of Northern Ireland had known peace during those few months, and did not want to go back to how things had been for the past thirty years. Sensing this feeling I wanted to be a symbol of the hopes of all mothers who wanted an end to the violence. I also wanted English people to take an interest in the suffering that had been allowed to happen in Northern Ireland, instead of only taking notice when the violence crossed over to England. I don't know how far I succeeded in those aims. In the two years after Stephen's death events in Northern Ireland were momentous. Throughout those two years, I felt that Stephen was with me every step of the way, pushing me on when the situation seemed so bleak, telling me to speak out to stop other young lives like his being thrown away.

It has been for me a crash course in the history of Ireland and the background to the conflict. I believed that if I was to put forward my views on what I thought about the situation in Northern Ireland, I had to do so with some basic knowledge of the events that had led to the present situation. Like many English people, I didn't even know the names of the six counties of Northern Ireland before Stephen's death caused me to take a deeper interest.

The last time I saw Stephen alive was on Boxing Day 1996, Saint Stephen's Day. This led me to use as a guiding light the words spoken by Saint Stephen when he was killed: 'Don't blame them.'

I

THE KNOCK ON THE DOOR

'MRS RESTORICK, IT'S ABOUT your son Stephen. Can we come in?'

It was a quarter to eleven at night on 12 February 1997 when we heard the knock on the door. Mark, our elder son, was watching TV with me. He was three years older than Stephen and still lived at home with my husband John and I in Peterborough. I was glad of his company as John worked in Nottingham during the week. As Mark went to the door, he said, 'Who can that be at this time of night?' I wondered why they hadn't rung the doorbell, why knock? After a few moments I went to see what was happening. A policeman stood on the doorstep. Behind him was another man in a light, ribbed pullover. As soon as I saw the policeman I realised something serious had happened. Then he said those words: 'It's about your son Stephen.' As we walked up the hallway I asked, 'Has he been injured?' The policeman asked me to sit down and I knew then what was coming. But first he introduced the other man, a major from the local Territorial Army depot. Then came the knife in my heart as he said, 'Stephen was fatally shot earlier this evening at a vehicle checkpoint in Bessbrook.' Instantly my mind locked onto that word 'fatally'. I can't remember him saying, 'Stephen is dead.' But if it was 'fatally', then he was dead. Everything stopped. I just kept saying, 'It's not true, it's not true, it's not true. I don't believe it'. He couldn't possibly be dead. There were thousands of soldiers in Northern Ireland, how could it be Stephen? That sort of thing happened to other people, not ordinary people like us. If I denied it over and over again, perhaps it wouldn't be true and I would wake up from the nightmare. But slowly, the tidal wave of my emotions beat itself out on the shore of reality. And I calmly said, 'But it must be true because you are here.' I hadn't seen the announcement on the news that night that a soldier had been shot in south Armagh. No names were given but at least a little seed of dread would have been planted in my mind. But I had no warning at all of what was to happen to our lives.

Stephen had been at Bessbrook in south Armagh with the 3rd Regiment Royal Horse Artillery since the end of the previous September. South Armagh, on the border with the Republic of Ireland, was a hotbed of IRA activity. It was his second six-month tour there so I was less worried about the dangers he faced than I had been during his first tour four years earlier, when he was straight out of training. The IRA sniper who had killed eight soldiers and policemen during 1992 and 1993 had not been active since the breakdown of the IRA ceasefire the previous February. I had been more worried about Stephen's plans to buy a motorbike. For weeks I had tried to show him the disadvantages of a motorbike, saying that in an accident motorcyclists come off worse and girls don't want to sit on the back of a motorbike going to a nightclub on a cold, wet winter night. But he had to make his own decision. Stephen had phoned the previous Sunday from his barracks in the old flax mill to tell me he'd decided to keep his car and not buy a motorbike. A feeling of relief swept over me. That was the last time I spoke to him. Now, on the table in front of me lay the letter I had been writing to him that evening. I'd written that I would send him a parcel for his birthday, in twelve days' time, with chocolate, biscuits and perhaps a miniature bottle of his favourite whisky. But how could I not have known, as I wrote, that he was already dead? I had read of mothers who had felt that their child was no longer alive even before they had been told. Why hadn't I?

I desperately wanted the policeman and army officer to see exactly who this young soldier was. So I showed them two photos of Stephen, taken just after his army passing-out parade, when he was nineteen years old. The smile lighting up his face showed his joy at getting through the training.

Mark phoned my husband's elderly parents, who he stayed with during the week, so they could tell him what had happened, but John had gone to the local pub that evening and wasn't back yet. About a quarter of an hour later he returned, and his mother had to tell him that Stephen had been killed. She says it was the hardest thing she has had to do in her life. In the meantime, Mark phoned my two brothers, Raymond and Neil, with the news.

The policeman asked if there was anyone who could be with me. I phoned my friend Sue and just said, 'I need you, can you come over? Stephen's been killed.' She arrived about twenty minutes later with her husband Mike who then, with Mark as navigator, went to bring John home – neither John nor Mark were in a fit state to drive. Shortly afterwards the policeman and army officer also left.

With Sue beside me I hugged the photos of Stephen as the tears flowed. I wanted to hold him once more but all I could do was hold those photos to me. The pain of my grief was as bad as when I gave birth to him almost twenty-four years previously. Sue and I had gone to school together in my home town in Shropshire but had lost touch after I left school at sixteen. It was through working in Peterborough that, incredibly, we met again after thirty years. Both our husbands had been in the RAF. We sat together for quite a while, the silence only broken by my crying. Sue knew there was nothing she could say to help me, that I needed her just to be there. I had a desperate need to feel part of the continuing life of nature and that Stephen was still around in some way. So although it was past midnight on a fairly cold February night we sat in the garden, looking up at the stars. I felt so insignificant. My son was one of probably thousands who had died that day throughout the world, why should I expect him to live on in some way, somewhere? Suddenly, I saw a shooting star flash across the sky – a piece of rock burning up in the atmosphere but to me a symbol of Stephen's short life and my loss. He had lit up our lives with his happy personality.

Now that light had gone out and we had to find a way through the darkness. Feeling chilly, Sue and I returned to the warmth of the house. At about 2 a.m. Mike and Mark returned with John. Mike and Sue then left us, promising to return later that morning. John and I held each other tight, as the tears overwhelmed us. This young man, who people would see as a tough soldier, was our Stephen, who we knew was only tough on the outside. We had guided him through childhood to adulthood, with the changes in relationship that brings. Now in one short moment all had been taken from us. So the nightmare began.

My mind was confused, but I knew Stephen carried an organ donor card. Now I needed to know if his organs had been taken for transplant. I wanted something positive to come from his death. The police gave me the phone number of the Daisy Hill Hospital in Newry, where Stephen had died. The hospital said that Stephen's remains (how that word cut through me) had been moved to Craigavon Hospital after his death, as soldiers had to guard his body at Newry. No one seemed to know if his organs had been used. (Later that day I was told they could not be taken as his death was looked upon as murder. So Stephen's strong, young body had been destroyed by one bullet from a sniper's gun, and we were robbed of the consolation of his death helping someone else.)

There was nothing more we could do that night so we went to bed, but with no expectation of being able to sleep. We lay there, numb, crying, hugging one another, unable to say anything, as the hours ticked by. I stared at the ceiling for the three hours that remained of the night. At 5.30 I went downstairs to see if there was any mention on the news of what had happened. There might be nothing at all or a short statement at the end about a soldier being killed.

The first news was at 6 o'clock on GMTV, and I was surprised that the main item was Stephen's murder. They gave his name and said he came from Peterborough. There was an interview with a young mother from Bessbrook called Lorraine McElroy. She sat on a sofa, her husband beside her holding her hand, as she told how Stephen had been smiling at her when he was shot. She pointed to a graze on her forehead caused by the bullet after it passed through Stephen. From this interview I learned graphically exactly what had happened. On the previous night I had only been told that he had been shot at about 6.30 p.m. at a checkpoint in Bessbrook. Now I was hearing all the details, and yet the news item seemed to be about someone else, not our Stephen. Lorraine told how she and her husband had gone to buy ice cream for the children. She was surprised when Stephen stopped her. Going through the checkpoint quite a few times each day she had got to know Stephen, though not his name, and would often chat with him. Perhaps he hadn't recognised her car on that dark night. She said, 'The soldier took the licence off me and was smiling and handed it back to me. When it happened I don't even think he had the licence out of his hand. There was what I would describe as a flash and a crack and there was blood pouring from my head. I heard the soldier groaning. He was on the ground but there was nothing I could do. The hospital is only down the road but the journey was probably the most horrific thing I've ever endured because I was watching a young man dying. I just wanted to hold him because his mammy was not there and he was dying. So often you hear on the news that a soldier was shot, but he was a man, a young man, a person. He was smiling at me when it happened. He was just there and so nice and somebody killed him. Last night all I could think of was his face smiling at me. My heart just breaks for his family.' Today I still burst into tears when I hear her words. Lorraine made all but hardline republicans see beyond the uniform of a British soldier to the person within and a family who would be devastated by his death. But just as important to me, his mother, was that this woman was with him when I couldn't be. As a mother herself, she was angry because her child too might have been killed if he had been in the babyseat in the back of the car. She said there was no regard for what lives were going to be taken so long as they killed the soldier. Her final words echoed what we felt: 'And it's awful to think, is this the start of it all again?'

The situation in Northern Ireland was on a knife edge. Loyalist paramilitaries were being goaded into retaliation by IRA violence. But innocent Catholics would be the targets for this retaliation, rarely IRA terrorists. John and I decided to speak to the press as we wanted maximum publicity. We wanted the world to know that Stephen had been killed. We didn't want his death to be a minor paragraph hidden on an inside page – Stephen was too special for that. We wanted people to stop and think, here was a British soldier dead, next time it might be ordinary people in Northern Ireland. Something had to be done to stop this downward spiral of violence. We were in a state of numb shock, it still didn't seem real that Stephen was dead. But we wanted to make it clear that we didn't want his death to be the cause of retaliation and the death of even more innocent people in Northern Ireland. That would have been the last thing Stephen wanted. He believed he was there to prevent violence and to protect Catholics and Protestants. From 7.30 that morning the media were knocking on the door asking for interviews. Fortunately, reporters arrived usually one at a time. Neither of us had been interviewed before by the press, so for us this was a baptism of fire. We made no political statements or condemnations, just stressed that we wanted people to think where the situation in Northern Ireland was heading. The words came from our hearts, and I think people in Northern Ireland realised that and were moved.

The telephone and doorbell rang all morning. It was painful going over what had happened first with one reporter, then another, and another. But how could we speak to one and not the others, especially when they had driven up from London? Most were very sympathetic and tactful. Some asked irrelevant questions such as how many GCSEs Stephen had and what grades. One reporter even rang back to double-check this, and I told him in no uncertain terms to get his priorities right: Stephen was dead so what did it matter how many GCSEs he had? I kicked the wall in sheer anger as I said this which must have shocked the lady reporter standing next to me. By 2 p.m. we were emotionally drained. A reporter from BBC TV was interviewing us when the Sky TV team arrived. I just couldn't face any more interviews. So the BBC TV reporter had a chat with the Sky team and they agreed to take what she had recorded.

While we were being interviewed, photographers were clicking away at photos of Stephen in the album I had planned to give him when he married. It was a comfort to have this record of his life, especially the photos of him in his number one dress uniform taken two years earlier when he was best man at his friend Robin's wedding. Wearing this black uniform with its gold buttons and lanyard and red piping, he looked so smart and handsome. Holding his hat under his arm, his whole face was visible. (Usually photos are taken with the cap on, hiding the face.) It was these wedding photos the press mainly used. Unfortunately a few used a photo taken after his passing-out parade in which he was wearing a peaked hat and looking sideways. He disliked this photo intensely as it made him look too serious and solemn. I made many phone calls to newspapers and TV stations in the next few days and weeks asking them not to use this photo.

I desperately wanted to talk to the lady Stephen had been talking to when he was shot. I could have hated all the Catholics in Northern Ireland because an IRA man had shot my son, but she showed that not all Catholics supported them. How could I contact her, though? I only knew her name, Lorraine McElroy, and that she lived in Bessbrook. Later that day I was given her phone number. We spoke for a while and I immediately felt a closeness to her. Pressure was put on both of us by the press to meet, but we didn't want to become part of a media circus so we agreed to wait until the publicity had died down. Lorraine and I were invited to appear on television chat shows but we refused: no matter how well-meaning the programme, I felt Stephen's death was too serious a subject to be followed by an item on the latest diet or fashion.

Sue and Mike returned late that afternoon, insisting we eat something, though neither of us wanted to. We fluctuated between feeling hungry one moment and sick the next. They stayed with us until early evening, and over the next few days and weeks they could not have done more for us. As we had no family in the area we were grateful for their support. A couple of our neighbours called round to say if there was anything they could do, just ask. This was the start of a difficult time when people did not know what to do or say, and so often kept their distance. I felt like a leper with a little bell ringing to warn people to keep away. Things are very different in Ireland, where communities are closer and friends and neighbours are expected to visit after a death.

The national and local television channels and the local newspaper featured our interviews that evening but the national press coverage was not until the following day. The articles were very moving and were made even more poignant by Lorraine McElroy's words about Stephen smiling at her as he was shot and about being in the ambulance with him on the way to hospital.

With the help of sleeping tablets prescribed by our GP, we slept on Thursday night. But we awoke on Friday to find that it was all still true; it was not a terrible dream. That morning we were visited by a captain and regimental sergeant-major from Stephen's regiment. They would arrange the funeral and be our contact with the regiment, who had to continue their duties in Northern Ireland despite the trauma of Stephen's death. As Stephen had died on duty, the army would pay for the funeral, but we were not forced to have a full military funeral and the form of service was left to us. We definitely did not want a gun salute over the coffin, or a bugler. But we did want the pallbearers to be his army comrades wearing number one dress uniform. We also wanted some of his comrades in Bessbrook to attend the funeral, but not in uniform.

Later on Friday the undertaker, Mr Claypole, visited us to discuss our wishes for the service at Peterborough crematorium. After the post-mortem in Northern Ireland, Stephen's body was flown to Stanstead airport where Mr Claypole collected it late that evening. (A newspaper in Northern Ireland tried to make an issue of the fact that Stephen's coffin was flown on a scheduled flight, not a military one, and phoned to ask our views on this. I told them bluntly that it was of no importance to us what sort of flight it was, what mattered to us was that Stephen was in a coffin.) We arranged to visit the chapel of rest on Monday as we would be away over the weekend. We wanted to see Stephen, partly in order to make what had happened seem real, and partly because there were things we both needed to say to him. Even though we knew he was no longer there, his body provided a focal point for our feelings.

We had to decide on the date for the funeral. Only the following Wednesday, or Monday, 24 February, were available. Wednesday seemed too soon for the arrangements to be made and Stephen's army friends to come from Northern Ireland. So we decided on the 24th, which would have been Stephen's twenty-fourth birthday. By choosing this date we wouldn't have to face his birthday shortly after his funeral. Also, partly because it would be on his birthday, we decided that the service would be a celebration of his life and that no one was to wear black. We wanted a nonreligious service, partly because we ourselves have no strong religious beliefs and partly because we felt that religious differences, as well as political ones, lie behind the situation that led to Stephen's death. The crematorium manager gave us the phone number of Mr Pearce, a local member of the British Humanist Association authorised to take services. He kindly visited us at short notice with examples of services. Unfortunately, he was going on holiday until the following Saturday so I would need to have all the input to the service ready for his return, which didn't leave much time to discuss matters before the actual day.

Friday was the day when the messages of condolence started to arrive, not only from relatives, friends and neighbours but also from the general public, including Protestants and Catholics in both parts of Ireland. There were even cards from Catholic priests and nuns. Many of the ordinary Catholic people did not sign their names but wrote 'Catholic mother' or 'A Catholic family', and many sent Mass cards showing that prayers would be said for Stephen. All the Catholics said that they did not support the violence and that the IRA did not act in their name. There were also cards from the parents of other young soldiers who had been killed, in Northern Ireland and Bosnia. They gave their phone numbers and offered the understanding of someone who had already gone through that nightmare.

There were letters from a number of high-ranking army officers, and from the officers in Stephen's regiment. The major in charge of Stephen's battery in Bessbrook wrote, 'The battery has been completely numbed by what has happened, but has been greatly moved by the amazing courage and dignity shown by your family, and by the very brave reaction shown by Mrs McElroy.... . We have been greatly supported by the response of the local community who have been deeply affected by his death. We have received hundreds of messages

11

of condolence from residents in the area from all sides of the community and this has helped us to recognise the importance of our work in protecting the public from terrorism.'

There was a lovely letter from Stephen's battery commander over the previous two years in which he said, 'I would like to let you know the impression that Stephen made within the battery and regiment. In my mind he is characterised by his enthusiasm. Nothing was ever too difficult or too much trouble, and he always kept a positive spirit which was a tonic for morale. I was not at all surprised to hear that he had made an impression on the locals in his smiling, courteous way; it is a tribute to him that Mrs McElroy should be making that point so courageously. One of my lasting memories is when I told Stephen that he was to be promoted to Lance-Bombardier, the joy on his face made it look as if Christmas and Easter had arrived together. Stephen had a very promising future and his loss is truly a tragedy.' Stephen's troop commander wrote, 'We feel his loss very personally and he will be sorely missed by all of us. Stephen was a friend to us all and his great sense of humour kept us going through many a tough moment. I hope it will be some comfort for you to know that in his last moments Stephen showed immense courage and strength, insisting that first aid should be directed to the injured lady driver.'

The padre at Bessbrook Mill wrote, 'I first met Stephen last October when he arrived here in the Mill for his tour of duty. He struck me then as a very kind, strong, quality soldier. I was asked to go straight to the Daisy Hill Hospital on Wednesday evening. I arrived about thirty or forty minutes after Stephen died. I would like you to know that as he lay there calm and still I was able to pray for him and to commend him to Almighty God. I also prayed for you too with him nearby.'

The commanding officer of the battery in which Stephen's best friend Robin was serving at Keady in Northern Ireland wrote saying, 'I hope that you will find some comfort in the fact that the majority of local people in my area, which is a Catholic community, are shocked and revolted by Stephen's murder. Many local people have approached my soldiers, including Stephen's friends from J Battery, to offer their sympathy and shame that such a thing could happen. A nun broke down in tears at one vehicle checkpoint because she was so upset over Stephen's death. I hope that in some way this awful and tragic incident can become the catalyst for all sides to talk peace so that Stephen's death will not have been in vain. Mrs McElroy has been absolutely fantastic and between you and her you have made an enormous impact on the local population, with exactly the right words and articulating what all honest, decent people think.' Similarly, an officer commanding a regiment in Belfast wrote, 'The loss of your son has affected all of us in my regiment, even though we did not know him. It might in some small way be comforting to you to know that whilst out on patrol in the Ardoyne, one of the hardest republican areas in Belfast, the night after his death, a number of the locals expressed their sorrow for his death. They are not usually very talkative towards us, as you might expect, but on this occasion it seemed to me that there was genuinely a feeling of sympathy. I doubt this would have happened in former times. It indicates to me that the majority of the people here are sick and tired of the violence.'

One of Stephen's closest friends and his wife wrote, 'He was always so happy with such a positive outlook and was very special to both of us; this has all been such a terrible shock and we will miss him dearly. He was such a loyal friend and was always caring and generous with such a bubbly personality, he will always be in our thoughts and our hearts.' Stephen's room-mate during his spell at the regimental barracks at Topcliffe wrote: 'I have known Steve since April '93. We shared a room together for six months and in that time we got to know each other quite well. I will always remember Steve for his cheeky grin and his baby face. As you can imagine we never always saw eye to eye; when we fell out with each other we would take the mickey out of each other. To me he was a southern shandy-drinking puff, and to Steve I was a big thick northerner. Most of the time we would fall out with each other just to cheer ourselves up. There are a lot of things I could say about Steve but these two words somehow say everything – my friend. I will miss him.' A lance-corporal attached to Stephen's battery wrote, 'Your son was a really close friend not just to me but to everybody. Every time I saw him he always had a smile on his face or he would crack a joke or two. I will never forget your son.' Yet another wrote, 'I knew Steve well, I had been on a course with him and on many duties with him. I just can't believe he has gone. He was the nicest, happy-go-lucky bloke I've ever met. I was involved in the immediate follow-up and found myself on one of the other vehicle checkpoints the following day. It was quite moving when people stopped and left flowers and cards, the majority of the people were really disgusted and upset, they just want it all to stop and I think that goes for all his soldier friends including myself . . .'

The father of one of Stephen's army friends wrote to the *Daily Mail*. His letter, published on 19 February, shows the anger and frustration felt by many who knew Stephen and had sons in the army: 'I knew "Asterix", as Stephen Restorick, the British soldier shot dead by the IRA, was known to his friends. He impressed us with his warmth and humour and will be remembered with respect and pride as a young man any parent would feel proud to call their son and any country proud to call its citizen. Who are you, the faceless assassin, reviled by all decent people, hiding your shameful deed in a cloak of anonymity? Who applauds what you have done? . . . Are you killing for a "united Ireland"? Most people in Northern Ireland don't want to be part of a united Ireland. The Irish Republic may want the land but it doesn't want the financial burden. If being British is so dreadful, why do thousands of Irish choose to live in Britain? Terrorists, of whatever religion, are not wanted in any decent country. Were Ireland to be unified tomorrow, what would you do? You and your friends would continue your gangster activities, robbing banks, stealing and extorting protection money, intimidating and brutalising your own people with "punishment beatings". You shame those decent people who live and work together despite cultural, racial or religious differences. The world needs people like Stephen Restorick. There's no place on earth for cowardly nonentities such as you and those with whom you associate.'

There were letters from a number of Royal Artillery Association branches, but the most touching came from one in Northern Ireland. The secretary wrote, 'The Officers and Committee have asked me to write this letter; in all my years as secretary this is the hardest order I have been asked to carry out. I don't know where to start, what to say that will give you comfort, only don't judge all of us the same as the lost souls who carried out the premeditated, cold-blooded murder of your son Stephen. If you can find it in your heart to forgive us, please try, for in some way we are all guilty of what's happening in Northern Ireland . . .'

2

STEPHEN

'YOU HAVE A BABY BOY,' the midwife said as Stephen came into this world at twenty minutes into a Saturday morning. I burst into tears and said, 'I wanted a little girl!' Our son Mark was nearly three years old and we had hoped for a daughter this time. We'd only really thought about girls' names and had chosen Claire, after the song by Gilbert O'Sullivan which was popular at that time. But now the name Stephen came into my mind and always seemed totally right for him.

Stephen's birth on 24 February 1973 in Ripon, Yorkshire, went smoothly. John had driven me to the maternity unit and then returned home to await the good news. The 1970s were when fathers were being encouraged to be at their baby's birth, but John has problems with blood and injections. At Mark's birth he had rushed out of the room at a critical moment rather than faint, and only returned when it was all over. So this time there was no way he was going to be there. I would have to mop my own brow! Although this was my second baby, it was still a new experience for me as my labour had been induced with Mark and further helped with a glass of castor oil and orange juice. And there was me thinking such antiquated methods were only used by mothers themselves. But Stephen's birth was to be all my own work. I was surprised that my waters still hadn't broken although the pains were pretty frequent now. A short while before Stephen's birth I heard a crack. I asked the midwife what it was. She said that my waters had just broken. To me, that crack has an echo in the gunshot half an hour before his death.

The midwife took him straight to the nursery so I never got to hold him after the birth. Perhaps they were worried by what I had said about wanting a girl. Later that Saturday morning, while I was waiting for John to visit me, my GP arrived and asked if I had seen my baby. I told him that I hadn't even held him since he was born. He told the midwife to bring Stephen and as we waited the doctor said, 'I'm a little concerned as there seems to be a line missing from his hands. I'd like the paediatrician to see him on Monday morning.' He did not explain his worries to me and it was only later I learned this can be a sign of Down's Syndrome. So from that moment until the Monday, John and I feared that there was something wrong with our new son. But after seeing Stephen, the paediatrician said, 'There's nothing wrong with him, he just has very chubby hands.'

John and I met in 1965 when he was stationed at the RAF base close to my home town. We married in October 1967 when I was nineteen and he was twenty-two. The first two years of married life were spent at RAF El Adem in Libya and we were there when Colonel Gaddafi deposed King Idris. We returned to England in January 1970 and Mark was born the following April. We lived in RAF married quarters at Dishforth, three miles outside Ripon, from where John made a daily journey to RAF Linton on Ouse near York, where he was a corporal in the workshops. In 1973 he was twenty-eight and I was twenty-five. Due to world overpopulation fears, parents were encouraged to have only two children. So with Stephen's birth we felt our family was complete – unless someone could guarantee that the next baby really would be a girl! We took our new son home and introduced him to his 'big' brother. Mark never showed any jealousy to his baby brother, though they had the normal fights as they grew up. When Stephen was born he had a fantastic amount of black hair, which seemed to stand on end, but this soon disappeared and blond hair grew in its place. His eyes at birth were blue but turned the most beautiful brown. I hadn't realised that all babies are born with blue eyes. Before long he was smiling, then

Stephen aged six

Mark and Stephen
feeding pigeons in
Trafalgar Square

sitting up, and then crawling, whereas Mark had shuffled on his bottom. From then on there was no stopping Stephen, and he was walking by his first birthday. But he was very late teething; his first tooth didn't appear until he was over a year old. I began to wonder if he would have any teeth.

When he was eleven months old we moved to married quarters at RAF Wittering in Cambridgeshire, and he was christened at the parish church by an RAF padre who originally came from Ireland.

Stephen was a normal, mischievous little boy. He was always on the go. He'd stand in his highchair, rocking it back and forth, held in by his baby harness. He was fascinated by the television, walking up to it and touching the screen. We have a lovely photo of him touching the screen as he smiles at us. But he was also strong-willed and there was many a tantrum during the 'terrible twos', and even later. He was also very inquisitive. A lady doctor at the children's clinic became most indignant when he wanted to touch everything on her desk. He was totally different in temperament to Mark who was placid and would sit quietly, just watching what was going on.

Stephen's first lucky escape of many was when he was about a year old. I went into a baker's shop, leaving Stephen in his pushchair outside. As I came out of the shop some men were delivering huge sacks of flour. Suddenly one of them dropped the sack he was carrying. It hit the handle of the pushchair, tipping it up. Fortunately the sack did not fall onto Stephen or I am sure he would have been killed or badly injured. I gave the delivery man a piece of my mind but I think the poor man was as upset as me.

When Stephen was three years old we moved to our own house in a village called Ryhall. The main road from Stamford bypassed the village so its roads were relatively quiet. There was a village square with sycamore tree, pub and village shop, and a short road leading to the church and manor house. The Victorian school was now the village hall where the playgroup was held, and nearby was the primary school next to the village playing fields. A shallow river meandered around the village. It was an idyllic place for Mark and Stephen to grow up.

It was not long after this that Stephen got the cut on his left cheek. He

19

tripped over a rug and went head first through the glass doors of a low-level bookcase. Fortunately as the glass shattered it missed his eyes but it made a deep cut on his cheek. I rushed him to Casualty at Stamford Hospital where a doctor put three stitches in without anaesthetic. This was done by wrapping Stephen tightly in a blanket and quickly inserting the stitches while I held his top half and a nurse held his feet. The noise he made can be imagined. The stitches weren't even done properly: the cut grew together but left a noticeable scar. No doubt the scar later gave him a chat-up line with girls about how he said he'd got it. Another cut, this time on his forehead, was a result of him going head first over the back of the settee.

Stephen was the original disappearing child. If you turned away for a second, he was gone. This happened three times before he started school, once in the sand dunes at the seaside, once at Oulton Park during a grand prix, and once at Stamford street market. Each time we were frantic with worry. But a little later Stephen would reappear with a policeman, chatting away without a care in the world. Childhood illnesses were rare: he never caught any from his brother or school friends except chickenpox. Croup was a different matter. Every time he had a cold, his breathing would become very rasping. Bowls of hot water were placed in his room for him to inhale the steam and ease his breathing.

He loved the sun and tanned easily. We usually holidayed in Wales or Cornwall, but one Easter we went to Crete where Mark and Stephen enjoyed the candlelit procession carrying a saint's statue from the church through the village and the fireworks afterwards. Shopkeepers were enchanted with his blond hair and happy smile and gave him and Mark traditional hard-boiled eggs painted red. Considering Stephen's love of chocolate, he probably thought these a poor substitute for our Easter eggs. Another year we went to Spain, where he experienced his first paella. He sat picking out all the bits of fish until he was left with just the rice, and even then he was not impressed. He was a very fussy eater. In fact even as an adult he never ate fruit – he said it made his mouth itch – and his choice of vegetables was limited to potatoes, peas and carrots, but he always drank lots of milk. Despite my worries during his childhood, this limited diet did not seem to do him any harm.

Stephen in Air Cadet
uniform with his
Best Cadet award

When he was ten years old we sold our house at Ryhall and returned to married quarters at RAF Wittering for a year until we could move into our house in Peterborough. It was during this time that my mother died suddenly and Stephen had his first experience of the sadness that death brings. Four years later my father died, but I think Stephen accepted this more as he knew Granddad had not been happy since Granny died and now they would be together again. He was very close to all his grandparents, but as we lived quite a distance from them visits were limited to school holidays or occasional weekends.

We moved to Peterborough in March 1984, and for the first time Stephen had a bedroom of his own. In his teens his hobby was making model aeroplanes which he hung from the ceiling. In time there were so many I worried that the plaster on the ceiling might come down. He took great care making these models and painted them meticulously. Some were used in displays by the Air Cadets during his time with them. He enjoyed visits to Gibraltar and Germany with the Air Cadets and went gliding a few times. He even won the Best Cadet prize one year. He wanted to follow his father and grandfather into the RAF, preferably as a pilot. But to be a pilot he would have to work hard at school and pass exams. He'd learned to read and write at the normal ages but like most boys he did not read many books, preferring comics and magazines. He was intelligent and could learn facts that were important to him, such as details about aeroplanes, but he never excelled academically. So he never achieved his ambition, although he stayed on at school for two years in the sixth form to improve his GCSE grades. Leaving school in 1991 at eighteen years old, recruitment had been cut back severely, and the trades offered him in the RAF did not appeal to him. Now he was too old for youth training schemes, so on leaving school he took temporary jobs. John had left the RAF in 1985, and after a number of jobs in small engineering firms he was made redundant in 1991 from a firm training the long-term unemployed. By the following year, the recession was biting. Stephen also found himself unemployed. After a few months on the dole he felt there must be more to life, so he went to the army recruiting office and joined up. He knew I did not want him to do it, but it was *his* life. Thankfully we cannot see what the future holds, so he was not to know that by signing his name that day he set in motion a chain of events that would lead to his death almost five years later.

He joined the Royal Artillery, by coincidence my father's regiment during the Second World War. Initial training was at Woolwich on the south bank of the Thames in London. During the first few weeks recruits are not allowed out of barracks but after that we travelled down to see Stephen some Sundays. He suffered from homesickness at first, so there were a few unhappy phone calls until he settled in. Not being the strongest-built of lads, he found the physical training hard. So he was really proud when he completed the training as many fell by the wayside. The day of his passing-out parade came but despite it being early June, the weather was atrocious. The rain poured down and there was a cold wind. The previous day had been sunny so few people who had travelled to London then, as we had done, had brought umbrellas – and none were provided. So we sat there at the ceremony getting soaked to the skin, except for the VIPs and senior officers who sat beneath an awning. During the ceremony, a smile came to our faces when we saw that one of the officers in the parade was standing in a puddle and every time he stamped to attention a spray of water shot up. The parade went smoothly but the new soldiers' uniforms were soaked. However, this didn't dampen the joy they all felt as they threw their hats in the air when they had left the parade ground at the end of the ceremony. A few months after Stephen's death, when the captain who had been in charge of arranging the funeral came to deliver Stephen's Northern Ireland medal to us, we realised that his son had been in the same passing-out parade.

Stephen was selected to join the 3rd Regiment Royal Horse Artillery, who take the top 10 per cent of those passing out in the Royal Artillery. In celebration we held a party at home with family and friends. It was a passing-out party in more than one way for the younger generation, especially since Stephen's cousin Christopher, who was thirteen years old, decided to sample what was left in the glasses and ended up feeling very unwell all that night. Stephen joined his regiment at Colchester and was trained on the AS90 self-propelled gun. He was told that his first posting would be to Northern Ireland. Not only Northern Ireland, but south Armagh. He was stationed at Bessbrook near Newry. During his first week there, two helicopters collided at the heliport within the barracks, killing all on board. I knew helicopters transported the troops around the area because travelling by road was too dangerous, so I was afraid Stephen might have been involved. I was relieved when he phoned to say he was all right. He told me there wasn't a fire engine at the barracks so the soldiers fought the flames with fire extinguishers until a fire engine arrived from Newry. I could tell that he was very shaken by what he had seen and upset that they had not been able to save the lives of those on board.

During this tour of duty I was in tears one day at work and my boss asked me what was wrong. I told her I had an awful feeling that I would never see Stephen again. Looking back, was this a premonition of what was to happen on his next tour? Thankfully Stephen did return safely from that first tour, but we were very aware of how he'd changed. It made me angry that their lives were in danger over there but no one in England seemed to want to know what was happening in Northern

Ireland or to care about what our lads had to do and the dangers they had to face. Bessbrook itself, Stephen told us, was a place where Catholics and Protestants got on together, and if any trouble happened it came from outside. He was there at Christmas that year and told us people had brought them Christmas dinners as they manned the checkpoints.

Soon after his return, the regiment moved to Topcliffe in North Yorkshire, not far from Ripon where he was born. He took part in exercises in Oman, Jamaica and Canada. The Canadian exercise was in September 1995 and John and I met up with him at Red Deer in Alberta during our first holiday in North America. Together we visited a huge shopping mall in Edmonton which has fairground rides indoors, including a very tight loop-the-loop roller coaster. Needless to say, Stephen and his dad challenged each other to go on the ride. They both came off feeling rather shaky. The next day John and I had to leave for the airport at Calgary and onwards to Ontario, but Stephen stayed with our relatives, Pearl and Sherri, for a few more days and they took him to the Lake Louise area to see the mountains.

Back home, one day Stephen presented me with a kitten. It was such a pretty tabby kitten, with white shirt and socks. He assured me it was a lady cat as we already had a neutered male. He decided to call it Widget (from the beer cans) but I said Suki was a better name for a lady cat. When we took it for a check-up and injection the vet told us that although it was only small he was certain it was a male cat. So Suki reverted to Widget and I told Stephen I hoped he was better at telling the girls from the boys in the nightclub on a Saturday night. I took a lovely photo just before Stephen left for Northern Ireland of him holding Widget in our garden.

While he was based in Yorkshire Stephen came home most weekends, but we saw very little of him. After dropping his bag of dirty clothes on the kitchen floor, he was soon out of the door again to visit his friends. He always told me to leave his washing and I asked him when he had intended to do it as he was never there. But he always did his own ironing – we have a photo, taken during the last Christmas he spent with us, of him ironing, wearing only check bermuda shorts and a red Santa Claus hat. Saturday nights meant the nightclub until the early

24

hours, and he would often return having met yet another girlfriend. I jokingly asked him one day how he expected me to remember the right name if he brought a girl home. His good looks and happy, easy-going personality ensured there was a string of girlfriends. All fell by the way-side. He was only in Peterborough at weekends, and most girls want their boyfriends around all week. But he was never heartbroken, so it was obvious he hadn't met the right one yet. Plenty more fish in the sea! Late Sunday afternoon he would return from visiting all his friends just in time to do his ironing and enjoy a meal with us. Then it was two hours belting up the A1 back to Topcliffe.

We joked that Stephen was a 'dedicated follower of fashion'. He spent quite a lot of money on clothes, some of which soon went out of fashion and were only worn a few times. He took great care about his appearance, both about how he dressed and his personal hygiene: you could always tell in the nicest possible way when Stephen was around. Many soldiers have tattoos but I always hoped he would never have one, I just hate them. So when one day he asked if I wanted to see his new tattoo, I feared the worst, knowing how garish some of them are. But when he took off his shirt I saw on his upper right arm a Celtic band in black. Even I could not find fault with it.

Stephen's taste in music was broad; he liked excerpts from classical pieces and also the latest techno-rave synthesised music of the night-clubs. Some of it I liked because of the beat, telling him I'd be dancing to it if I was his age. His response was a look of total disbelief. Other tunes were too repetitive for me and I would jokingly ask him if the needle had stuck. Now, however, when I hear this type of music it re-minds me of him.

Like most young men, Stephen drove fast. His first car was a black Ford Fiesta XR2 which we lent him £2,000 to buy. Early one morning about a month later John woke me and told me not to get upset but Stephen had crashed the car. He was all right but feeling very sorry for himself. Stephen told us he had been driving down the A1 near Peterborough when he hit some debris on the road and the car rolled over. We've heard other versions since which involve speeding. The car was a total write-off, and as he'd only been able to afford third-party insurance he got nothing back. To replace it he bought a white Vauxhall Astra only to find that the speedometer wasn't working. He ordered the part but needed to use the car in the meantime. I asked him how he knew what speed he was doing if his speedometer didn't work. Grinning, he said he could tell by the number of cars still overtaking him.

Stephen's other love was his mountain bike. He had a top-of-the-range Marin bike which he told me he bought secondhand for £500. According to his friend Colin it actually cost £1,000. He even bought special front forks which cost another £300. I still have a sweater of his with on the back the slogan 'Danger, Psycho Biker – Do not Feed the Animal'. He took the bike to Topcliffe and helped to form a regimental mountain bike team. At least in North Yorkshire there are some hills, if not mountains, whereas Peterborough is on the edge of the flat expanse of the Fens. In his will he left his bike to Colin and his car to Asa; Colin and Asa were his two best friends.

Stephen was promoted to lance-bombardier in 1995 and was due for promotion to bombardier, having passed the course in May 1996. He was looking forward, after his Northern Ireland tour, to a two-year posting to the sales team for the AS90. But he was becoming dissatisfied with the army due to manpower shortages. In his last letter to his grand-dad he wrote of both the long hours and the constant shift changes in Northern Ireland, saying, 'My body clock is in total turmoil. I am doing three days of 16 hours on and 8 off, three days of patrols, then three days of 12 on and 12 off. I am knackered.'

He spent a week's leave with us from 18 December 1996. As soon as he arrived in Peterborough he came to my workplace with a huge bouquet of flowers for me. Most of this week was spent visiting friends, and he told some that he wished he didn't have to return to Northern Ireland. We spent Christmas Day with John's parents, Stephen keeping us laughing with his jokes. He had to return to Northern Ireland on Boxing Day, the day dedicated to Saint Stephen, but there were no trains so Mark drove him to Heathrow to catch his flight to Belfast. I gave Stephen a big hug as he left our house and told him to take care, as I always did.

3

SHARING OUR GRIEF

THE TWO DAYS SINCE Stephen's death had been emotionally draining for us. Realising this, my elder brother Raymond insisted we went to stay the weekend at his home in Shropshire to escape the media pressure. Mark, however, preferred to stay in Peterborough with his girlfriend. Our journey to Shropshire was terrible; I don't know how John managed to drive with the pain we were experiencing. It took far longer than the usual two hours as we had to stop now and then to get out of the car and release our emotions. We held each other tight as we looked out across the rolling countryside. How could everything still be so beautiful, how could the birds still sing and the sun still shine? Stephen, our smiling, fun-loving son, was dead and yet everyone still rushed around. Life goes on but how could it?

After lunch at my brother's house, John and I went for a walk along a nearby country lane. It was a beautiful, spring-like afternoon and we needed to be on our own for a while with our thoughts. Mine turned to Lorraine. I decided to send her some flowers to show our appreciation for her words of compassion. We found a florist's shop and I told the assistant we wanted to send some flowers to a lady in Bessbrook, south Armagh. Checking her list of florists in that area, she said the nearest one was in Warrenpoint – a chill went down my spine as I remembered the eighteen soldiers killed there by the IRA on 27 August 1979. We told her the flowers were for Mrs Lorraine McElroy and were from

John and Rita with the message 'Stephen is now back in Peterborough, thank you for being there for him when we couldn't.' The assistant made no connection with the murder of a soldier in Northern Ireland, despite Lorraine and Stephen having been mentioned in every newspaper and news bulletin for the past two days. This was our first experience of something that had shattered our lives not even making an impact on other people. The same thing happened to us in Peterborough, so it was not just because we were in a small Shropshire town.

That night, tired from the travelling and emotionally spent, we soon fell asleep. But I woke up at 3 a.m. and tried desperately to think what I could do to prevent Stephen's murder leading to retaliation and spiralling sectarian violence. I decided to write to President Clinton in the USA as there had been such high hopes when he visited Northern Ireland in 1995. On 30 November he had told a cheering Belfast crowd: 'You must say to those who still would use violence for political objectives: you are in the past; your day is over.' Still shaking from the emotions surging through me, I could barely hold the pen but I managed to do a rough draft which I wrote out again later that morning. Outlining what had happened to Stephen, I told the President I was writing in desperation and hoped that he could help. I begged him to do all he could to bring all sides together round the table to start talking, and to keep them there. The peace process had ground to a halt, and hardliners were trying to incite the violence again. I said, 'I am writing this at 4 a.m. as I cannot sleep for if I sleep when I wake up the nightmare of Stephen's death will be true but I so want to sleep because the pain of knowing I will never see him again is too much. I will never again be able to feel him hug me, see his smiling face or hear his voice.' I told him of the messages of sympathy people had sent from Northern Ireland saying that they did not want the violence to start again, they had known peace for a while and did not want to go back to the horrors of previous years. I ended by saying, 'Please, please, please do all you can to make sure no other mother has to go through the hell I am going through at the moment. As a father yourself I am sure you can imagine how I and my family are feeling at the moment.'

Emotions flowed over John and myself in waves. Despite being with my brother and his family, sometimes we just had to be alone together, holding one another close and crying. Later that morning I told my brother that I felt I was going mad, that I was imagining everything that had happened, it did not seem real, could not be real. He reassured me, saying even he had difficulty believing it at times. To reinforce the fact, I would read over and over again the newspaper articles about Stephen's murder. But even then it seemed to be only his name on the page, it hadn't really happened to him. Later I explained this feeling by saying how long can a dream last? Could you dream seeing your son lying in his coffin? Could you dream going to his funeral and meeting all the people there? Then could you wake up and say, 'I had a terrible dream'?

My younger brother Neil, his wife Janet and their sons Andrew, David and Christopher arrived later that morning and tears were shed between us. The boys were all stunned by what had happened, death being a rare visitor to young men. They had many a struggle trying to come to terms with Stephen's death. As we sat talking, memories of Stephen's antics with his cousins came to mind, such as the time Stephen presented his uncle Ray with an ashtray from a pub and said that he would have brought a bar stool as well but his brother wouldn't help him carry it. Such were the harmless, laddish things he got up to. We were soon even laughing a little – such were the memories of Stephen's personality.

When we returned home on the Monday morning, I started to put the service together. John's father and my nephews Paul and Christopher wrote anecdotes about Stephen, as did his friends Colin, Lisa and Asa. There was the music to choose as we were not, of course, having hymns. We had wanted an upbeat number to finish the service, the type of tune Stephen would have been dancing to at a nightclub. We chose 'Born Slippy', a typical techno-rave number with a driving beat. Unfortunately we had too much music, even though the other tunes were edited halfway through. So 'Born Slippy' was dropped, to the disappointment of Stephen's cousins and friends, but probably to the relief of the older people at the service. Whenever I hear that tune it epitomises the energy and pure zest for life that Stephen had. I can see him dancing away with a smile on his face as he chats up a possible new girlfriend.

More cards arrived on Monday, many only addressed to 'The Parents of L/Bdr Stephen Restorick, Peterborough'. But two letters didn't arrive – those I had expected from the prime minister, John Major, and our local Conservative MP, Dr Brian Mawhinney, who is himself an Ulsterman. Perhaps I was naïve to expect them to write so soon. But it made me very sad and angry that there were no letters from the very people whose policies Stephen had been carrying out, yet people who did not know us had written. In frustration I phoned our MP's office, asking if he had been out of the country in the past few days. His secretary said he hadn't, so I told her how hurt I was that I had not heard from him. I also asked her to contact the prime minister's office with the same message. We received their letters in Wednesday's post, a full week after Stephen's death. Without my knowing, my seventeen-year-old nephew Christopher also phoned the prime minister's office on Monday. Having heard me express my feelings about not receiving a letter from the prime minister, he rang 10 Downing Street to say how upset his Auntie Rita was.

That evening we went to the chapel of rest to see Stephen. Some people would say that you should remember someone as they were and not see them after their death. I had followed this advice when both my parents died, despite my need to see them as I had not been there when they died. John's parents are both still alive, so Stephen's death was the first time he had faced this dilemma. Apprehensively, we went in to see Stephen. I saw a very plush coffin with a white satin lining; Mr Claypole said the army had done us proud, it was a very expensive coffin. I said, rather abruptly, that it was the least they could do as he had died for his country. Stephen was dressed in his number one black dress uniform, as I had requested. He looked as if he was asleep and I was surprised at how long and beautiful his dark eyelashes were. But something seemed different about his hair. Then I realised: there was no wet-look gel on it.

I told Stephen how much I loved him. Silently I told him I was sorry, sorry that people in power had allowed this to happen, had allowed young men to lose their lives when a lot of people in England couldn't care less about what happens in Northern Ireland, and many of those in Northern Ireland would not compromise in order to find peace. After a while we left Mark alone with his brother for a few private moments.

During that week we received hundreds of cards and letters. There were messages of sympathy from the principal Church leaders in Northern Ireland. The Archbishop of Armagh, the Most Reverend Dr Robin Eames, wrote, 'I have just returned from visiting your son's colleagues at Bessbrook. All I spoke to in Bessbrook referred to your son with pride and respect. His young colleagues are devastated. All I can add to those words you have already received is this: you must be proud of your son. You will remember him with pride. He died serving this community at a time when ordinary decent people here need protection. He was doing his duty with great professionalism. Your sorrow and anguish is shared by us all.'

The Most Reverend Sean Brady, the Catholic Archbishop of Armagh, wrote, 'Your lack of bitterness and noble sentiments have edified very many people. Among many others, the parish priest of Bessbrook has acclaimed your tremendous generosity of spirit and nobility of heart in a recent interview. I hope that Stephen's death may not have been in vain, but may hasten the day of lasting peace and reconciliation in this troubled land.' He issued a press release on the day after Stephen's death in which he said, 'I am totally appalled by the shooting of Stephen Restorick, the young soldier murdered in Bessbrook last night. Mrs Lorraine McElroy, the young wife and mother who was injured in the incident, has spoken poignantly this morning of the horror she experienced at witnessing a life taken so cruelly. I offer my profound sympathy and prayers to the soldier's grieving family. This shooting is an evil deed. Its only purpose can have been to undermine the already-fragile peace. Unquestionably, it increases a sense of fear and horror. The desire for peace is very deeply felt throughout the whole community. I appeal to all right-thinking people to reject out of hand whatever could in any way favour or support this return to violence. Violence is the enemy of peace.'

The Moderator of the Presbyterian Church, the Right Reverend Dr D.H. Allen, wrote to express the sympathy of the whole Presbyterian

Church: 'It deeply grieves us that lives are lost in this pointless war which the IRA has waged in our land for many years. It is even more so when young men like your fine son Stephen, who give themselves to serve and protect us, are so viciously and callously murdered. . . . We are in debt to your son and will always be. He gave his life for our country and we thank him. We thank you for all you gave to him to make him such a wonderful person who was so well liked by all who knew him. We know that you will miss him very much and we want you to know that we shall not forget him.' Another message came from a Methodist church in Belfast: 'Our hearts have been hurt and saddened by the death of your son Stephen. I would ask you to forgive us for the loss of your boy. Please forgive us. We all must bear some of the guilt. Thank you for your impassioned plea to those who would plan to do further evil deeds. I pray that God will use your words to touch the hearts of those who plan and carry out these evil deeds.'

A Catholic priest in Belfast wrote, 'It is with deep sadness that I write this letter on the occasion of your young son's death. By all accounts Stephen was a fine young man who has become one more of the victims of a senseless "war". I have had the sad duty of being with many young men who were slaughtered like Stephen, I have buried them and have seen their poor parents like you left to grieve their memory. Thank you for your appeal that more violence will not come from Stephen's murder; those words are a light amidst the darkness. I pray that the person who shot your son will be caught and brought to justice. There are many mothers and fathers here in Northern Ireland who have gone through what you are experiencing and are holding you very much in their prayers.' A sister from a convent in the Republic wrote, 'All the members of our community were deeply shocked at this awful deed and we abhor the actions of the IRA and what they stand for. I do so admire your nobility and dignity all through this terrible tragedy. You have shown you are able to forgive and also to plead for peace in Northern Ireland. Hopefully your shining example will be instrumental in furthering the cause of peace there.'

Every death causes a ripple of emotion amongst family, friends, work colleagues. With Stephen's death that ripple spread to people who never knew him personally but were moved by his smiling picture in their morning newspaper and Lorraine McElroy's moving words. These people sent cards and letters from towns in Britain, Northern Ireland, the Republic, and other parts of the world. A letter came from the widow of Lieutenant-Colonel David Blair of the Queen's Own Highlanders, who was killed with seventeen other soldiers on 27 August 1979 at Warrenpoint. She wrote, 'I just wanted to say how much I admired the wonderful way in which you bravely expressed all that my family and I felt in similar circumstances years ago and still feel today. My husband used to say that it's the ones who are left behind who suffer, and your wonderful son suffers no more. You must be very proud of him, he has become part of history and his death, I am sure, has not been in vain because people have been so outraged by his murder. I had been so encouraged by the peace that has lasted for a while in Northern Ireland. Let us hope and pray that the peace will return, perhaps as a consequence of your son's death.'

Some of the messages from Northern Ireland and the Republic showed what people thought about Stephen's death and the political situation there. A Bessbrook grandmother wrote, 'We are all very, very disappointed that another young life has been taken away, by some person who is not worthy to be called a human being. How can they do this kind of thing? I am a Catholic and I am disgusted that this evil is in our society and we do not know who this person is. We do not want this happening in our country as then we are all thought of as being the same as these murderers. My daughters grew up in the troubles and it is still going on for their children. I felt I must write to you and let you know there are a lot of good people over here in Ireland.' A lady from Newry wrote, 'I could only imagine that in your position I would be full of hatred and bitter beyond belief. I just hope you realise that at least 90 per cent of the ordinary, decent people have nothing but the utmost sympathy for you and all the other innocent people who have suffered at the hands of these mindless monsters. I assure you although we share the same religion they by no means speak for the ordinary people.'

Many more wrote saying that the majority of Catholics did not support the IRA. A man from Bangor, County Down, said, 'His life was taken so suddenly by a cowardly act in the name of Irish freedom. Many people believe this is supported by Irish Catholics. I, being an Irish Catholic, totally condemn this despicable act. Stephen came to Northern Ireland to protect the people of both communities and he did this to the best of his ability and his life was taken while doing his duty. I hope no more lives have to be lost before these sick people realise that no one in Ireland, North and South, wants any part of it. I thank you for the protection your son provided to the people of Northern Ireland.'

A grandmother from Derry wrote, 'I am so sorry your beautiful son had to come to this country to lose his young life in the awful cruel way he did through the awful hatred and bitterness that the people of this beautiful country have for each other. I myself am a Catholic but that never made any difference to me or my sons and daughters, as we did our best to bring them up in that way and some of my very best friends are not Catholics. Words fail me to explain the disgust I feel for people who do such awful things. Deep down they really are cowards in my mind. Please don't judge us all as being such awful people.' In similar vein, a Protestant lady from Belfast who signed herself 'A very sad and sorry old lady' wrote, 'This terrible deed is condemned by 95 per cent of the citizens of Northern Ireland. We who have lived here all our lives cannot understand the terrible evil. I am a Protestant but many of my friends are Catholic and we all condemn these killings and bombings. As I look at the lovely colour picture of your "little boy soldier" in to-day's paper, I feel sick at the thought of the hatred and bitterness that leads men on to evil deeds. I have three grandsons of around Stephen's age so you will know that I understand.'

A man from near Belfast thought there was a higher purpose behind Stephen's death. He wrote, 'You must feel very proud of Stephen. Please try to draw comfort from the certain knowledge that from this awful tragedy will come good – his death will not be in vain. God moves in mysterious ways which are sometimes hard for us to grasp and understand. Your dignity and restraint in these circumstances was noted and talked about by many of my friends. You have set a worthy example for us to follow.' Similarly, some saw Stephen's death as a turning point; a lady from near Dundalk wrote, 'Personally I think that Stephen's death may not have been in vain. It could I think be the key to the peace we are all seeking. I really believe that out of his death could rise the peace.' I hoped so much this might be so but also wondered how often people in Northern Ireland and in the Republic had seen such hopes destroyed by yet another murder.

'An ordinary housewife in Northern Ireland' said she had grown up in the troubles and had always been thankful for the peace-keeping forces, adding, 'I am often struck by how young the soldiers look and when we sometimes exchange a "Good Morning" I tend to think of their folk over in the mainland and their concern for the safety of sons serving in Northern Ireland. For every parent in that position, it must be their worst nightmare that some day they'll receive news such as you got last week. All I can say is that the ordinary people of this Province are in a situation over which they have no control and although there is relative peace at the moment, no one doubts that violence could erupt again very soon. There is no simple answer to the Ulster problem – the vast majority of people really want peace and are grateful for all that the security forces have done to keep ordinary people safe.'

Many who wrote did not sign their names but they indicated, or we presumed, that they were Catholics. One, who just signed her letter 'A Mother', wrote very movingly: 'I have sons of my own and I can't even begin to know how you must feel but I shed tears for Stephen and then again I cried with gratitude when you appeared on TV and said you wanted peace in Northern Ireland. We are just ordinary people who want to live our lives in peace but we are being destroyed by terrorists like the evil, cowardly man who took your son's life. Over the years I have cried many times about the young English soldiers whose lives have been taken away and during these past months I thought maybe they had stopped shooting soldiers in cold blood. Stephen was a lovely lad, it is such a tragic loss.'

There were many letters from the Irish Republic. A couple from Santry expressed their sympathy and added: 'Many others from this side of the Irish Sea share our sentiments when I say we were shocked, horrified and disgusted to hear the news on TV of another brutal, cowardly murder in Northern Ireland. Poor lovely Stephen killed because he happened to be a soldier doing his duty trying to protect others but caught up in political turmoil which has caused so many heartaches in so many homes both in Britain and throughout Ireland. We both originated from Northern Ireland and shared different religious beliefs. We have lived in the Irish Republic for the past twenty-four years. Each time we hear or have heard of another atrocity we are so saddened at the futility of all this loss of innocent lives. We were particularly touched by the pictures of such a handsome young man as Stephen whose life has been so prematurely taken away from him.'

A few were a little more forthright in their condemnation of Stephen's murder. The sender of one card from Northern Ireland wrote, 'He died at the hands of scum who hide and creep around. Please do not think all people in Ulster are such lowlifes, we try to live as normal lives as possible. I know that people on both sides of the divide are shocked and sickened at this cowardly act. Please be strong, your son was a hero and died trying to protect the good respectable people of Ulster. And for that we are forever in both his and your debt.'

Some spoke out against the politicians. An Irish Catholic mother who wrote after it became known that I had sent a letter to all the politicians involved in Northern Ireland said, 'I want to congratulate you on your very courageous gesture in sending letters to John Major and Gerry Adams as they are the main ones who need to talk and get the peace for all of us established on this island so all of the young English men who are sent here in the army can go home and be safe. The cease-fire was here two years ago and John Major, Paisley and Trimble et cetera did nothing about it. I hope you can find some comfort from the fact that you are trying to help us all over here and that your dear son did not die in vain.' A man from County Westmeath in the Republic wrote in similar vein: 'This killing (and the manner of it) has further alienated many, many Irish people from giving any support whatsoever to the "republican" solution to the Irish "question". Too many people in high places are so entrenched in their own personal and party positions and ideologies that it is no wonder no progress is being made. All the "participants" seem to do is blame the "others" to justify their own lack of action. They are therefore happy justifying their centuries-old prejudices and see no reason whatsoever in making even one step forward in progress for fear also of "losing their traditions".' A man from Limerick wrote, 'When I reflect on the senseless protracted violence that has prevailed in Northern Ireland down the years, I ask the rhetorical question why or how can the political leaders within Ireland and the United Kingdom continue to allow the present situation to drift endlessly on. Despite the convening of the all-party talks unless there is a Christian willingness by all sides to conduct these on an unconditional all-inclusive basis, underpinned by a spirit of mutual forgiveness for all previous unjust maiming and taking of human life, and a determination to negotiate a new and lasting peace in Northern Ireland there can be no realistic prospect of having the problem finally resolved. It is a stark fact that throughout the past twenty-five years this conflict has resulted in the death of at least 3,000 human beings, including your own son. I am heartened that there are people like yourselves, the parents of the late Tim Parry, the late Senator Gordon Wilson, who can visibly display such practical Christianity at a time of such personal pain and suffering caused directly and arising directly from the conflict in Northern Ireland. Hopefully your forgiveness and prayers along with those of the peace-loving vast majority of the people within the islands of Ireland and Great Britain will help to expedite a final peaceful resolution to this conflict.'

Young people also wrote. One, now a Methodist Youth Pastor in Lurgan, said: 'I am a 23-year-old young person living here in Northern Ireland. Your son was a fine young man, almost the same age as myself which makes it hard for me to comprehend. This is my land your son was bravely defending, and that bravery contrasts with the cowardice of the person who shot him. Your words of hope echoed across Northern Ireland and serve as a reminder to us all who live here of our obligation to play our part to bring about a new future, a new day of hope. That requires all the people of Northern Ireland. As a young person I will play my part.' A nineteen-year-old man from the Republic wrote, 'What appalls me are these men of violence who spread this misery to innocent people like you and your son. I can only say that you have the support of millions of Irish people not just here but throughout the world. We all completely reject this mindlessness. We all wish we could live in peace with our Northern Irish neighbours and we all wish that the tragic history of these islands could be forever consigned to history. I know you, like many English people, wonder why your sons have to be on this island in the first place, why they have to risk their lives. I can only say that without them Northern Ireland would be in a worse state than it already is. I can only pray that your son's death was not in vain, that it will drive the effort towards peace and one day bring reconciliation to this divided island.'

A lady from Belfast gave us advice on how we should react in our grief, which I have tried to follow: 'May I just say never let bitterness or hatred ruin your lives; your anger may be overwhelming and justifiably so, but dwelling on thoughts of the perpetrators will only cause you to become more embittered, and your son would not wish that.'

One particular Mass card was very special for me as it was just signed 'A Crossmaglen Family'. I knew that Crossmaglen was one of the staunchest republican areas in County Armagh and a place where many soldiers had been killed. To receive such a card truly said to me that not all Catholics in that area were celebrating Stephen's death. We had been warned by the army that we might receive some threatening or triumphant letters from republican sympathisers, but this did not happen. Those with such views perhaps felt they had achieved something with Stephen's death and there was no need to further hurt his parents.

Some people sent us very moving poems they had written. One of these poems, 'My Son' by Elsa Summers of Burnley, speaks for all mothers who have travelled through the 'valley of tears' after the death of a son they loved more than words could ever say. She wrote it following the death of her 24-year-old only son Stuart in May 1996.

> The tears they flow
> They would fill a lake.
> Your friends they cry
> But not for your sake.
> They cry for their loss

They cry in their pain
They wet my shoulder
I grieve once again.

Like pebbles on a beach
They ebbed and flowed.
They contained my grief
With their tears on show.
I grieve for you always
No tears ever shown
My heart is broken
Only you and I know.

That week is something of a haze. I remember going into the centre of Peterborough and seeing all the people rushing about their daily lives: I just wanted to stand there and scream, to tell them to stop and listen to what had happened to my son. Did they not know or care? I could not cope with all the people rushing around. I was in a daze. It was painful to have people near me, as if I had lost a layer of skin. Peterborough is so big that many people do not know us. John's mother had the opposite problem. Living in the small town where she was an infants teacher, she is well known. She was upset by all the people who stopped her to say how sorry they were about her grandson's death.

We visited the crematorium. Never having been there before, we wanted to see the layout before the day of the service. In the chapel, one long wall is a huge window, and I hoped the army would check the grounds in case a sniper decided to fire on the soldiers in the chapel. We decided we wanted the coffin to remain on the dais when we came out of the chapel. Also we wanted the cross to be left on the wall for those with religious beliefs and to symbolise our hope that if there is a God he would understand why we had chosen a nonreligious service. Should we have an urn or a casket for Stephen's ashes? We expected to move to Nottingham in the future and we didn't want Stephen to be left in Peterborough. So we chose a casket: then we could either scatter his ashes or inter them later.

Some news reports of Stephen's death said that he had hoped to get engaged soon. A woman rang to say that Stephen and her daughter Lindsay had talked about getting engaged although they had only known each other since Christmas. She said Lindsay wanted to see Stephen at the chapel of rest, would it be possible? For us this was a very difficult decision, Stephen hadn't said anything to us about her, and although her family lived locally we had never met. We felt very protective towards Stephen, and the undertaker had advised us to accompany anyone wishing to see Stephen. Wanting to meet Lindsay first, I asked her mother to bring her to our house the following evening. When I met Lindsay, I could understand why Stephen had been attracted to her. She was very pretty, blonde, and petite. As she too was in the army, Stephen probably thought she would have more understanding of life in the services, how people have to leave at a moment's notice and be away from home for long periods. She showed me Stephen's letters which showed his feelings for her. She came with us to the chapel of rest the next evening. We led her into the room where Stephen lay and stood with her for a few moments. I told her that if she wanted to kiss him it would be better to do so on his hair (I didn't want her to feel how cold his skin was). Then we left her on her own with him. Lindsay came to the funeral but we did not hear from her again. A year later in the local paper I saw a photo of her wedding to another young, smiling soldier. It was very painful for me, thinking what might have been.

The parents of another girl wrote saying how much Stephen had meant to them and how he had continued to visit them and her grandparents even after the relationship had ended. They asked if they could visit Stephen at the chapel of rest. We met them there and were very moved by the feelings these people, who we had never met, showed for Stephen. He had certainly touched many hearts.

Wednesday was one of the two days when the funeral could have been held. It was the most awful day, with gale-force winds and rain lashing down, so I was glad we hadn't chosen that day. It was also the day I wrote to the prime minister, the Northern Ireland Secretary and all the Northern Ireland MPs, and the leaders of the Labour Party and the Liberal Democratic Party asking them to do all they could to find a peaceful solution in Northern Ireland and make progress towards talks. I also wrote to Gerry Adams, president of Sinn Féin, asking him to pressurise the IRA to call a ceasefire from Easter. I was struck by the fact that Stephen had died on Ash Wednesday, the first day of Lent, and in the letter I emphasised that people give things up for Lent. Stephen had given up his life, couldn't the IRA give up their refusal to call a ceasefire? At that time I knew very little of Irish history and especially the Easter Rising of 1916. Now I realise that Easter wouldn't be an appropriate time for republicans to call a ceasefire. With the letters I sent a photograph of Stephen in his army uniform and asked them to keep it on their desk until Easter. I realised a couple of days later that perhaps a photo of Stephen in army uniform wasn't suitable for Gerry Adams so I sent one of Stephen with his friends in a nightclub so that Adams could see him as a young man full of life. Would my letters have any effect? Why should Stephen's murder make any difference when so many others had been killed? But I had to try.

These letters led to a terrible family row. Our emotions had been building up like steam in a pressure cooker since Stephen's death. I was rushing to get the letters in the post that evening as the local paper wanted to print the text the next day. Addressing the envelopes, I asked Mark to help by putting the letter and photo of Stephen inside. He did this for a few moments and then left the room. I, in my haste, thinking he just didn't want to help, became angry. John came in, and as I told him what had happened, I lost my temper and threw a cup across the kitchen, smashing it. All the pent-up emotions flooded out. Mark told his dad it was too upsetting to see his brother's face each time he put the photo in the envelope. Mark, being the sort of person he is, hadn't felt able to explain this to me. I, being the type of person I am, was dealing with my loss by sending these letters. I hadn't realised it would affect Mark differently. I doubt if the politicians thought for one moment about the sheer emotional cost of those letters. Later that evening we went to Sue and Mike's for a meal but we just picked at the food. I was in tears because of the argument over the letters, so Mike took John and Mark to the sitting room to talk while I poured my heart out to Sue. She and Mike were very supportive at this very difficult time for us all. Referring to these letters, the Ulster Quaker Peace Committee in Londonderry wrote after Stephen's funeral, 'We very much appreciate that in the midst of your bereavement you found time and courage to write to our political leaders to encourage them to keep open channels of communication between all parties. You have added significantly to the work being done to try to heal the divisions within our community. We would endorse your vision that Stephen's death may "be a catalyst for peace".'

That week, Colin and Lisa, Stephen's friends since schooldays, came to see us. It was good to have young people in the house. They were very upset about Stephen's death but soon turned our sadness to laughter as they told us of their memories of him. I said that the neighbours would be knocking on the door complaining at the laughter when we should be tearful. Colin, jokingly, said there would be lots of girls at the crematorium, some of them with prams. Getting his meaning, I told him I hoped there would be a pram there with Stephen's baby in it. At least then there would be a little bit of him left for me to love. But on the day there were no prams and no babies.

What should I wear to the funeral? One night I woke up knowing the answer, my apricot-coloured jacket with a flowered skirt. I woke John up and told him. After he had fallen asleep again, I suddenly thought that some people in Northern Ireland would see apricot as orange and my attempts to be neutral would be defeated. So I woke him again and explained to him why I could not wear my apricot jacket after all. I thought to myself, I've lost my son, I shouldn't have to worry about what clothes I wear at his funeral.

I wanted people to have a memento of the funeral. As it was not a religious service there would be no printed hymn sheets with Stephen's name on. We decided to have a card with Stephen's name and the date of the service on the front. On the reverse John wanted the poem 'Do Not Stand at My Grave and Weep'. It seemed to express how Stephen would want his family and friends to see his death in the future. John didn't know all the words, but out of the blue two copies of the poem arrived in that morning's post. One came from a nun in southern England who said it was found after the death of Lance-Bombardier

Stephen Cummins near Londonderry in 1989 in an envelope addressed to his parents. The other copy came from Stephen Cummins's parents saying they knew what we were going through; their son had been twenty-four when he was killed in Northern Ireland. The poem seems to touch a lot of people – it was sent to us many times over the next few days:

> Do not stand at my grave and weep.
> I am not there. I do not sleep.
> I am a thousand winds that blow.
> I am the diamond glints on snow.
> I am the sunlight on ripened grain.
> I am the gentle autumn rain.
>
> When you awaken in the morning's hush
> I am the swift uplifting rush
> Of quiet birds in circled flight.
> I am the soft stars that shine at night.
> Do not stand at my grave and cry.
> I am not there; I did not die.

I had a constant pain which felt as if my heart had been torn in two and that I was crying tears inside that could not or would not come out. When people talk of a broken heart the phrase is now all too real for me. I knew Stephen would not have wanted us to be in floods of tears but to remember the happy memories, but it was so hard at times. I thought of all the other parents of soldiers who had travelled this road before us. Was it worse to lose a soldier son when so many others like him were being killed, as in Northern Ireland in the past? More people would be in the same situation as yourself so you could share your grief, but any significance to his death would seem to disappear. Or was it worse to be like us, where there was no one in exactly our position and few parents locally had lost a son or daughter?

Two of our Irish friends visited us that week, keeping up the Irish tradition of visiting the bereaved to say 'sorry for your troubles'. Columb, a former work colleague, is an architect and comes originally from Belfast. Eamonn, from Londonderry, lived near us. His son

Bernard and Stephen were friends together in the Air Cadets but had lost touch since. Eamonn said he presumed we knew about his brother's past. Realising we didn't, he told us that in the early seventies his youngest brother became involved in the IRA at fifteen years old, had been arrested for sending letter bombs to prominent people in Britain (none of whom, fortunately, were killed or seriously injured) and was sentenced to a long prison term. Since his release he had turned his back on the IRA. His father, a teacher at a Catholic school in Londonderry, and his mother had been totally unaware of their son's involvement until his arrest. It really showed us how the tentacles of the IRA permeate the Catholic community.

John and I visited the chapel of rest again on Sunday, the day before the funeral. Mark had made his last visit on his own two days earlier. I took with me a small spray of silk flowers sent to me by a mother who had kept them from her soldier son's wreath, and a single red carnation from the wreath sent by STOP 96, a peace group in the Republic of Ireland. These were placed in the coffin with Stephen as symbols of our hopes for peace in Northern Ireland. I gently touched Stephen's dark-brown hair and said goodbye to him. I told him that we would never forget him. Again I told him that I was so sorry that my generation and my parents' generation had not been able to find a solution to the problem in Northern Ireland and that the situation had been allowed to drift on so long at the cost of so many young lives like his. I looked for the last time at my handsome young son, not wanting to leave that room but knowing I had to and that I had to be strong for him tomorrow.

4
THE FUNERAL

If I should die and leave you
Be not like others, quick undone
Who keep long vigil by the silent dust and weep.
For my sake turn to life and smile,
Nerving thy heart and trembling hand
To comfort weaker souls than thee.
Complete these unfinished tasks of mine
And I perchance may therein comfort thee.

Thomas Gray

So came the day of Stephen's funeral and his birthday. For twenty-four years our small family had celebrated this day with a card and present and, when he was younger, a party. Now we were formally to say goodbye to him. Hundreds of people would be with us: some had seen him grow from childhood to maturity and had celebrated those birthdays with him, some knew him from schooldays, others since joining the army; a few only knew him from the accounts they had read or heard after his death.

During the morning, my two brothers and their families arrived with John's elderly parents and sister Jane. We all waited awkwardly, wishing we did not have to face the next few hours. A few minutes after midday, the hearse and two funeral cars arrived. I was strangely calm, even when I saw the coffin. It was not that I was being strong – I still felt detached, as if I was in a dream. The undertaker quietly passed to me an envelope containing a lock of Stephen's hair which I had requested the previous evening before we left the chapel of rest. It is now with a photo of Stephen in a gold locket which I wear as a bracelet on my right wrist: in that way I feel he is always with me.

We left in good time for the five-mile drive to the crematorium and the 12.30 service. As we pulled out of our road, an elderly ex-serviceman stood saluting the coffin. Further down the road, at the entrance to our small shopping centre, a Boddington's beer lorry waited as we passed by and at the roundabout a little further on yet another beer lorry was stopped by a policeman to let us through. I thought how Stephen must be looking down on us and laughing. Two beer lorries waiting for him, he truly was in heaven!

The police escort cleared a way through the traffic and we were soon at the crematorium. As expected, there were a lot of people there; a public address system had been set up for those who couldn't be seated in the chapel. They were all gathered around the doorway as we pulled up in front of the chapel. All I saw was a sea of faces as I stepped out of the car, holding John's hand tightly as the coffin was lifted from the hearse. Our family formed up behind the Union-Jack-draped coffin carried by eight of Stephen's comrades. On top of the coffin was a wreath of flowers from his regiment, his black peaked cap with red band and gold Royal Horse Artillery emblem and black shiny belt. We entered the chapel to the moving sound of the *Adagio for Strings* by Samuel Barber, which Stephen first heard as the theme to the Vietnam War film *Platoon*. The coffin was placed on the dais as John and I took our seats in the front row with his parents and sister, and Mark and his girlfriend. Stephen's army comrades from Bessbrook stood to my left in front of the large window forming one wall of the chapel. Behind us, people took their seats but I was oblivious to them.

We wanted the service to celebrate Stephen's life, which was why we had chosen a humanist service. Humanists think that this world is all we have, and can provide all we need, that we should try to live full and happy lives ourselves and, as part of this, help to make it easier for other people to do the same. People who have strong religious beliefs would argue with these views, but they are still a good basis by which to live. Mr Pearce began the service saying, 'We cannot come to the funeral of any young man or woman, however the death may have been caused, without questions in our hearts and minds. What had young Stephen done to deserve this? we ask. Why must we conduct our public affairs at the expense of incomplete and promising lives? I do not have answers to these questions, any more than do the philosophers or the churches. What we can answer is the question as to how we should respond. The rejection of vengeance, an absolute refusal to be provoked, is a principle by no means confined to religions. No answer to that question, of how to respond, is more courageous or more telling than that of Stephen's own mother. Her clarity of mind and firmness of spirit in this time, of all times, will live in many hearts for a long while.' I had expected the whole service to be about Stephen and was surprised at this reference to my words on the morning after Stephen's death.

He gave a short account of Stephen's life and read a poem sent to us by a lady from Northern Ireland, which typified Stephen and told us to remember the good times:

> Remember me by the laughter, not by the tears.
> Remember me by the joy and the fun we shared
> Through all the happy years.
> And think of me, if you will, with a smile,
> When we all shared jokes and laughed
> At things we did a wee bit daft.
>
> We sometimes gave the world a shake,
> And when others stood and said
> 'Oh what a way to carry on,
> I'm sure their senses must be gone,'
> It only made us laugh the more.
> So when you've laughed until you're sore
> Or when the tears run down your face –
> These are the things that brought me joy.

So if you have some love for me,
Then that's how you'll remember me.
For when you smile, then I'll smile too.
But if you cry, I'll cry with you.
So keep me happy, let me see
A happy joy that's just for me.
And as I sleep, I'll smile with you,
I'll share the past and future too.

Major Mark Milligan gave a brief outline of Stephen's career in the Royal Horse Artillery and the circumstances surrounding his death. He said, 'Lance-Bombardier Restorick recognised Mrs McElroy in her car at the checkpoint, and, typically, he smiled at her and passed the time of day. Despite being fatally wounded, his one concern was that his colleagues should be looking after Mrs McElroy as well.' His account was followed by 'Search for the Hero' by M People. The words say that 'you must search for the hero inside yourself, for the secrets you hide until you find the key to your life'. It seemed very appropriate now applied to Stephen, and the drumbeats of the introduction remind me of the sound of the helicopters based at Bessbrook.

The rest of the service consisted of the anecdotes of his family and friends. These were read by Mr Pearce because they themselves would have found it too emotional. Mark's memories of his brother came first. He told of the sadness of knowing that he himself had taken Stephen to Heathrow to catch the plane to Belfast, and said that it was hard for him to accept that he wouldn't ever be coming home again. But the memory he wished to share was a happy one: of a night when John and I were out and he was watching *Top of the Pops* with his brother. Steve turned off the sound on the TV, turned it full up on the stereo, and came back to the washing-up in the kitchen. A few seconds later there was an almighty crash. All the pictures and ornaments over the fireplace had been thrown to the floor, fortunately unbroken. They picked them up, put them in place, and turned down the volume, laughing their heads off and hoping we wouldn't find out.

John's elderly parents recalled arriving at Peterborough station to spend Christmas with us when Stephen was about ten years old. He was waiting for them in the ticket office area. As they came through the barrier he raced across and threw himself at his Gran with a hug of love and affection and took Granddad's hand. They said there was always plenty of fun and noise when he was around. Granddad had encouraged his ambitions in the army and had wanted to be able to enjoy a pint of beer in the mess when Stephen became a sergeant, though the old man doubted he would live long enough. Sadly Stephen's death was a tragic and unforeseen end to that idea. Stephen, they said, certainly gave them a lot of love and a lot of happy memories.

Stephen's cousins Christopher and Paul, both seventeen years old, told of escapades with him at their local nightclubs. Both these accounts ended in quiet laughter from many in the chapel. As did Colin's account of a night camping when, after numerous cans of lager, they pretended to be vampires by hanging from the underside of a nearby bridge ten feet above the river. After a while Colin saw sense (and felt cramp) in time to clamber to safety, but Steve found the situation hilarious – until the pain got to him and, giggling, he found he couldn't move. Colin had to pull Steve back onto the bridge, where the two of them began laughing helplessly all over again.

Stephen's friend Lisa described a different Stephen, who was like a brother to her, and she the sister he never had. She told of his lack of tact and sensitivity in expressing within their hearing his opinions of young men she was beginning to think she fancied. But he had, to her relief, approved of her fiancé.

The only formal part of the service, the committal, was very simple but moving: 'In sorrow at his passing and delight and thankfulness for his life, we commit his body to its natural end. We commit his force of character and range of friendship to our memories. We commit his joy in living and vitality of spirit to our hearts. We commit his body to be burned, that it may return to the cycles of nature whence it came.' This was followed by the haunting song 'Belfast Child' by Simple Minds. The words 'One day we'll return here, when the Belfast child sings again' spoke of all those who had left that city because of the troubles. As the song died away, Asa's simple poem telling how much Stephen's friendship meant to him was read out.

The service was now almost over. Mr Pearce read a piece by the poet Brian Patten in which he says a man lives as long as people remember him: 'For as long as we carry him inside us, for as long as we carry the harvest of his dreams, for as long as we ourselves live holding memories in common, a man lives. And the days will pass with baffled faces, then the weeks, then the months, and there will be a day when no question is asked, and the knots of grief will loosen in the stomach, and the puffed faces will calm. And on that day he will not have ceased, but will have ceased to be separated by death.' Mr Pearce concluded the service by saying, 'Stephen would have marked his birthday with some kind of party with friends, many of them are here today. They know that he would have wished us to strike an upbeat note.' We left the chapel with 'Don't You Forget About Me' by Simple Minds playing, and I cast a final glance at Stephen's coffin.

Outside, the February sun was gently shining: I had so hoped it would not rain on this day. We read the messages on the three wreaths: from his regiment, Peterborough City Council, and STOP 96. These were the only wreaths, as we had said we would prefer donations to his memorial fund. We were introduced to the young soldiers who had been his pallbearers, most of whom we'd not met before. They looked so smart in their black number one dress uniform. Next came a long line of dignitaries. During the previous week I had asked if the taoiseach (prime minister) of the Republic of Ireland could be contacted to see if he would send a representative following his condemnation of Stephen's murder. Now before me stood the tall, bespectacled figure of the Irish ambassador in London and his wife. It meant a great deal to me that they were there. Next came our local Conservative MP, Dr Brian Mawhinney, representing the prime minister and the Northern Ireland Secretary. I realised they themselves could not attend at such short notice but was disappointed they hadn't sent separate representatives. After dignitaries from Peterborough City Council came our relatives and friends. I was handed the folded Union Jack, Stephen's hat and belt. There was a sudden clamour from the ranks of press photographers kept at a distance by the police. They wanted to take photos of me holding them, with John beside me. We agreed to the photos being taken as they had agreed to our wish for no interviews. They did, however, interview the Irish ambassador, Dr Mawhinney, and Mr Pearce.

At the buffet after the funeral I rather neglected many of those attending but hoped they understood, because I so wanted to talk to Stephen's comrades from Northern Ireland, especially those who had been on duty with him at the checkpoint when he was shot. I spoke to two young army officers who gave Stephen first aid, one having travelled in the ambulance with him to the hospital. They had been talking to Stephen just before he had gone out onto the road and asked him what the situation was like in Bessbrook. He had told them in the colourful language that soldiers use amongst themselves, 'F — all happens here.' I kept thinking, Famous last words, Steve.

I also spoke to Stephen's bombardier (corporal) who had been on duty with him and had taken control of the situation when Stephen was shot. I asked him how long Stephen lay on the ground before they reached him. Lorraine, who was injured by the same bullet, had said it was for quite a few minutes. He told me he had to ensure the overall situation was safe before they went to Stephen's help. If they had all rushed forward it might have been a trap and more lives would have been lost. It only took about a minute, but seemed longer as time seems to slow down at such times. We also spoke to his lieutenant-colonel who a few days previously had visited our home to express his condolences, as had the previous major of his battery, Major Milligan, who knew Steve well (the current major was still in Northern Ireland). It was a sad thought for me that it was only because of Stephen's death that we were meeting these high-ranking officers. They were, however, very kind and not at all aloof, though I doubt if Stephen ever saw them in the same light. Stephen was the first soldier the regiment had lost in many years, he was a popular soldier, and I know they were all deeply affected by his murder. So was a young RUC policeman who attended and who had often been on duty with Stephen.

Soon it was time for his comrades to leave. They formed up in a long line and as each one came past they gave me a hug and shook John's hand. It was so sad to think they had to go back to Northern Ireland and carry on as if nothing had happened. We returned home with our

51

close family, Sue and Mike, Colin, Asa and Lisa. Having faced a very emotional day, we were all downcast and exhausted. It was still hard to believe it was true. But it was and we had to live through it and come to terms with Stephen's death. I was determined that I was going to fight back. I was going to make sure people remembered the young soldier who was shot as he smiled at a Catholic mother. I would do all I could to make the politicians and people of Northern Ireland take note of his death, despite it being only one of many in that troubled land. I would make people see that if they did not want the violence to go on for another century they had to start to do something now. But so often in the past such deaths had been quickly forgotten. Would interest from the press last long enough to give me the chance to speak out? And, just as important, would people listen?

5
GRIEF FILLS THE ROOM

Grief fills the room up of my absent child,
Lies in his bed, walks up and down with me,
Puts on his pretty looks, repeats his words,
Remembers me of all his gracious parts,
Stuffs out his vacant garments with his form:
Then I have reason to be fond of grief.

King John, William Shakespeare

In the weeks and months after Stephen's death a maelstrom of emotions
swept over me. There are many stages of grief: shock and disbelief,
yearning, anger and guilt, followed by depression with its sense of iso-
lation, futility and loneliness. Oh so slowly do these give way to acceptance of loss and a life of new circumstances and purpose. The pain of
grief has to be suffered; there is no escape or avoidance. It can, however,
be shared: people can help just by being there, offering a caring presence
and a listening ear. But death is the great unmentionable in our society,
and most people do not know what to say to a bereaved person. I felt
people were avoiding me, perhaps worried that I would burst into tears
at the mention of Stephen's name. But I so wanted people to talk about
him, otherwise it was as if he had never existed. People underestimate
the depth of sadness in bereavement and think you should soon get over
it. It is only when the shadow is cast over you personally that the black,
deep depths of grieving can fully be known.

After the funeral, wanting to be on our own for a few days to come to terms with our loss, we decided to go to Brixham. It was the last week in February so this Devon town, noted for its picturesque harbour and fishing industry, was very quiet. We've always loved Devon, perhaps because the Restorick family roots lie in Devon and Cornwall. The surname comes from the old Cornish language and is the name of a small farm, Restowrack, near St Austell in Cornwall, from which the family took their name in the thirteenth century. At the beginning of the seventeenth century, John's namesake was a yeoman farmer at Axmouth in east Devon. Everyone in Britain with our surname is descended from his three sons – John's ancestor was the eldest son.

The small hotel where we stayed, originally a Victorian villa, had wonderful views out to sea. Apart from a couple of nights, there were no other guests, so we were on our own most of the time, which was what we wanted. We couldn't have coped with a lot of people around us enjoying themselves. We went for walks round Brixham harbour with its replica of Drake's ship the *Golden Hind* (in which he sailed round the world) and small fishing boats in the inner harbour, beyond them the quay for larger fishing boats, and the yacht marina. On the quayside is a statue to William of Orange who landed here from Holland in 1689 to take the throne, at parliament's invitation, from his wife's father, James II.

Another walk was to Battery Gardens with its views right across Tor Bay to the holiday towns of Paignton and Torquay, while at the other side of the harbour was Berry Head, a headland with Napoleonic fort and lighthouse. We would sit up there and hear the seagulls calling, the sea pounding against the rocks below and look at the fantastic views along the coast to the south or across the vast expanse of the bay to Portland Bill in Dorset. Cocooned in our sorrow, we felt far away from other people rushing about their everyday lives. Solitude was what we needed. One day we drove to a seal sanctuary a few miles away, but when we arrived there were several cars in the car park so we left. I couldn't face being with a crowd of people. We drove along country roads instead, stopping at a little bridge over a stream. Snowdrops peeped through the grass in the weak February sunshine. Spring was not far away. Walking along the road we could hear the stream rippling over stones and the birds singing. It was totally peaceful, as if nature was wrapping us in a protective blanket and healing our hurt. We just needed to feel our grief and not have to conceal it or deny the very real pain we were going through.

Later we arrived at a pub beside a river, bought a drink and sat at a picnic table on the river bank. A few other people were there but we now felt better able to cope. A couple sat at a table not far from us. They had two young boys, about six and four years old, very similar to ours at that age. They were feeding the ducks on the river, going right up to the edge without any fear of falling in, and laughing at the ducks arguing over a piece of bread. The younger boy reminded me so much of Stephen. The pain struck again and I was in tears thinking of him. The crocuses and daffodils were flowering. Spring truly was in the air, everything was bursting with life once more. I felt so sad that Stephen would never again experience this, and I knew that in future the first hints of spring would always remind me of his death. Life seemed so very, very cruel.

Some days were less spring-like, with lashing rain, so I began to reply to the many cards and letters. Those from his mates and the general public were very moving and meant a great deal to us. Parents of other soldiers serving in Northern Ireland wrote of their fear when they heard a soldier had been shot that it might be their son and the relief when they knew it wasn't, but also the sadness of knowing some other parents were not so lucky. Many wrote about our words during the various interviews; one mother sent a 'Thank you' card, writing in explanation: 'I wanted to thank you both for the wonderful words that you have spoken about not wanting Stephen's death to cause any more problems in Ireland. To have said this at a time when your hearts are breaking makes you very special people.' There were letters and cards from parents of soldiers, RUC officers and civilians killed by terrorists in Northern Ireland. The parents of Lance-Bombardier Stephen Cummins wrote, 'We cannot promise you anything but a very hard road ahead. Try to forgive neighbours and friends who can't face you and seem to deliberately avoid you – they just have no idea what to do or say.' (We remembered those words in the weeks and months ahead. Bereavement is a very lonely time.) The mother of a soldier killed by a bomb in Armagh on 9 February 1993 voiced the topsy-turvy world of our feelings of gratefulness that Stephen died quickly, writing, 'My own son Michael had his arm and leg amputated, also one side of his face was gone. He lived eleven hours after. I only wish he had been killed instantly to have saved him the suffering – indeed our boys shouldn't have been killed at all, my boy was twenty-one.' I believe the way in which Stephen died touched far more hearts than would have been the case if he had died in a car crash back home or from some illness, and in that I feel fortunate.

Those wild, wet days also gave me time to look back. In a strange way, I began to see events in the previous two months as symbols of what had happened since. First, there was our holiday in December to Egypt, a country we'd always wanted to visit. The majority of the tourist sights are connected with death, from the richly decorated tombs in the Valleys of the Kings and Queens to Tutankhamun's treasures and the burial chambers within the pyramids. The other symbol lay in my visit to Brixham only a month previously. I had reached a stage in my life when I needed time on my own to think things out. I knew I wanted to go to Devon but had no idea of exactly where. Through pure chance, I found myself in Brixham. I had been there only once before, while on holiday just up the coast at Dawlish Warren with John and our boys in 1982, but couldn't remember anything about the town. I stayed at a lovely little guesthouse, the harbour master's home in days gone by. My room on the top floor at the front had a fantastic view across the harbour. It was the type of place I needed to be, where I could think things out and come to a decision. Over the next few days I went for many a long walk, despite the freezing weather. One day I sat on Berry Head in the biting wind totally surrounded by fog, another day I walked along the top of the breakwater on the outer harbour not caring if the wind blew me off. I suppose I was saying that if there was a God, it was up to him what happened to me. I found the Blue Anchor pub on the quayside near the statue of William of Orange and was made to feel welcome by the bar staff and regulars. The landlady was very kind to me – perhaps she could sense what I was going through – and the pub became my haven.

There were many symbols in Brixham that later had a relevance for me. There was the statue of William of Orange, the hero of so many Protestants in Northern Ireland. At the Blue Anchor there were two ladies with Irish accents. One, the barmaid, came originally from southern Ireland whilst the other's father had brought the family to Devon from Northern Ireland when the troubles were at their worst. She and her husband provided the music one night at the pub, calling themselves Southern Comfort – the name of an American drink. But the name also reminded me of the refuge provided by some in the Republic of Ireland to IRA men. With both ladies I discussed my son being in the army in Northern Ireland and the situation over there, though evermindful of Stephen's safety I didn't give them any details. Another night, music was provided by a man playing guitar and synthesiser. He sang a couple of Irish songs, although he was not Irish himself. He intrigued me as he had a bad stammer but when he sang it totally disappeared. He called himself Sniper. The final symbol was the tune the bells of the church clock rang on the hour – the hymn 'Abide with Me', whose composer, the Reverend H.F. Lyte, was the vicar of Brixham in Victorian times. That hymn is used at many funerals. After a couple of weeks in Brixham, mainly spent walking round and round the town lost in my thoughts, I decided it was time to return home. I left behind so many things that only after Stephen's death I saw as forewarning me. But in January I was too wrapped up in my own problems to see them.

Now back in Brixham with John, I returned to the warm welcome of the Blue Anchor's landlady and, one night, to the music of Sniper. That name had far more significance for me now.

Our stay in Brixham lasted just over a week and gave us the space and privacy we needed to start to accept our loss. But now we wanted to be back home. It would still be another two months before John returned to work, though Mark went back within a month. I never returned to my secretarial post at Peterborough City Council. I knew I couldn't cope with the workload and the pressure. Also I felt that if I returned I would be accepting what had happened. I would be saying that Stephen, my lovely son, was dead but I could still go to work and type letters and answer the phone as before. Deep inside I knew my life would never be the same again. I even changed the way I dressed, feeling I had to go back to basics, jeans and a shirt, hair naturally straight and no makeup. I had to show people the real me, no pretence. I felt that smart clothes and makeup would somehow prevent people from seeing that.

I had to make Stephen's death a focus, if only for a year, and do my utmost to make it mean something, to be a symbol of all the other victims in Northern Ireland. I didn't want any other parents to go through what we were suffering because of the situation in Northern Ireland. So many had experienced this grief over the past thirty years – and who now remembers the names of most of the victims except the immediate family? I wasn't going to allow Stephen to be forgotten.

Never for one moment had I thought that one of my children would die before me. My mother died in 1983 and my father a few years later. It was part of growing older myself – I accepted it though it did not lessen the sadness at the time. When I was told that Stephen had been killed, I was hit with a total feeling of shock and disbelief, only slowly followed by acceptance. But it was the acceptance of fact, it was not emotional acceptance. There followed a period when I still couldn't believe Stephen was dead. I would read the newspaper articles about his death and although I was reading his name it was as if I was reading about someone else. I had made a tape of the music used at his funeral and I would play that to reinforce in my mind the reality of his death. The music caused the tears to flow. I cried and cried until I was exhausted. But it helped release the terrible pain inside. It is not an exaggeration to say that I felt as if my heart had been ripped out and yet I was still living. Some days the feeling of sadness welled up inside me and overflowed in tears. Some days the tears did not come, but I felt a deep well of tears inside me. Months later when people saw I had been crying they would ask what was the matter. I couldn't believe they could ask such a question – wasn't it obvious? John wasn't with me during the week because of his work, so for much of the time I had to grieve on my own, just as he did. Only at weekends were we together to comfort each other and hold each other tight in our sorrow. John, like many men, keeps his emotions deep inside, so when he cried I really knew he was hurting. But he wouldn't talk about how he was feeling, so I sometimes felt he wasn't hurting as much as me. Mark too grieved inwardly, and I felt I shouldn't expect him to comfort me.

In my case, the anger that comes with bereavement focused on the fact that the situation had been allowed to go on for so long with the loss of so many young lives. I thought, if politicians' sons were on the front line they would try harder to end the conflict. I felt anger at what I saw as intransigence on the part of some Protestants in Northern Ireland over what they saw as a right and tradition, ignoring the feelings of the nationalist community. I never wanted revenge or to show hatred. The love I feel for Stephen made me want to understand how someone could be motivated to kill another person to try to achieve political aims. But still the anger welled up inside me and I had to let it out. In the early days, the anger and pain were so bad I tried to numb it by drowning my sorrows in alcohol. When the anger got too much I would throw my glass across the patio, shattering it, just as my hopes and life had been shattered. But this was nothing to what I did to my golliwog. I don't have soft toys around the house, but a golliwog had special significance for me. At about three years old I had to go into Shrewsbury hospital, twenty miles from my home, for an eye operation. My parents didn't have a car so could only visit twice a week – an eternity for a small child. They gave me a golliwog to keep me company but it went missing while I was in hospital. Forty years later, I bought another golliwog at an antiques fair. He had a red jacket, white shirt and black-and-white-striped trousers. I felt that everything would be fine now that I had 'my golly' again. After Stephen joined the army I put two photos of him on either side of golly's arms on my dressing table. Somehow I felt that he would be safe. But he wasn't. So, a little while after his death, I took the golliwog into the garden and stabbed it over and over again with a carving knife, pinning it to a tree. I felt as if I was killing someone, I was so full of anger. In a silly, childish way I had trusted that golliwog and it had failed me, just as my old golly had left me on my own in hospital. John found the golliwog the next morning. He took it down, saying people would think we were racist. I didn't try to explain to him why I'd done it as I didn't think he would understand.

Just as I had loved my golly as a child and lost it, I began to think I had lost Stephen because I loved him too much. I was too close to him. It wasn't logical, but that was what I felt. I find it difficult to make lasting friendships, to let people into that private little part of myself. In contrast, I am able to go up to complete strangers and chat to them. As well as the anger, there was guilt. I felt guilty when I could get through the day without crying for him, even months after his death. Guilty when I realised I hadn't been thinking of him. Guilty that my life continued when I had far rather it was his.

I wanted time to stand still. I wanted to be able to say, 'This time last week he was still alive.' But it doesn't stand still. The longer the time since I last heard his voice or felt him hug me, the further I felt from him. Now it will always be so many years since he died, not 'this time last year he was . . .' It will be that 'today was his birthday', 'today was the day he died'. Now I have to be content with his photo and the memories.

The world seemed suddenly to be filled with people called Steve, on TV and in the newspapers, but not the one who mattered to me. It was so painful to see and hear that name so often. I felt a terrible need to see him again. I would suddenly be reminded of Stephen when I saw young men in the street with hair like his or wearing their shirt outside their trousers like he did. I wanted so desperately to go up to them, put my arms around them and hug them so tight. But I knew I couldn't. Then a terrible pain would pierce my chest and the tears would overflow from the terrible emptiness inside me. I'd go into his room and smell his clothes, trying to capture his smell, that lovely fresh smell of body spray or even the sweaty smell from his keep-fit run. But the clothes had all been washed, so all I could do was hold them to me as I cried. They had been returned by two of his army mates, neatly packed with his CDs and other belongings in two large boxes. I knew they had to be returned, but I felt as if the army was saying 'Thank you, we've finished with him now.' His mates stayed too long as people often do, not knowing when to leave, and I know it was hard for them but I just wanted to be on my own to release my tears.

I desperately wanted Stephen back. Soon after his death, Dolly, the cloned sheep, hit the headlines. If they could clone a sheep surely they'd be able to clone another Stephen. I had a lock of his hair – and that would have DNA in it. But so many things in our lives had changed since 1973 when Stephen was born. I soon realised that this clone might grow up to be totally different, perhaps making us hate the name Stephen and destroying the happy memories we had of the original. Every person is an individual – even identical twins have different personalities. The scientist who cloned Dolly was a guest of honour at a Nottingham University graduation ceremony six months after John left his employment there; the other guest was Mary McAleese, President of the Republic of Ireland but originally from Northern Ireland. I thought back to my wild hopes for a cloned Stephen and felt a link between Stephen and these two people.

Dreams suddenly became very important to me. Usually I don't remember my dreams, but after Stephen's death they were so emotional that I would wake up crying, with them still vivid in my mind. In one I was hurrying to put the letters and photos of Stephen into the envelopes to the politicians on the Wednesday after his death. Looking up, I saw Stephen and Mark looking in at me through the window. I called to Stephen asking him to help me, he just smiled and shook his head to say no. I said over and over again, 'Please come here, please come here,' and I was crying and crying. In another dream he was about four years old and enjoying bathtime. As he stood up for me to dry him, I wrapped the towel round him and hugged him so tight to me. Again the tears flowed and I woke up. In the December after his death, I dreamed I was in a kitchen with my mother. She told me I had to put what had happened to Stephen behind me and get on with life. I burst into tears and said, 'How can I?' Again I woke up crying. My mother had suffered two stillbirths – perhaps I had never fully realised the grief she must have experienced. A year after his death I dreamed of Stephen again. Now he was adult, wearing his mustard-coloured pullover: it was lovely to see him again as I last remember him. I put my arms round him and hugged him. This time I didn't cry but felt such a warm feeling of love for him.

Certain pieces of music have a special significance for me because they were used at Stephen's funeral, or because they remind me of him or because the words say something special to me. One of these special songs is 'Search for the Hero' by M People. This song, used at his funeral, really made us feel that in a way Stephen was still around. On 6 July the *Sunday Times* Magazine carried an article about Stephen's death and its effect on a wide range of people. John and I read the article over breakfast and, starting the washing-up, I asked John to phone the author, Michael Bilton, to thank him. Suddenly the phone rang and it was Michael phoning us for our opinion. At that exact moment, 'Search for the Hero' came on the radio. It was as if Steve was saying he approved as well. Similarly, when visiting Stephen's mates at Top-cliffe barracks, as we walked to Splash's house (he was with Steve when he was shot) we heard the tune coming from one of the houses. It was as if Steve was saying he was still there with his mates. About eighteen months after his death I was feeling very low one day having read again the *Sunday Times* article. I wanted to feel Stephen still existed in some form that I couldn't understand. So I said, 'Show me if you are around.' I switched the radio on. It was tuned to the channel I usually listen to, but for some unknown reason I changed to the local station. The second song was 'I Will Always Love You' by Whitney Houston, which kept going through my mind when Stephen left for his last tour. It was not a scheduled record – someone had phoned in only a moment before to request it. I collapsed in tears. A few minutes later I phoned the DJ and told him how much the record meant to me. I asked if he could play 'Search for the Hero' sometime. His response was that it was scheduled in half an hour's time. Pure coincidence, perhaps, but to me it meant far more.

Stephen's death has caused me to question my religious beliefs, or lack of them. I have great difficulty in believing in God, who I cannot see. I suppose I am the original doubting Thomas. Yet I accept that the air around me is made up of nitrogen, oxygen and carbon dioxide even though I can't see those gases and wouldn't know how to prove they are there. I cannot decide whether God created man, or man created God to fill a need in his life. Still, I have often wanted to cry out, 'If there is a God, why are you doing this to me? Why did my son have to die?' Some might see a religious dimension in Stephen's death. Was it meant to be that the same bullet injured a Catholic mother? Was that meant to make both communities think about where they were heading? Or was it just pure chance?

Since Stephen's death I have been questioning and searching, and many people have tried to help me in my search. But I still feel nearer to a Creator, if there is such a being, on a sunny day in the countryside or on a starry night than I ever do at a church service. So many questions run through my head: Were ancient peoples wrong to worship nature or a multitude of gods? Why did God only show himself to the Jews and not all races? Religion seems to cause so many divisions and even hatred between people. Some cannot accept that Catholics, Protestants, Jews and Muslims worship the same God but in their own ways; Protestants and Catholics disagree on their interpretation of Holy Communion.

Before Stephen's death I was sure this life was the only one. Now I hope it isn't. I so hope that, as others say, he is happy in a better place. If there is life after death, can you communicate with the dead? I have my doubts. However, I was made to look at this more closely. A few months after Stephen's death our neighbour Gill visited a medium. She believed Stephen had made contact with the medium and she came to tell us, not sure how we would take it. I am sceptical about mediums, believing they have good memories and take a special interest in local news. I'd never been to a medium before but I decided to visit this one. I only gave my Christian name, and decided to reply just 'yes' or 'no' to her questions, determined not to give any information to help her. I arrived at her house in a small town twenty miles from Peterborough and was led into her sitting room. I sat opposite her at a table covered in a black cloth with symbols embroidered in gold thread. She put my tape in the recorder and her watch on the small cushion in front of her. It was not eerie, but just like a normal conversation between us. She rubbed the watch gently for a few moments and gave some information which seemed to be about my father. The information turned to a young man, it might be about Stephen, but I said nothing to lead her on and didn't give his name. Gradually more and more was revealed, but she could have remembered it from newspaper and TV reports. She said that two cars were involved. At first she thought he had been hit by a car but said she could hear a noise, she clapped her hands once. Then she said, 'Was he shot?' I said yes. She said that a woman in a car had also been injured but was all right now. 'Have you met her?' she asked. I said, 'Yes.' She said, 'He's glad you've met her as he thought you would like her.' (I presumed she could tell from the tone of my voice that our meeting had gone well, but I was surprised that she had the connection between two cars as the gunman had been in one car out of sight of Stephen.) She continued, 'He was good-looking, conscious of his looks, very particular about his hair.' I thought, aren't most young men? About halfway through I said his name before I could stop myself. She replied, 'He hasn't given me his name.' She asked if we had a black and white cat which wasn't very well. (We did: it was old and had lost weight – the vet said it had the start of kidney failure.) I had one question that would prove to me whether she was in contact with Stephen. I said, 'What was the name of the kitten he brought home?' She asked if it was a tabby kitten and I said yes. However, she wasn't able to tell me, although Stephen had chosen its name, Widget.

Much of what she had told me was accurate but general so I was still sceptical, believing she probably had recognised me. Had she? A few months previously my photo had been in the press. Did she know Gill was my neighbour and purposely mention Stephen in order to get me to come? At the end of the session I paid in cash rather than by cheque to conceal my name in case I decided to visit her again. She still insisted she did not know me. My next visit was about six months later. The same young man came through and said he was my son Stephen. She said that I was wearing a ring of his which I fiddled with at times and that pleased him. This surprised me as she'd said it wasn't Stephen's when I'd asked her the previous time whose ring it was, though not telling her I had found it in his bedroom. At the end, showing her a photo of

Stephen and Mark I asked if the young man was either of them. She pointed to Stephen and said it was him. She of course had a fifty per cent chance of being right.

I would like to believe that Stephen lives on in some way but I can't help thinking the medium has a good memory and is a clever, perceptive reader of people. Perhaps I am fortunate in that I am not desperate to make contact.

Not wanting Stephen's ashes to be interred in Peterborough, we found it very difficult to decide what to do with them. After the cremation, I placed the small wooden casket in his bedroom, where I made a little memorial with the Union Jack from his coffin, his Northern Ireland medal, the peaked cap and belt from his dress uniform, and his cycling helmet. At first we thought of scattering his ashes, but then we decided we wanted a grave to visit in years to come. It was early autumn before we decided he should be in Market Drayton, my home town, where my parents and great-grandparents are buried. The place is marked by a white military headstone bearing the emblems of the Royal Artillery and 3 RHA with Stephen's details between them. At the foot of the headstone are the words 'For my sake turn to life and smile' from the poem by Thomas Gray. We knew Stephen would have wanted us to carry on with our lives and smile, but it is very difficult at times. Looking at his headstone, I think of the rows and rows of white headstones in the beautifully maintained war cemeteries outside Tobruk where we lived in the late 1960s. I never expected that one day my son would have a similar headstone on his grave.

November came. Remembrance Day now had a personal meaning for us. Each year I had bought a poppy, placing it in the grass beside the war memorial after the wreath-laying ceremony. Now I wore a poppy in remembrance of my own son. As I read the words 'We will remember them' on the war memorial I often thought, do we? Only on one day a year, and many no longer attended the wreath-laying at the war memorial, which we now attended in remembrance of our own son. Shortly afterwards, I placed a spray of poppies on Stephen's grave. Nearby I noticed the graves of some Polish and Czech airmen from the Second World War. I placed a spray of poppies on each to show that someone still cared about these young men so far from their own countries and families.

There came the time to face 24 February without Stephen; it would have been his twenty-fifth birthday. Our friends Sue and Mike invited us to their house for a meal as they knew it would be a difficult day for us. It was Shrove Tuesday, so we had pancakes. The previous year Shrove Tuesday had fallen two weeks earlier, on the last full day of Stephen's life.

My birthday and Mother's Day are both now difficult times which emphasise Stephen's absence. My fiftieth birthday came eleven months after Stephen's death. I didn't feel like celebrating, but to mark the day we had a quiet meal in a Shropshire pub with my brothers and their families. But we were all too aware that Stephen wasn't with us. Having a drink in the bar before the meal, I noticed the beer mats were for Bombardier beer. I kept one beside me all night and brought it home afterwards, feeling that Stephen was with me.

As the months passed, the terrible initial pain of knowing that I would never see Stephen again lessened. But I had been told that the grieving process is two steps forward and one step back. How true this was. Just when I began to think I was coming to terms with what had happened, suddenly I would be flung to the depths again. The sadness came in waves with troughs between – each trough lulling me into thinking things were getting better, only for me to be drowned in tears when the next wave hit. Apathy is another stage in the grieving process. I found it so hard to do anything; everything seemed so pointless or such an effort. There was no enjoyment to be found in anything. I didn't want to go to the cinema, to a restaurant or even on holiday. Grieving is a long, hard road, which has no end though perhaps the journey will get easier with time.

My feelings were echoed by the poem 'Perhaps' by Vera Brittain, dedicated to her fiancé who had died of wounds in France in 1915. It was included in a book of poems written by women during the First World War. I had bought the book a few weeks before Stephen's death. It is called *Scars Upon My Heart*. Three verses of Vera Brittain's poem put into words my own feelings:

Perhaps some day the sun will shine again,
And I shall see that still the skies are blue,
And feel once more I do not live in vain,
Although bereft of you.

Perhaps some day I shall not shrink in pain
To see the passing of the dying year,
And listen to the Christmas songs again,
Although you cannot hear.

But, though kind Time may many joys renew,
There is one greatest joy I shall not know
Again, because my heart for loss of you
Was broken, long ago.

The Restorick family stand in silence at the checkpoint in Bessbrook, County
Armagh, where Stephen was shot dead by an IRA sniper on 12 February 1997

MARTIN McCULLOUGH

6

WE WILL REMEMBER HIM

AFTER STEPHEN WAS KILLED, I didn't want his name forgotten
by all except our immediate family. In a way, we were fortunate that Stephen was the only soldier killed in 1997: it meant
that his death attracted more publicity and his name was more widely
remembered especially by people in Northern Ireland, at least during
the year after his death. So many people have been killed in Northern

Ireland, and like most people I only remembered the few who stand out such as Lord Mountbatten, Airey Neave MP, Marie Wilson and Tim Parry (though I could not remember the name of the three-year-old boy who was killed at the same time as Tim). I now have a book listing all those killed in the conflict, whether in Ireland, England or on the Continent. There are over 3,500 names so it is little wonder that no one can remember them all. The violence has gone on for almost thirty years; a whole generation has grown up during that time and to them news of bombings and shootings became normality.

In the week after Stephen's death I had asked his regiment if there could be a memorial to him at Bessbrook. It was now in place and they invited us to the dedication ceremony on Tuesday, 18 March 1997. Only a month after his death, this would be the first time we had visited Northern Ireland. We, like many British people with no family or business connections there, had never visited on account of the violence. Our visit only lasted twenty-four hours and was under strict military protection as there was no IRA ceasefire then. As a result, there was no opportunity to meet the people of Bessbrook, but at least it enabled us to see for ourselves the beautiful countryside in which Stephen had served.

Our son Mark, my two brothers, their wives, and Stephen's two youngest cousins, Paul and Christopher, came with us. We flew from Stanstead to Aldergrove airport, not far from Belfast, where we were met by a captain from Stephen's regiment who would be looking after us during our stay. We spent the night in the safety and luxury of the officers' mess at RAF Aldergrove, where John and I had been given the VIP suite. I thought how Stephen would be smiling at that.

After breakfast the following morning we were driven south to Bessbrook through the beautiful rolling countryside. Arriving at the Mill, we passed through high metal gates; in front of us was a long, tall building that reminded me of a Yorkshire woollen mill. Built in the nineteenth century by Quakers, who abhor warfare, but now home to soldiers, this mill mirrors the situation in Northern Ireland. The commanding officer and major of 3 RHA gave a short briefing about the regiment's work in the area, then drove us in an army vehicle to the

The checkpoint at Bessbrook: the shield on the right was only erected after
Stephen's death, and the sniper shot that killed him came from
200 yards up the road beyond the sangar on the left.

checkpoint. I saw a crowd of press photographers, TV cameramen and
reporters hovering around. Although they were kept at a distance I still
felt they were denying us the privacy we so badly needed at that very
emotional time. Suddenly I saw that now there was a high metal screen
half across the road, shielding the soldier checking the cars from the direction the sniper had fired from. I felt so angry. The army knew there
was a sniper in the area. Why hadn't they foreseen what had happened?
Why hadn't they erected the screen when the ceasefire broke down a
year before, not when it was too late?

The flowers caught my attention. There were dozens of bunches
from local people on the wire fencing at the exact spot where Stephen
had fallen. My mind went back to the photo in the newspapers of
Lorraine placing a flower there from a bouquet she had received. There
had been lots of flowers then, and more recently others had replaced
them. I held John's hand tightly as the commanding officer led us and
Mark to the spot, the rest of my family following behind. After John
and I had placed our bouquet, my two brothers and their families placed
theirs next to it beside the fence. We all stood for a few moments in

70

silence alone with our own thoughts.

My thoughts were of the waste of a young, vibrant life and the futility of the situation but also of the many cards we had received from people in this area, people we did not know but who remembered Stephen's smile and happy personality. One family wrote, 'We only knew him through the checkpoint going in and out of the village, but he was a warm and friendly young man with a very friendly smile and I saw him half an hour before he was shot. I will always remember him in my prayers.' A lady wrote, 'I knew your son from the checkpoint and always found him a pleasant young man with a smile and a cheery word and you can justly be very proud of him. I speak as a Catholic mother and these people do not act on our behalf. We are totally against violence.' Another lady, from Green Road in Bessbrook, the road on which Stephen had been killed, wrote: 'I had been through the checkpoint about three times that day and spoke to him each time. He was lovely and very well-mannered. I am a Catholic but I hate the IRA, most of us do, they're cowards and I'm so ashamed that this happened where I live.' A lady from Dundalk, a town just south of the border said to be a haven for the IRA, wrote, 'I just had to write to you as one mother to another and let you know that not all Irish people are anti-British. I cried for your son and all your family. . . . I was lucky enough to have met him at a roadblock that day. It was raining and I told him he should not be standing out in the wet. He laughed and I said, "Your mother would not let you stand out here getting wet if you were at home." He gave me his wonderful smile and said I was right. So I just had to write and let you know he was thinking of you in his last few hours. I feel it was a privilege to have met him. He put sunshine into my life in those few minutes we spoke together, and you as his mother must be so proud to have such a wonderful son. He was a credit to both you and your husband. . . . I just don't know what to say to comfort you but just think of that handsome boy with the lovely smile. He was a special person.' I wondered if it actually was Stephen she had spoken to – the soldiers work shifts so it may have been another soldier, and they are all told to be courteous to the people they stop at checkpoints. However, I like to think it was Stephen who touched this lady's heart so much.

71

The commanding officer took us a few yards past the screen towards where the shot had been fired from. He said they believed the sniper had fired from the back of a car near where the road dipped by a white house. It still seemed so unreal to me, as if I was still in that dream. I remembered the officer was concerned we should not stand there for long, aware that we could become targets. I suddenly thought, I couldn't give a damn if an IRA man shot me now. I felt he had killed a part of me already.

We went into the guard post beside the checkpoint, and I remembered the young officer telling me at the funeral that Stephen had been in there only a couple of minutes before he was shot. In all, we spent about half an hour at the checkpoint. As we were about to leave I saw a middle-aged couple standing a little way off. I went over to them and the wife hugged me and said most of Bessbrook condemned the murder. She also said that Stephen was a lovely boy and would wave at them as they passed by.

We returned in the same army vehicle to the Mill. There we met many of Stephen's comrades. They joined us for a delicious buffet lunch and I joked that Stephen always said army food was terrible. Soon it was time for the dedication of the memorial. In those first few days after Stephen's death I had envisaged a granite boulder with a brass plaque, and basically this is what I now saw in front of me, though the stone was smooth, mottled-grey marble. A short service was held on the lawn in front of it, accompanied by the clatter of helicopters landing and taking off from the helipad a few yards away. The chaplain said the army had an essential role in protecting the community from terrorism, his words mirroring what I believed about army withdrawal. 'If you take the troops out, there would be mayhem, and people who live here would live in fear and intimidation. Stephen's life was lost fighting for the freedom of others.' Nevertheless, at times I had felt in frustration that we should pull our troops out and let the people of Northern Ireland get on with it. Towards the end of the service we said the Lord's Prayer and the lines 'Forgive us our trespasses as we forgive them who trespass against us.' I wondered not for the first time whether I could forgive the man who had killed Stephen. At the close of the service, we placed our

wreaths against the memorial and planted a flowering cherry tree behind it, the commanding officer, myself, John, and my two brothers in
turn placing a spadeful of soil around its roots. We had been lucky with
the weather; it hadn't rained all day except for a few spots during the
service. They seemed symbolic of the many tears shed by Stephen's
family and friends since his death.

We travelled back to Aldergrove airport in silence; even the captain
and driver said nothing. All of us were lost in our thoughts about the
situation there, whether they would ever find a solution, and how
many other young men like Stephen would have to lose their lives before one was found. We said our farewells to our escorts at the airport; it
was not until we were checking in that my tears began to flow. I had
been so detached all day, but now suddenly I had the thought that this
was where Stephen had landed on Boxing Day and this was where his
coffin was flown from. It had been a long emotional day for me and for
a moment feelings of bitterness got the upper hand. My son had come
to protect all the people of Northern Ireland, whether Protestant or
Catholic, but they had sent him back to me in a coffin. As the tears
flowed, these feelings passed and the bitterness did not return; only the
futility and sadness remained.

I was surprised to learn that a few days earlier, on 4 March, Stephen
had been mentioned during the Irish radio station RTÉ's *A Thought for
Today* programme. The piece was written by Eamonn Conway, a
Catholic priest and theology lecturer at a Dublin college. His thoughts
probably reflected those of many people in the Republic. 'To be honest,
Northern Ireland doesn't impinge much on me. I half-listen to the
news, but it might as well be about a different country. It's only when
I go abroad and people ask me to explain why Catholics and Protestants
so hate each other that I really have to think about it. Then I become
defensive. I want to make it clear that it's not because of religion people
are killing each other. At home, generally, the north slips into the back
of my mind. But for some reason the recent murder of Stephen
Restorick did impinge on me. He was the British soldier shot dead by
a sniper in County Armagh, just a few weeks ago. I was struck by the
photos of him in the paper, his youthful yet serious expression, and also

by the calm and dignified way his father spoke about him on the radio. Stephen was only twenty-three. I have already had twelve more years of life than Stephen will ever have. And I wondered about the man who looked down the barrel of the rifle, carefully selected Stephen, adjusted his telescopic sight, and then gently squeezed the trigger. Did he realise that Stephen was smiling when the bullet literally ripped through him? I am trying to understand. Could I kill? Probably, given the right or wrong circumstances. And that's frightening. It's easy to hate people you never really get to know. It's easier to kill a British soldier than to kill Stephen Restorick, aged twenty-three, with a family who loves him. When you get to see people as people it's harder to hate them. And yet even in our day-to-day [lives] how often are we advised to "keep your distance", "be objective", "don't get involved". This morning I am aware of my own power to give life, and also to take it. I am also aware that the north, which in reality is only a few miles down the road, *is* my problem.' His words echoed my feeling that Stephen's death had given people the opportunity to look at where the situation was heading and what their own stance in the future should be.

Almost a month after our visit to Stephen's regiment at Bessbrook, we joined them again for a Service of Memorial and Thanksgiving for their safe return from Northern Ireland. It was Thursday, 10 April, and we had travelled to Ripon's imposing cathedral for the service. I felt almost as if Stephen's life had come full circle as it was in Ripon twenty-four years before that he had come into this world at the local maternity hospital. I had many memories of struggling with pushchair and shopping bags on the bus to Ripon market with both the children, and of picnics at the nearby ruins of Fountains Abbey.

With us at the service were my two brothers and their wives with their sons David, Christopher and Paul. John's elderly parents had not felt strong enough to come. Just before 11 o'clock we approached the huge west door of the centuries-old cathedral and were greeted by the regiment's commanding officer. Ahead of us were two field guns and behind them, standing on the steps on either side of the main doorway, two gunners in full ceremonial dress and beside them two representatives from the British Legion carrying the regimental standards.

Walking up the nave between row upon row of soldiers in camouflage uniform, we reached our seats on the front row. Beside us were the family of Gunner Jon Cooper who had died a few days after Stephen, though not in action. I sat next to his mother, with John and Mark to my right, and with my two brothers and their families immediately behind us. Across the aisle were senior officers of the regiment, their wives and other senior officers linked to the regiment.

The first hymn was 'Praise My Soul the King of Heaven'. I tried to sing but couldn't, and when we came to the verse that says, 'In his hands he gently bears us, rescues us from all our foes', I thought, He didn't save Stephen from his foes, did he? The Reverend David Coulter began the service: 'We have come together to give thanks for the successful completion of the tour of duty and to pray for the bereaved and fallen. With thanksgiving we come before God and pledge ourselves to the continuing service of our Queen and our country and, under the guidance of God, to work for peace and justice in our world.' The Lord's Prayer followed, challenging me with the same question about forgiveness as at Bessbrook Mill. Since then I had read Saint Francis of Assisi's prayer inspired by the Lord's Prayer which goes even further: 'Enable us to forgive perfectly and without reserve any wrong that has been committed against us. And strengthen our hearts truly to love our enemies, praying for them and striving to serve them.' I hope I'm doing this in my own way, also that I don't have any enemies among the people of Northern Ireland, though some would see me as the mother of an enemy – a British soldier. As to serving them, the only way I could do that was by supporting the peace process.

After a short reading and the hymn 'O God Our Help in Ages Past' there was a reading by the commanding officer, followed by prayers for peace, for Queen and country, and for those who mourn, ending with Saint Francis's prayer 'Make Me a Channel of Your Peace'. The sermon was followed by the Act of Remembrance:

> They shall grow not old as we that are left grow old.
> Age shall not weary them nor the years condemn.

At the going down of the sun and in the morning
We will remember them.

The haunting notes of the Last Post rang through the cathedral and was followed by two minutes' silence, and then the Reverend Coulter said a Prayer of Dedication, 'Today we commend to God's care and keeping the memory and the names of Lance-Bombardier Stephen Restorick and Gunner Jon Cooper. Let the memory of their sacrifice and loss be always an example to us.' Finally came the hymn 'I Vow to Thee My Country' to the stirring music by Elgar, containing the poignant words

The love that never falters, the love that pays the price,
The love that makes undaunted the final sacrifice.

Stephen had certainly paid the price of love for his country. We had both paid that price: Stephen had made the final sacrifice, and I as a mother had paid my sacrifice in losing him, just as our family had. I was not sure if my love asked no questions. I certainly had questions I wanted the politicians to answer, such as why the situation had gone on so long, why they seemed unable to make the necessary compromises to bring it to an end, and why even after so many innocent deaths they still seemed unable to see each other's point of view.

The service ended with the National Anthem and we left the gloom of the cathedral and returned to the warm spring sunshine. I was wearing the same summer suit of blue jacket and floral print skirt that I had worn at Stephen's funeral so I was glad of the mild weather as we stood talking to some officers, waiting for the car to arrive that would take us to the regimental barracks at Topcliffe.

On the way there we came to a narrow bridge where there were road works and traffic lights. Just in front of us on the opposite side of the road was a broken-down lorry with a man looking under the bonnet. Immediately I felt the officer in the front of the car stiffen and noticed him anxiously looking to both sides across the fields as if there was danger present. I suddenly realised that they had not yet returned to normal reactions although they were back home. It would take time. In Northern Ireland a broken-down lorry next to traffic lights could be an IRA ambush. Here in North Yorkshire it was something we would not normally take much notice of.

At Topcliffe, after drinks at the officers' mess, we went for lunch in the junior NCOs' mess. Here we met again Stephen's mates Mark (known as Splash, as his surname is Fountain) who had been with him when he was shot, and his mate Tommy from Newcastle. We also met their wives for the first time. Many of his comrades came up to us to say hello and then went back to sit with their friends or wives. It was strange; Stephen had been in the regiment for four years but before the funeral we had only met a couple of his mates. They all went their separate ways at weekends, Stephen sometimes going to their home towns to experience the nightlife. These were the young men who had known Stephen as Astro from his nickname Asterix, rhyming with Restorick. They had faced the dangers of duty in south Armagh with him, the dust and mud of manocuvres on Salisbury Plain, and shared the fun of a few free days at the end of their overseas exercises. It was many years since the regiment had lost a soldier, and I know all the officers and men were affected by Stephen's death.

We were presented with a beautiful statuette of a gunner in full ceremonial dress and blowing a bugle. It is jokingly known in the regiment as a chocolate soldier as it is dark brown. It now has pride of place next to Stephen's portrait.

I wondered if Stephen's mates questioned my composure. Did they think I didn't care about him if I could chat to them and not burst into tears? The emotional strain of realising he was no longer with his mates built up inside me and I left the room for a little while. The wife of one of his mates came out and I told her I cared so much about him and missed him so much. The tears flowed and she could see, as all the others could see when I returned to the room, that I was hurting inside even though I didn't always show it. It is strange how much one can be suffering and yet the tears don't always come.

Stephen's regiment founded two trophies awarded annually in his memory, the first for the winning team of the leadership competition, competed for by the lance-bombardier and bombardier leadership course; and the second for the junior NCO who has shown the most promise. This second trophy is presented annually on Sidi Rezegh Battery Day, 21 November, when his battery remember their comrades who died in that battle during the North African campaign of the Second World War.

After a while it was time to leave Topcliffe and Stephen's friends. We knew that their lives would move on; only those who had been closest to him would keep in touch, and in time even they would stop. Perhaps only we would always remember him. Only on Remembrance Day would his mates think of Astro and the time they were at Bessbrook.

Not only had it been the memorial service that day, it had also been Stephen's granddad's eighty-seventh birthday. In a way, the security forces presented him with a birthday present, for that evening we learned that a number of men had been arrested in south Armagh in possession of a Barrett .50 bolt action gun, the same type used to shoot Stephen. A week later, forty-year-old Bernard Martin McGinn, from Castleblayney, just south of the border in the Republic, appeared in Banbridge magistrates' court charged with Stephen's murder. He was also charged with the murders of Gilbert Johnston, a former member of the Ulster Defence Regiment (UDR) in August 1978 and Lance-Bombardier Paul Andrew Garrett in December 1993. I had written to Paul Garrett's parents with my condolences immediately after his death, although I did not know them personally. I felt a link as he was in the Artillery like Stephen, who had returned safely from his first tour in Northern Ireland earlier that year. But there was also a connection in his name as my maiden name was Garratt and I have two nephews called Paul Garratt and Andrew Garratt. This was the only time I had written to the bereaved parents of a soldier, and now a man had been charged with the murders of both him and my son.

A month later we paid another visit to Northern Ireland. It was the early May bank holiday weekend, and we were visiting Northern Ireland as ordinary people would, not shielded by the army. Gary Trew, our host, could not have done more for us. We met his wife and children and enjoyed a meal at the home of some of his friends who have a mixed-religion marriage, learning of the problems they had faced. One couple had moved to England for a while to get away from sectarian attitudes to their marriage. We also enjoyed a meal with Margaret, a member of a Belfast group called Women Together for Peace. She had written to us after Stephen's death saying, 'We are an organisation which has been working hard for peace and reconciliation for twenty-seven years. We were devastated on hearing of your son's murder. .... The courage and compassion you have shown whilst enduring such grief is like a candle burning in the darkness. It has given some hope to those in Northern Ireland who have peace in our hearts and who join with you in mourning the tragic loss of your son.' During our visit we went to the Bushmills distillery and the Giant's Causeway, that line of volcanic rocks linking Northern Ireland under the sea with Scotland. It is to me symbolic of the rock-hard determination of the descendants of those people who came to Ulster from Scotland in the early seventeenth century to remain British.

On the Sunday, Gary took us on a bus tour of Belfast, taking in not only the imposing buildings in the centre but also a 'tour of the troubles' through Protestant and Catholic inner-city residential areas. First we went through the Protestant Shankill area, down the Shankill Road and up the Crumlin Road past the prison and courthouse. Here we saw the red-white-and-blue-painted kerbstones, while hanging from flagpoles and lampposts were the Union Jack and the flag of Ulster – a red hand and gold crown at the centre of the red cross of Saint George on a white background. On the gable-end walls of terraces were expertly painted murals, an art form which was born during the troubles. In this Protestant area the Red Hand of Ulster, William of Orange on his white charger, and gun-carrying, black-clad paramilitary figures featured in many murals.

There were not only murals but also political slogans. One said something like 'Remember Carson and 1912'. At that time I had no idea who Carson was, but I now know – as any Protestant would have told me straight away – that he led opposition in the north of Ireland to the inclusion in Home Rule of the six northern counties of Londonderry, Antrim, Down, Armagh, Fermanagh and Tyrone. In 1912, 100,000 men attended a rally in Belfast against Home Rule for the whole of Ireland, marching past a saluting base on which stood the leader of the British Conservative Party, then in opposition. The following year a quarter of a million of Carson's followers signed a Covenant, some, it is said, in their own blood, against the British Liberal government's plans to introduce Home Rule. This opposition within the six northern counties led to the organisation of the original Ulster Volunteer Force, armed with guns bought from Germany.

From the Shankill area our bus crossed the river to another Protestant area, on the Newtownards Road, with similar signs of territorial allegiance and murals. Surrounded by this area was a Catholic one, the Short Strand. Here the green, white and orange Irish tricolour flew in place of Union Jacks, marking this out as a Catholic/nationalist area. Travelling around these areas we saw the high 'peace walls', built to keep the Catholic and Protestant communities apart and prevent easy access for men of violence from the other community. Many of the connecting roads between these neighbouring areas were blocked by such walls. The few roads still open had huge gates, manned by soldiers and RUC officers, which could be closed in times of trouble. On our tour we saw many of the grey, armour-plated vehicles that carry soldiers and policemen while now and then an army helicopter clattered overhead.

The bus returned to the city side of the river, going along the Protestant Sandy Row towards the town centre. From there the bus normally goes along the Catholic Falls Road, but the tour was cut short because a commemoration was being held there. When we returned to Gary's car he asked if we wanted to go down the Falls. We were a bit wary but decided that if the police at the end of the Falls Road let us through then we'd go. We really felt we were going into enemy territory when the policeman waved us through. Most people were making their way home from the commemoration. The men and women might almost have been returning from a football match as they walked away from the park where it had been held. Yet they had been attending a ceremony to mark the deaths of the ten IRA hunger strikers at the Maze prison in 1981, and in particular Bobby Sands, the first to die, who was elected MP during his hunger strike. The strike's aim was to gain recognition that imprisoned republicans were political prisoners and had the right to wear their own clothes. The hunger strike became a battle of wills between the IRA and the Conservative prime minister, Margaret Thatcher. But it was finally called off on 3 October by the

IRA and this was swiftly followed by the British government granting permission for the prisoners to wear their own clothes. At the Sinn Féin ard fheis (annual conference) later that month their Director of Publicity, Danny Morrison, reflecting on their election success during the hunger strike, spoke of taking power in Ireland with a ballot box in one hand and an Armalite in the other. They made this their strategy until the 1994 ceasefire, returning to it in February 1996 when the ceasefire broke down. Our visit was only a few days after the UK general election on 1 May, and passing Sinn Féin's headquarters I saw a number of election posters saying 'Vote Sinn Féin, Vote for Peace'. I felt it was now time for Sinn Féin to deliver on its slogans.

We passed a heavily defended RUC station protected by its high metal walls and guard tower. This really was a fort in Indian territory, with Irish tricolours and tricolour-painted kerbstones everywhere. The murals here were about the hunger strikers, about freeing the 'political prisoners', and about the fight for a united Ireland. The slogan 'Brits Out' was scrawled on many walls. I thought, I wish we could get out but what would follow if we did?

We came to the park where the commemoration had been held. Most of the people had left now, and Gary asked if we would like to go in and have a look. I don't know if he is braver than us or if he was just teasing, but there was no way we were going to leave the car. We had no idea how these people would react if they discovered we were the parents of a British soldier, and we weren't going to give them the chance to find out. So we stayed in the car. My thoughts went back to the television pictures of the two soldiers who in March 1988 had driven into a road along which crowds were following the coffin of a man killed when a loyalist gunman fired on mourners at an IRA funeral at nearby Milltown cemetery. The soldiers had been dragged from their car, taken away, brutally beaten and then murdered. I remembered the picture of a Catholic priest praying over one of the bodies. He was Father Alex Reid and those events led him to work behind the scenes with nationalists and republicans to progress the peace process. With these thoughts we drove away from this republican area and out of Belfast. It had certainly been an experience for us.

The main reason for our visit was an invitation from Ardnaveigh High School in Antrim, to the north of Belfast, to plant a flowering cherry tree there in memory not only of Stephen but of all the victims of violence in Northern Ireland. The school is attended mainly by Protestant children, whilst the school next door, St Malachy's, is Catholic. Close links had been formed between the two schools, especially by Gary Trew, the religious education teacher at Ardnaveigh, and Seamus McNeill, his opposite number at St Malachy's at that time. In recognition of their work, Gary and Seamus were awarded the President Clinton Peace Prize in 1997, its first year. Later that year they travelled to the USA, where they were presented with the prize by President Clinton himself at the White House.

Gary came into our lives a few days after Stephen's death when he phoned to tell me of a poem about Stephen's murder written by one of his girl pupils. I was very moved by the simple but heartfelt poem, especially when he told me that Shauna, the girl who had written it, was the daughter of a mixed-religion marriage. The poem was called 'Death of an Innocent Soldier':

> I have to confess I felt really sick
> When I heard of the murder of Stephen Restorick
> A young soldier from England, here to help bring peace
> Brought home to his family, sadly deceased.
> Due to our troubles and bitter strife
> This young vibrant soldier had to give up his life.
> His parents appealed 'Let our son's sacrifice be the last.'
> Why can't we let our bitterness be a thing of the past?
> He was one of many who tried to help our land
> But his life was cut short by an evil hand.
> Don't let Stephen's death be another one forgotten
> Open your eyes, to see how our country is rotten.
> We're disgracing our country, we're hurting ourselves.
> It's time we stopped hiding behind these violent shells.
> The people of Ireland need to come forward and say
> The fighting must stop, not tomorrow but today.

Gary told me that they had built a path between the two schools so the children didn't have to walk along the busy road. It was through Gary that we were invited to plant the tree beside this path, which had been dubbed the Peace Path. He told me about Education for Mutual Understanding (EMU), a compulsory part of the curriculum, through which pupils learn about the traditions and beliefs of both communities. He also told me about Corrymeela, a Christian community on the north Antrim coast, where as part of the EMU course he and Seamus took groups of children from both their schools to learn about each other, accept their differences, and see the many things they have in common.

On the day of the dedication, Tuesday, 6 May, we woke to snow showers which were covering with a white blanket the fields around the farmhouse where we were staying. But by the time Gary's car arrived the snow was being melted by rain. With Gary was Shauna, a pretty, blonde fifteen-year-old. It was only a few minutes' drive to Ardnaveigh. Gary introduced us to the headmaster and some of the staff, then took us into a couple of the classrooms to meet the children. We tried to encourage them to talk about how the violence had affected them, but they were very reluctant, which was understandable in the circumstances. They learn to be careful and not voice their views immediately to strangers.

St Malachy's School was still on holiday after the May Day weekend so we were not able to visit its classrooms. However, the headmaster, a teacher and some of the pupils from the girls' football team attended. (Gary had told us about this football team, which comprised pupils from both schools, and the invitation they had received from Celtic football club to visit Glasgow. In Northern Ireland, as in Glasgow, Celtic is supported by Catholics whilst Protestants support Rangers. However, both teams were now trying to overcome these divisions. Gary said the girls needed a football strip for the visit so we made a donation from Stephen's memorial fund to buy it. I joked to Gary that Stephen would approve as long as the shorts were short enough.)

The dedication of the tree was simple. The headmaster, Gary and a few pupils from both schools stood in a group as I read out an extract from the book *Pig in the Middle: The Army in Northern Ireland 1969–84* by

Desmond Hamill, which I had bought only a week before Stephen was killed. In the extract a secondary schoolboy in Belfast recalled:

> On Monday 12 February, it started to snow. It had snowed all night and in the morning it had settled on the roofs and trees and cars. At morning break we had a snowball fight with the prefects and the masters. We rolled Big Ted, the woodwork master, in the snow. Every day there is a running battle between us and the Protestant school across the road. The police escort the Protestants and the Army escort us down the road. But that day I saw a very strange thing. Catholics and Protestants, police and soldiers, were all snowballing each other happily. But I don't think I'll see anything like it again.

After the light snow showers earlier that morning, the extract seemed very appropriate. I pointed out that the event happened in 1973, the year Stephen was born, and on 12 February, the day he died. It showed that things had improved in that time – schoolchildren no longer had to be escorted to school by soldiers and policemen. There was still a lot more to be done, however, and the children at Ardnaveigh and St Malachy's were showing the way forward.

We placed soil around the already planted tree, photos were taken, and a reporter interviewed us. I told him that we felt it was important for young people to understand one another and that we hoped that in the future people would be able to come to an agreement to settle their differences without guns and bombs. I also said it was encouraging to see what was happening here and that one of the things Stephen told us was that he was sorry that while he was in Northern Ireland he had only been able to meet people going through the checkpoint. I added that we had met Shauna's parents the previous evening and discovered we had a lot in common. Her mother's name was Rita and her father was a welder like John, and they also had a son who had been in the army. Shauna told the reporter, 'In a way I thought I knew how they felt because when my brother was serving in the Gulf War, there was a time when I didn't know if he was alive or not. I just thought it would help them if I wrote a poem and sent it to them. I also wanted to let them know that most young people don't want violence and killings, but peace.'

Perhaps even during this visit we were protected, for we certainly only met people with moderate views and not hostile to ourselves or to the British in general. But I believe they are the majority who just get on with their lives, not wanting to become involved and fearful of speaking out against the gunmen, which is totally understandable when it could place your family at risk. It takes a person with very strong ideas of right and wrong, against humanity in general or friends and neighbours, to speak out if his family would suffer as a result of his actions. Most people, understandably, keep their heads down, get on with their everyday lives, and hope the evil does not touch their family. When it comes to election time they mainly vote along traditional lines, the Catholic/nationalist vote going to the Social Democratic and Labour Party (SDLP), the Catholic/republican vote to Sinn Féin, with Protestants mainly voting for one of the unionist parties. It is very hard for cross-community parties such as the Alliance Party and the recently formed Women's Coalition to reach across the divide.

Following our visit, we founded a Stephen Restorick Prize at each of the two Antrim schools, to be awarded for a project on peace, whether a poem or an essay. The first year the winning entry at Ardnaveigh High School was by a girl pupil and contained her poem 'Peace Is All Around Us'. The simple sentiments spoke for so many young people. The first verse was:

> Peace is all around us, if you would just let it happen.
> Ardnaveigh and St Malachy's will help us if you let them.
> No more bombings or shootings, wouldn't that be a
> lovely world.
> It's up to our generation to make sure that things change now.

If all schools could provide such a good example as Ardnaveigh High and St Malachy's there was hope for the future. But in some cases the influence of family and neighbourhood could destroy all their good work. Nevertheless, we left with feelings of hope and of admiration for the young people of Northern Ireland who live in such difficult times.

Another cherry tree was planted in Stephen's memory later that month, in England, and the ceremony brought together people from England, Northern Ireland and the Republic. It was suggested by another person touched by Stephen's death, Tim Coglan, the owner of Braunston Marina on the Grand Union Canal, near Daventry in Northamptonshire, which is twinned with Ireland's Grand Canal. We had not known Tim previously nor had we ever been to Braunston, but we were delighted with his idea of planting a cherry tree in Stephen's memory at the marina on the day of the marina show, 24 May. Tim had an Irish Catholic father and a Scottish Presbyterian mother, a parentage reflecting both sides of the community in Northern Ireland. The theme of the show was building bridges, and in his press release Tim said:

> I believe I have felt more acutely than some the bitter divide that finds its fullest expression in Northern Ireland. In my own small way, I have been trying to assist the movement towards peace by building bridges between the boaters of both countries – getting people together, and moving forward from suspicion and mistrust to understanding and friendship. Lance-Bombardier Restorick's tragic death underlines how elusive that peace remains.

Senator Pat Magner of Seanad Éireann, who had responsibility for Irish waterways, planted the tree with us as a symbol of hope in the midst of suffering and as a message of his sympathy to our family. He said that as the father of two sons of similar age to Stephen, he was only too aware of our grief, and also of the suffering the conflict had caused to thousands of other families in Britain and Ireland. He was determined to do all in his power to hasten the search for peace, which would take root in a just and lasting settlement to the present conflict, and said that the violence must cease. A minute's silence was observed for all the families bereaved by the conflict in Northern Ireland. The ceremony was also attended by the Right Reverend Ian Cundy, Bishop of Peterborough, and Father Jerry White, the Catholic priest of Daventry, who comes from Ireland. We were very pleased that Stephen's friends Colin, Lisa and Asa were able to be with us that day.

These events, together with the seats that were later placed in Stephen's memory, help us to hope that people will remember Stephen in the future and the sacrifice he made.

7

WHEN MOURNING COMES

IN MAY 1997 A RESEARCHER ON *World in Action*, the Granada ITV series, phoned me about a programme they were planning to make about the effect of recent deaths in Northern Ireland on the families concerned. They intended to interview Diane Hamill, whose brother Robert had died recently after a beating by a gang of Protestant youths in the centre of Portadown, and Marie Wicks, whose son Ivan was attacked in Londonderry by a gang of Catholic youths. The researcher asked if I would be willing to take part. The programme would be filmed in Belfast but all expenses would be paid. Never having been in front of a TV camera before, except for the interviews immediately after Stephen's death, I was nervous about taking part in the programme. I am not very good at expressing myself, so wondered if I would find the right words. My feelings and beliefs about the situation in Northern Ireland were one thing, but actually putting them into words was something else. At the same time, though, I wanted to take part in such a balanced programme which focused attention on the deteriorating situation in Northern Ireland caused by the sectarian killings at that time. There was also the question of whether to allow the media to pry into my private life and thoughts. Sometimes, some might say often, the press is intrusive. But after Stephen's death we decided we wanted to speak about him and the situation over there, so we never felt the media interest as intrusive; instead we welcomed it. This programme would enable me to put into words my thoughts and feelings over the three months since Stephen's death.

The following Wednesday I stepped out of a chauffeur-driven car at Birmingham airport for the flight to Belfast. Collecting my tickets from the airline desk I discovered they were Business Class, entitling me to wait in the Business Class lounge. However, I knew I would feel out of place there so checked I could wait in the main departure lounge instead. For the first time in my life I travelled 'first class', and I was amused to learn that during the short flight Business Class passengers were served with a full tray meal whereas the other passengers only had biscuits and tea or coffee.

Arriving at Belfast City airport I took a taxi to the hotel I had been booked into, the Culloden, and was amazed to see a five-star sign beside the entrance. I wasn't used to such luxury. My room was in fact a suite with views over Belfast Lough to the hills beyond. After unpacking and freshening up, I waited in the lounge for the producer and assistant producer who would join me after that day's filming. They were a little late so I ordered a gin and tonic and was surprised to find that a small plate of canapés and a bowl of cheese sticks accompanied the drink. These were delicious, and when I ordered another drink more arrived with it. I was beginning to think I wouldn't need any dinner. Eventually the TV team arrived, apologising for their lateness, and briefly they went over their plans. We then adjourned for dinner. The producer ordered a French wine but after we had all tasted it he decided it was corked. I, in my ignorance, just thought it sweeter than other French wines – it certainly didn't taste terrible. However, the wine waiter agreed immediately that it was corked and fetched a new bottle. This tasted drier and I joked about drinking too much cheap wine recently as the original had seemed OK to me!

After dinner, we were all tired so we parted until the next day; I was told that a taxi would take me to the studio when they were ready to start filming. I couldn't get to sleep so I read for a while before falling asleep. I awoke, as normal during these early days after Stephen's death, to the dawn chorus. I turned over, fell asleep again and suddenly woke with a start at half past eight. In a mad panic in case breakfast finished at

9 o'clock, I hurriedly showered, washed my hair, dressed and put on my makeup. I raced downstairs only to find that I needn't have rushed – breakfast was served for another hour, though there was still the worry that the taxi might arrive before I was ready.

After breakfast I waited in the gardens enjoying the warmth of the sun. Suddenly I felt terribly sad. To me this hotel was luxury. But many of the people staying there were probably used to such surroundings and were on business expenses. I felt bitter at the personal cost of luxury that I couldn't otherwise have afforded. Bitter that many there wouldn't even remember Stephen's name and how he had died protecting them. Suddenly the tears flowed and I realised at that moment I felt bitter against the whole world. How could it continue as if nothing had happened, how could life go on as normal and the sun keep shining? I was not feeling sorry for myself. I was feeling sorry for Stephen. Could people forget him so easily, did they not care? Looking back, I realise that life had to go on normally around me, otherwise I myself could not stay in that hotel or fly by that airline. But this was only three months after Stephen's death.

Late that morning the taxi arrived and we drove through Belfast to the Laganside Studios. I was led into a large dark room and came face to face with a huge black-and-white picture of Stephen in his camouflage uniform. I sat on the cottage-style settee, beside a small round table on which stood a brass framed colour photo of Stephen and a flower arrangement. A small microphone was clipped onto my jacket and the sound level was tested. In front of me was a camera on a semicircle of tracking set into the floor. The camera moved along the track filming me from different angles while a static camera did close-ups. Powerful spotlights blazed down on me, making the studio feel as hot as an oven. A large fan stood nearby but it was noisy so couldn't be used during filming. I got hotter and hotter as the filming went on and on. The problem was that the interviewer wouldn't appear in the finished programme so I had to remember to incorporate the question into my answer. Sometimes I forgot to do this, so we had to repeat it. The filming began with questions about Stephen's birth, the special closeness I felt with him, and some anecdotes about when he was a child. I was asked how his childhood in England differed from growing up in Northern Ireland and my feelings when he joined the army and left home.

I spoke about the dangers he faced in Northern Ireland: it had always been at the back of my mind but I couldn't think of it all the time. This was his second tour at Bessbrook so I hadn't been as worried as before when he was straight out of initial training. He knew what he was doing, and although the IRA ceasefire had broken in February 1996, things still seemed relatively quiet over there. But you never know what is going to happen, and you never imagine that it will be your own family that is affected.

I outlined my lack of knowledge about Northern Ireland before Stephen was posted there, which I said was usual for English people. In response to a question about the political views Stephen and I had on Northern Ireland, I said that Stephen, as a soldier, had to carry out the policies of the government in power at the time. He had no choice about that just as he had no choice about going to Northern Ireland. He certainly tried to carry out his duties in a manner sympathetic to both communities as was shown by Lorraine McElroy, who had told how he always smiled at her and talked to her two sons. It was sad that Stephen only met people briefly and artificially at the checkpoints, never socially. Turning to my political views I said: 'I don't think it relevant what my political views are on the situation in Northern Ireland. One way I look at it is that there are two and a half years to go to the turn of the century and that people have that time to try and make a difference or are they still going to be killing one another into the next century? Haven't enough tears and blood been shed already? I had a thought this morning. There is that big lake in the middle of Northern Ireland, Lough Neagh, and I thought, have enough tears and blood got to be spilt to fill that lough before people say enough is enough and we're going to sit down and talk and try to get an agreement that we're all happy with and not resort to violence. Stephen's death has made me more aware of the enormous sadness that both communities have suffered through violence and it can't go on, a solution has to be found.' I also said that because children go to separate schools, they are denied the everyday opportunities to get to know one another.

That helps to continue the problem, especially if they live in a predominantly Protestant or Catholic town or estate. Due to history, different political views and aspirations had become entwined with religion which in turn helps to continue these divisions.

In response to a question about whether Stephen had ever discussed the situation in Northern Ireland with us, I said that he hadn't. I didn't know whether he thought that we, like most people in England, wouldn't be interested, or whether he just wanted to forget about it when he came home. It must be very difficult for soldiers: they could be killed at any moment, whilst people back home don't want to know about the situation in Northern Ireland and probably don't care whether it is part of the United Kingdom or not.

Then came the difficult part. I had to say exactly what had happened to Stephen on the night he was killed and to us after we were told. It was almost as if the knife was twisting in my heart as I struggled to get out the words. I was soon wiping away the tears. I was asked why I thought Stephen's death was so significant in Northern Ireland. I said that it was mainly because he was the first soldier killed since the IRA ceasefire had broken down. Also I believed that people saw him not just as a soldier but as a young man and, more than that, one who had been smiling as he talked to a Catholic mother when he was shot. The hundreds of cards we received from Catholics in the north and the south of Ireland showed that his death had meant something to them.

In response to a question about who I thought was to blame for Stephen's death, I replied: 'The person to blame was the person who pulled the trigger. He aimed purposefully at Stephen, seeing him only as a British soldier, not as a young man. To me it was cowardly that he shot Stephen in the back, it wasn't as if it was a face-to-face shoot-out. He took aim and shot Stephen in the back without any chance. The gunman probably believed he had political views which justified that act. But the way I see it, no political aim justifies murder. This is especially so when the victims are civilians. Although I saw Stephen's murder as cowardly, to me it was far more cowardly to place a bomb in an area where you know civilians are, then walk away and leave that bomb to go off and not to personally see the consequences, not to see the suffering that it causes. At least Stephen was a soldier who some people would see as a legitimate target, a representative of their enemy, the British government. Stephen saw his role in Northern Ireland as stopping that type of person moving arms and explosives around Northern Ireland which they could use to shoot and bomb innocent people, and if it meant taking out men of violence who did that, then that was what he had to do.'

My reply had concentrated on the individual person, so now I was asked what my feelings were about the fact that a whole organisation was behind Stephen's murder. I said, 'I feel angry about what's happened. I'd see that as my main emotion, and sadness. In a way it's strange, whether it's just my personality or just the way I'm reacting at the moment, I can't feel bitter personally towards the man who killed Stephen. I just feel anger that the whole situation has been allowed to go on and on and more and more people have died and still people are so entrenched in their views, and they won't give an inch, and how many more people have to die before both sides give a little?' Perhaps I still hadn't looked at the fact of it being an organisation, my feelings still concentrating on the man himself.

What about vengeance, revenge? 'No, I thought about vengeance. Wanting revenge just ties you up in knots inside, makes you bitter. To me, the fact that somebody has been arrested and charged with Stephen's murder has helped a lot; whether he is found guilty remains to be seen. Vengeance leads to what is happening now in Northern Ireland. A Catholic is killed so a Protestant is killed in retaliation, so then a Catholic is killed and it goes on and on. You just can't do that, that's why laws were brought in, so that it is taken out of personal hands and you have to prove you have the right person for committing a murder. Innocent people aren't killed because somebody of the opposite religion has been killed. You find the person who did the crime and they are punished, not innocent people. So there is no room for vengeance.'

What about forgiveness? I replied that at one time, when we were hoping that the ceasefire would be introduced at Easter, I said that if it meant that no more people would be killed in Northern Ireland, I would be willing to meet Stephen's killer face to face and tell him I forgave him. There would be no court case. But that was only if there was a ceasefire, no more people were killed and positive talks took place. (I doubted at the time that the man would ever be arrested, so the court case was hypothetical.) Now I was not so sure I could forgive the person. I could in a little way perhaps understand the way his mind was working, I could understand his aims. I could to some extent sympathise with and understand those aims, but I couldn't agree with the way he went about trying to achieve those aims.

The interviewer asked what did I see as a way forward, what about a united Ireland? I said that the people of Northern Ireland had to decide how they want to go forward, what sort of political set-up they want, what sort of link they want with the Republic, if any. They had to do that by sitting down and taking part in serious talks, probably hold a referendum to get a clear view of what people feel. It wasn't for me to say how I thought things should go forward or what sort of political solution they should have in the future, it was for the people in Northern Ireland to really think about it and talk about it and stop shooting one another in the meantime. I added that if someone had asked me ten years earlier what three things in the world I thought impossible, I would have said Russia would no longer be communist, that the Berlin Wall would come down, and that Nelson Mandela would be president of South Africa. All of these had come about. Now there was a fourth 'impossibility': that there would be no more fighting over what the future in Northern Ireland was going to be, and that instead the people would be able to sit down and sanely discuss the way forward together.

The interviewer said I must feel a lot of bitterness that, of all the soldiers in Northern Ireland, it was my son on this occasion who was killed – it could have been any one of those soldiers at the checkpoint but it was my son. I told her that when I was told of Stephen's death I said over and over again, 'Why Stephen, why?' There are so many soldiers in Northern Ireland, why was it he who was in the wrong place at the wrong time? But at the same time, especially around the time of the funeral, our feelings were so intense and painful, that we wouldn't have wanted any other parents to go through our suffering. So it was two-edged. Why Stephen? but at the same time we didn't want any other parents to go through that as it just tears your heart out.

The next question had me in tears again: 'What does life seem like now without him?' I said, 'It's empty. Some days are better than others. I wake up in the morning and I don't want to get up. Everything seems pointless. Although I've another son and a husband, who I love dearly, it still seems pointless and every morning I hear the dawn chorus like I used to when he was first born and I had to get up and feed him at five or six o'clock. And every morning I see that bullet go through him. And then I see him lying in his coffin. Nobody should have to see their own son in a coffin. But I needed to see him. I had to say goodbye to him.'

After I had dried my tears, the interviewer asked, 'How do you remember Stephen and how would you like everyone else to remember him?' I said that to me Stephen will always be the madcap, happy, good-looking young man. A young man who in a photo taken on his passing-out day reminds people of the film star Tom Cruise. I would like everyone else to remember him as a young man who came to Northern Ireland to try to prevent violence, to stop innocent people being killed, and in doing so lost his own life and was denied the possibility of marrying, having children and the normal life other people take for granted. 'Did I feel cheated that there would be none of these?' I accepted when Stephen joined the army that if he married and had children I would see little of them because he would live away from us, but I never thought there wouldn't even be a marriage, that we wouldn't have grandchildren through Stephen. Yes, I did feel cheated. I also felt angry.

Again the tears came when I was asked what I missed about Stephen most. 'I miss his fun, his laughter, his arms around me giving me a hug, just him being there. Also I miss his friends coming round, because you also lose his friends when he's gone, they stop coming. There's just a whole gap in our lives that has opened up. It's like a light has gone out in the world, he was full of fun and full of the joys of life.'

In response to the next question I said I felt Stephen's death had brought my husband and I closer together; we were clinging to each other and fortunate that when one of us was tearful the other one wasn't, so we had been able to comfort each other, but there was still a huge hole in our lives. Also it was very difficult for our son Mark: he'd always had a 'little' brother around, and now he was like an only child and felt very lost. Even though the boys were very different in personality, they were there for each other. It had been hard to talk about what had happened within the family because you think you'll upset the other person if you talk about it. Also, other people think, that's life, you've got to get on with life. Referring to the differing reactions to Stephen's death in Peterborough compared to Northern Ireland, I said Peterborough is a large place, a new town which in my view didn't as yet have a close community spirit. Our neighbours and work colleagues were very shocked by Stephen's death, but others in Peterborough just noted the local connection. There seemed to be a far greater effect in Ireland, north and south. I spoke of the hundreds of cards from Protestants and Catholics and their condemnation of the IRA.

Finally I said, 'Some people might say I shouldn't be in front of a camera talking like this about what's happened but I want people to see not just what's happened to me but what's happened to the mothers, the sisters, the daughters, the fathers, the brothers of all those that have been killed through the violence in Northern Ireland. This is what it does and it's got to stop. How many more people have to go through this before people will sit down and talk and give a little on each side?'

On a lighter note, at the end of the interview I had to learn two separate introductions, one of which would be chosen to start the programme. However, I soon realised that I could never be an actress: there was no prompt board to look at, and if I remembered one part of the short introduction I forgot or stumbled over another part. I certainly admire actors who can learn a whole play.

I was exhausted emotionally and physically. I had opened my heart to the camera in that interview. Although the interviewer was sensitive, the questions themselves had at times been searching and painful. The programme has a large audience in Britain and Northern Ireland. I hoped it would have the desired effect on the viewing audience. At the end of filming, I was introduced to Marie Wicks, who told me she was torn between being there or with her son Ivan at the hospital as the attack had left him frightened of being on his own. He was still in a bad way, but fortunately a couple of days later he was allowed home to complete his recovery. The other person taking part in the programme, Dianne Hamill, had been interviewed the previous day so unfortunately I did not meet her.

As it wasn't yet time to leave for the airport, I went for a walk. Finding a park, I sat on a seat in the sunshine near the children's play area. I was so emotionally drained by the interview and everything felt raw again. I missed Stephen so much and I cried and cried. Fortunately there was hardly anyone else in the park. After a while I returned to the studio, and a taxi took me to the airport for my return flight to Birmingham. I arrived home exhausted at about 9 o'clock.

The programme was broadcast the following Monday, 19 May, and was called 'When Mourning Comes'. It was half an hour long, and my three hours of interview had been edited to ten minutes. However, it was a very moving programme showing the human cost of the violence. On 3 June I sent copies of the video with a covering letter to Tony Blair the new prime minister, the Secretary of State for Northern Ireland Dr Marjorie Mowlam, David Trimble, leader of the Ulster Unionist Party (UUP), the Reverend Ian Paisley, leader of the Democratic Unionist Party (DUP), John Hume, leader of the SDLP, and Gerry Adams, president of Sinn Féin. I hoped that even if my words had no effect on the politicians at least the raw emotions shown on the video of three women who had suffered recently might hit a nerve and speak for all the other women who had suffered over the past thirty years as a result of the violence in Northern Ireland.

8

DRUMCREE

SOME TIME AFTER STEPHEN'S DEATH I was told his regiment had been sent to Northern Ireland in September 1996, instead of April 1997 as planned, in consequence of the deteriorating security situation following the Orange Order march at Drumcree on the outskirts of Portadown, County Armagh, in July 1996. This made me feel that, to whatever small extent, Stephen's presence at that checkpoint in Bessbrook on 12 February 1997 was due not only to IRA violence but also to what I, as an outsider, saw as intransigence on the part of a section of the Protestant community.

I had seen TV coverage of the July 1996 stand-off on the Garvaghy Road between the Orange Order marchers and the RUC and soldiers. Although the Orange leadership repudiates terrorism, loyalist groups such as the Loyalist Volunteer Force (LVF) played a key role in stoking up the confrontation at Drumcree. Demonstrators blocked off the main road to Belfast International Airport and seventy other roads in Northern Ireland, including routes into ferry ports. Loyalists set fire to cars and a van close to the centre of Portadown as Orangemen blocked off the town centre. The culmination was the murder in Lurgan by loyalist gunmen of Michael McGoldrick, a 31-year-old Catholic who had recently graduated from Queen's University, Belfast. He left a wife five months pregnant and a seven-year-old daughter. His family issued a statement saying, 'The politicians must bear some responsibility for this.

Fire-and-brimstone speeches have featured too much in this situation. Their loose talk has cost this young fellow his life.'

At the end of five days' tense confrontation, the Orangemen in their black suits, bowler hats and orange sashes were allowed to march down the Garvaghy Road. Sir Hugh Annesley, the RUC Chief Constable, said that in order to prevent serious loyalist violence he had reversed his original decision to reroute the march. As the Orangemen marched, the RUC officers who had faced them across the barbed wire now protected them from the angry nationalist residents shouting abuse at them. In the violence that immediately followed, RUC officers fired plastic bullets at angry nationalist demonstrators in Belfast and Strabane as they vented their anger. In Armagh, fourteen buses were set on fire, the post office was petrol-bombed, and seven vehicles were destroyed. In Londonderry 500 people marched on the police station. Gerry Adams said the RUC's actions would make it more difficult to convince the IRA to restore the ceasefire. Cardinal Cahal Daly, the Roman Catholic primate of All Ireland, accused the RUC of capitulating in the face of violence.

Many people have said that the problem with Northern Ireland is that people not only know their history, they live it every day. Seventeenth-century events such as the Battle of the Boyne and the Siege of Londonderry are still sharp in people's memories. We never studied Irish history in my schooldays, it was all Empire and European history. To understand the present at Drumcree, it is necessary to know a little of Ireland's past. The roots of the situation lie in English rule in Ireland since the twelfth century which, due to the Reformation, from the mid-sixteenth century became Protestant rule of mainly Catholic Ireland. Following the flight from Ulster of the Irish earls of Tyrone and Tyrconnell at the beginning of the seventeenth century, Scottish Protestants settled in the Ards peninsula. Derry was settled with Protestants by companies of the City of London, hence the name Londonderry. During that century most Catholic landowners were removed from their land, and laws were passed against the Catholic religion. In the 1840s came the potato famine: a million died and many people forced by hunger to leave Ireland for England or America. In 1912 the Orange Order, the largest Protestant organisation, played a leading role in the mobilisation of loyalists under Edward Carson against the British government's plans for Irish Home Rule. Home Rule was put in abeyance during the 1914–18 war, but the 1916 Easter uprising in Dublin and the execution of its leaders led in 1918 to a war of independence. But in 1921 instead of Home Rule for the whole of Ireland, the British government partitioned the six northern counties to create Northern Ireland and Protestant rule for its Catholic minority. However, the constitution of the Irish Republic would still lay claim to those six counties.

The campaign for Catholic civil rights and the Protestant backlash to it led to thirty years of conflict from 1969, and the re-emergence of the IRA. This produced in the unionist community a siege mentality and an even stronger need than previously to show their allegiance to the British crown. Meanwhile it led republicans to seek an end to British rule and a united Ireland through force and through their political arm Sinn Féin, while nationalists sought to achieve it politically. By the 1990s unionists believed that decades of IRA violence and intimidation had encouraged the British government to consider the possibility of leaving Northern Ireland with as much dignity as possible. This belief was increased after the Anglo-Irish agreement of 1985, under which the Dublin government, as a guardian of Catholic interests, gained the right to be consulted on the routes of marches. Unionists saw this as evidence of ambitions on the part of the Republic to take an ever-growing role in the administration of the north.

Drumcree is one short word for an event held annually on the first Sunday in July which had become the touch paper for a powder keg. Members of the Orange Order parade from their Orange hall in Portadown to the little church at Drumcree for a service commemorating those killed at the Battle of the Somme. Afterwards they do not return by the same route but via the Garvaghy Road in Portadown – through a nationalist housing estate. Their fathers and forefathers marched down the Garvaghy Road and they believe they should do so in the future. It used to be a country road and when housing estates were built on it they were mixed, but now they are mainly Catholic with a small Protestant estate at the end nearest the town. The Orangemen see the route as traditional and their march as exercising their right 'to walk the Queen's highway'. The nationalist community sees the march as triumphalist and wants it routed away from there. But the Orange Order believe nationalist opposition to their marches is orchestrated by Sinn Féin, who encouraged the formation of residents' committees to make previously uncontentious parades a focus of discontent, and the order refuses to talk to the leader of the Garvaghy Road Residents' Coalition on account of his conviction for paramilitary activities. Nationalists would respond that the 'marching season' has always been a fearful time for them (therefore many go on holiday then). Portadown is a predominantly Protestant town and stands beside the River Bann which divides Protestant eastern Ulster from the overwhelmingly Catholic west. The Orange Order has always played an important part in the social life of the area, and its members feel their traditions are being eroded. Over the past ten years, of the ten routes they used to follow through Portadown past Catholic communities, only this one remains. The march has become a last stand for its members, especially those in Portadown itself, as the order was founded nearby in 1795.

In England we have no equivalent to these marches. The only parallel I could see was that if the National Front tried to march through inner-city Asian communities, they would be banned by the local police as inciting violence. Nationalists see Orange Order marches as expressing Protestant supremacy: Orange Order bands play tunes offensive to Catholics and some members make insulting gestures. The marchers believe that their tradition and right override nationalist objections. In 1995 Ian Paisley, leader of the DUP, was reported to have told the Orangemen, 'Win this battle or all is lost, it is a matter of life or death, freedom or slavery.' By 1997 virtually every senior unionist politician was a member of the Orange Order and it had 120 seats on the Ulster Unionist Council, the governing body of the largest unionist party, the UUP. The success of David Trimble and Ian Paisley in 1995 in securing the right of Portadown's Orangemen to walk their traditional route was seen as a rare victory and helped Trimble become leader of the UUP soon afterwards.

Following Stephen's death, I paid far more attention to events in

Northern Ireland and particularly to Drumcree. In 1997 the march was to be held on 6 July, just two months after the British general election in which Labour had defeated the Conservative Party. It really was a testing time for the new government, and both the Orange Order marchers and the Sinn Féin-led Garvaghy Road Residents' Coalition were eager to test them to the brink. This time the final decision on whether the parade went ahead would rest not with the new Chief Constable, Ronnie Flanagan, but with Mo Mowlam, the new Secretary of State. Elections in the Republic the previous month had brought Fianna Fáil to power, and the new taoiseach, Bertie Ahern, urged Tony Blair not to allow the march to go ahead. Once again Gerry Adams implied that the march decision would be seen by the republican movement as a test of British intentions which could affect a possible IRA ceasefire.

Words flew back and forth between the two sides. Joel Patton, the leader of the hardline Spirit of Drumcree faction within the Orange Order, said the issue at stake was whether the Protestant culture and identity would be allowed to survive. He said, 'Republicans want to control areas where there is a nationalist majority. If we concede that then large swathes of Ulster will *de facto* no longer be part of the United Kingdom.' Brendan McKenna, the leader of the Garvaghy Road Residents' Coalition, said, 'The Drumcree march is all about who runs the Six Counties. Is it the British government or is it the Orangemen?'

I was very worried about the situation. I knew that I had no influence over these people, yet I still felt compelled to let them know my feelings on what I saw as their intransigence. So, on 1 July I wrote to David Trimble, Ian Paisley, John Hume, Denis Watson (the County Armagh grand master of the Orange Order) and Brendan McKenna. I said it was exactly five months since Stephen was murdered by the IRA and I asked them, as representatives of the two communities, to use their influence to make the coming marching season a peaceful one. I questioned why Orange Order marches go through Catholic areas and whether tradition was a justifiable reason for providing the potential for ill feeling in the Catholic community. Couldn't the tradition be maintained but through Protestant areas only? In the rest of the UK such marches through areas of differing beliefs or cultures would be seen as inciting the population of those areas to violence and would be banned. They all had children, perhaps grandchildren – did they want their lives to be endangered because men of violence found justification for their acts through the discord in communities caused by their actions? I finished the letter by saying I didn't have a politician's gift of words but my words were sincere. They were not biased towards one community but written in love and understanding for the vast majority of people who feel powerless when events wreck whatever progress has been made towards peace and understanding between the communities, and reignite age-old misconceptions and hatreds.

David Trimble replied, enclosing a copy of a letter sent the previous month to Garvaghy Road residents by the Armagh County Orange Order grand master and grand chaplain. The order's letter stated that the parade was in commemoration of the Battle of the Somme and that attacks on the parade were seen as a denial of the marchers' civil liberties and as an attack on their religion. The letter acknowledged the objections raised by the nationalist community and said that only members of Portadown District would parade; they would walk four abreast so that the march would pass in less than five minutes, and only hymn music common to both traditions would be played. The letter said the order hoped 'the vast majority of the people of Portadown will work together in a new spirit of tolerance to defeat extremists who want confrontation this summer. As a matter of principle, we cannot be involved in talks with convicted terrorists because of what they have inflicted on our community. But we do want to listen to all those within the community who want to promote harmony and mutual respect among the people of Portadown and welcome constructive comments.' Trimble said that the response had been disappointing.

On 2 July senior Orangemen were said to be furious at comments by the taoiseach urging Mo Mowlam to block the march. In response to the taoiseach's intervention, the banned Loyalist Volunteer Force, which is based in Portadown, issued a statement warning that 'If the Orange parade does not go down the Garvaghy Road on Sunday, the Irish government may expect civilians to be killed in the Irish Republic. Once and for all, the Irish government has to learn that they will not interfere with the internal affairs of Northern Ireland. This threat will be carried out immediately if the parade is banned.' Ken Maginnis, the UUP security spokesman, said, 'Much of the aggravation which has led to this declaration by the LVF lies at the feet of Bertie Ahern, whose utterances imply a threat against the unionist tradition.' Security forces expected the IRA to carry out a terrorist attack if the march was forced down the Garvaghy Road.

As the tension mounted, I seriously considered going there myself. I didn't care about the danger, I wanted to stand before the marchers as they confronted the soldiers and police. I wanted to ask them why. Why couldn't they stand in the other person's shoes and see that to Catholics their marches brought fear of violence from loyalist hangers-on? Why couldn't they compromise and return from Drumcree church the way they came? Why did they cause a situation which each year seemed to destroy the work done over the previous months to try to bring Catholics and Protestants together? I admit sometimes I wondered why my son died protecting these Orange Order members who seemed so intransigent. However, as the day of the march drew nearer and the tension rose, my husband and elder brother eventually persuaded me not to go to Drumcree in view of the anticipated violence.

Mo Mowlam held 'proximity' talks with representatives of the two sides but to no avail. A possible compromise by which the Orange Order would have the legal right to parade but would do so at another time was backed by the order's grand master but was rejected by the local Portadown lodge. Police and army Land-Rovers were drawn up on the route leading from Drumcree church, and thousands of police and soldiers were moved into the area.

Yet again the decision was taken to allow the march to go ahead. In the early hours of the 6th, scores of police Land-Rovers and army vehicles swept into the Catholic area. Residents tried to block the road but RUC officers moved quickly through, clearing people out of the way. Masked youths chanted 'IRA' as rocks, bottles and petrol bombs rained down on the police and troops. By 6 o'clock the area had been sealed.

Mo Mowlam had promised no last-minute decision and that residents would be told personally whether the parade would proceed.

She failed to do so, fearing it would allow time for more petrol bombs to be stockpiled, endangering RUC lives. Immediately before the parade she said, 'This is a sad day for all of us. Many will be angered by what has occurred, but I appeal to them and to all with influence in their communities to exercise restraint.' She said that the vast majority of Northern Ireland people had hoped for a sensible accommodation, adding, 'I have done my utmost to achieve that, as has the Chief Constable. But where there is intransigence on both sides that becomes impossible.' She defended her decision, which she described as regrettable, and said she understood the anger of nationalists. She said that most people accepted the current way of dealing with disputes was inadequate, and legislation would be introduced later in the year to deal with the marching issue.

Shortly before 11 o'clock the parade left Portadown centre towards Drumcree church where the Reverend John Pickering told the Orangemen over the public address system, 'The eyes of the world are on you at this time. We want to follow the path of peace and justice for all.' After the service the Orangemen began their march from the church towards the Garvaghy Road. The Garvaghy residents began to gather again, women and children banging bin lids and biscuit tins on the concrete. Bottles were thrown at the Orangemen as they marched silently down the road, and children made two-fingered gestures. As the Orangemen marched out of the area, the nationalist crowd chanted 'No ceasefire now.' Lumps of concrete, stones and timber were thrown at the RUC. Masked figures fired ball bearings from catapults as more masonry was pelted at the soldiers. As the rioters advanced along the road, police fired plastic bullets. In the following thirty-six hours there were attacks on security forces, petrol bombings and hijackings; 80 people were injured including 46 police.

Now came the recriminations. Ronnie Flanagan, the new Chief Constable, faced criticism. He admitted that the threat of paramilitary violence had dictated his decision. He said that intelligence reports left police in no doubt that Catholics would have been murdered by loyalist terrorists had the Orange parade been banned, and that paramilitaries on both sides wanted to exploit the issue and that would have meant violence against the Catholic community. Meanwhile Bertie Ahern, who had called for the parade to be banned or rerouted, said he was deeply disappointed at the outcome. Gerry Adams claimed nationalist rights had been trampled in the interests of unionist domination. Martin McGuinness, Sinn Féin MP for Mid Ulster, said Tony Blair's government and Mo Mowlam had failed their first big test miserably. Brendan McKenna, the Garvaghy Road Residents' Coalition leader, said that Mo Mowlam had betrayed nationalists and should resign. Unionists attacked her for taking the decision on the grounds not of the Orange Order's right to march but of the threat of loyalist violence. For a time, the fact that she had allowed the parade through seriously damaged Mo Mowlam's credibility in the eyes of nationalists. Immediately after the march, she herself said, 'It will take time to rebuild trust and confidence in the nationalist community.' She added that she expected the Orange Order to reconsider marching plans for the coming weekend. 'There can and should be no triumphalism.'

In preparation for further trouble during the marches to be held in Belfast and Londonderry the following weekend, an extra infantry battalion was sent to Northern Ireland. Everything seemed on a knife edge. The Irish National Liberation Army (INLA), a hardline republican group, had said it was prepared to kill Orangemen throughout Northern Ireland if parades through contentious areas went ahead. However, at a meeting in Belfast on 10 July, county grand masters and their deputies were told by the RUC Chief Constable that postponement and voluntary rerouting of parades on the Twlefth would have to take place. The Orange Order agreed to this.

So the tension eased. Hardline unionists reacted angrily, however, Ian Paisley saying that the concession was a surrender on the same scale as the Munich agreement between Chamberlain and Hitler. He and Robert McCartney, leader of the United Kingdom Unionist Party (UKUP), called for unionists to withdraw from political talks. In response, Gerry Adams said, 'It would be immensely negative if unionists withdrew from talks. Without dialogue all dreadful sorts of things are possible. With dialogue everything positive and good and equal and just and peaceful is possible.' (In fact, Sinn Féin was not in the talks at that time as there was no IRA ceasefire.) David Trimble said, 'It really is a very sad state of affairs when the security forces can no longer guarantee the safety of people walking down a road.' Joel Patton called on members to ignore the cancellations and to turn out anyway to show their anger at the decision.

The final word went to Mo Mowlam who said of the Orangemen's agreement to voluntary rerouting, 'This is the beginning – we have a long, long way to go. But it's a good symbol of what we have got to do. An accommodation is not a dirty word where human lives are at stake.' It had all been a baptism of fire for her. Although she had been shadow Northern Ireland Secretary in opposition, Labour had only been in power for two months. One veteran Belfast political journalist was quoted in the *Daily Telegraph* as saying, 'She has a tendency to think well of everyone and has perhaps not realised how poisoned Northern Ireland is. I don't think she quite understands the depth of hatred and sectarian division.'

On 14 July I wrote to Robert Saulters, David Trimble, and Ian Paisley praising the Orange Order's decision on the Twelfth marches, saying it showed the Orange Order in a better light than the disastrous decision to go ahead with the Drumcree march. Traditions could be maintained but in a way that did not cause ill feeling within other communities which when fanned by extremists could lead to violence. It was not a sign of weakness to take account of the wishes of the Catholic community; indeed, doing so took the wind out of the sails of the extremists and helped the more moderate section within the Catholic community. At least that was how it seemed to me. I said that despite Stephen's murder, or perhaps because of it, I cared about what happened to the people of Northern Ireland. I ended my letter by saying I hoped they would help Mo Mowlam progress the peace process and that the decisions they had taken that weekend could only put even more pressure on the IRA to call a ceasefire. They would find public opinion very negative if they did not do so. (The ceasefire was declared on 19 July.)

The following year, Drumcree became a stand-off again, but this time the government had the force of law on its side. During the intervening months a Parades Commission had been set up to decide on such contentious marches, with the power to ban a march if there hadn't been consultation between the Orange Order and the nationalist community or if it was felt that a march would lead to violence. Legislation was passed to uphold the Parades Commission's decisions. The commission contained representatives from both political viewpoints but the Orange Order refused to recognise it or accept its decisions. In 1998 the commission banned the Drumcree march. This time the march became a test not only of the government but of the whole Stormont peace agreement, reached three months previously, which the Orange Order opposed.

Army reinforcements and RUC officers were drafted in again and huge barricades and ditches were built, cutting the Garvaghy Road off from Drumcree church. After their service, the Orangemen camped on a field beside the church, saying they would stay there for a year if necessary. Their cause was a magnet for those wanting to cause violence, not only at Drumcree itself but throughout the north. The RUC manning the barricade on the Garvaghy Road were attacked with bricks, wooden stakes and fireworks, and shots were fired at them on two occasions. Three police officers were injured in a blast bomb attack. The following night, police fired plastic bullets as the crowd tried to break through the barricade.

In the early hours of 12 July there was an arson attack on the home of the Quinn family in Ballymoney, which caused the deaths of three of their four young sons – Richard, Mark and Jason, aged ten, nine and eight. They lived on a Protestant estate with their Catholic mother who had raised them Protestant. It was not known for sure whether their deaths were linked with Drumcree, but a split began to develop between the hardliners and Orange Order moderates. Support dwindled for the hardliners at Drumcree. It did so especially after the County Armagh Grand Chaplain, William Bingham, said that no road was worth a life. He was heckled by Joel Patton, but a 'representative group of Orange Order chaplains' backed his stance, expressed revulsion at the murder, and extended sympathy to the parents and family of the boys. Their statement continued, 'We express to the Roman Catholic community in Northern Ireland our deep sorrow that so many of them have been intimidated out of their homes, and that several of their churches have been burned. The spectacle of people attempting to injure or murder policemen and soldiers in Portadown, and the intimidation of police families, has brought shame on the Protestant community, and all the more since it has been done under the guise of supporting the Portadown district's protest against the determination of the Parades Commission. We pray that the day may quickly come when all the people of Northern Ireland will be enabled to live in mutual respect and neighbourly harmony, each fulfilling the Redeemer's command to love your neighbour as yourself.' However, David Jones, the Orange Order's Portadown district spokesman, dismissed the statement saying they were not a representative group of chaplains. The Church of Ireland Primate, Dr Robin Eames, also called on the Orangemen and their supporters to end their protest and let those who were negotiating a solution get on with the job.

The Orange Order never did get to march down Garvaghy Road in 1998. Its presence on the hill beside Drumcree church dwindled, though there were rallies in Portadown centre in the months that followed, some of which led to violence including the death of a Catholic RUC constable. In 1999 the Parades Commission again banned the order from marching down the Garvaghy Road as it still would not meet with the residents' group. Nor did meetings with the prime minister achieve any compromise. In early June another death was linked to the stand-off when in Portadown the 59-year-old Protestant wife of a Catholic was killed by a pipe bomb thrown through her window by loyalists. Again in July the road was barricaded by the army and rows of barbed wire were strung out across the fields between the church and the Catholic housing estate. But this time there seemed to be a change of tactic by the Portadown Orange Order, which dispersed after their church service with no violence from loyalist hangers-on. The Spirit of Drumcree group was conspicuously absent and Joel Patton had even spoken about leaving Northern Ireland.

For many people, three small white coffins will always stand as an indictment of the hardline attitudes of the Portadown lodge of the Orange Order and the loyalist violence this can lead to. I felt that the words on a card sent to John and I after Stepehen's death by 'a Catholic mother of eight' from Portadown applied to those Quinn boys too: 'Your son's murder was so unnecessary, please forgive us all. Father forgive them for they know not what they do.'

9

CEASEFIRE AND TALKS

IN THE MONTHS IMMEDIATELY AFTER Stephen's death my sole aim was to do all I could to get the ceasefire reinstated so that inclusive talks could take place. The only way I could do this, as an ordinary mother, was to write to the politicians concerned. As mentioned previously, immediately after Stephen's death I wrote letters to President Clinton, to the prime minister and leaders of the Labour and Liberal Democratic parties, to all Northern Ireland MPs and the president of Sinn Féin, Gerry Adams, and to the taoiseach begging them to do all they could to get the peace process moving again and bring about an IRA ceasefire. These letters were written in the depths of grief; perhaps some of the hopes and sentiments in them were naïve, but they were what I felt and hoped at the time.

I wrote to Gerry Adams again on the day the IRA claimed responsibility for Stephen's death, saying we had presumed the IRA was responsible but did not believe they would admit such a cowardly act as shooting a man in the back, and wounding a young Catholic mother in the process. (This statement alone unfortunately shows how the depths of my grief made me forget the atrocities carried out by both sides in Northern Ireland.) I ended the letter, 'Although Stephen was a British soldier, he never harmed any Irish person and was carrying out duties aimed at preventing violence and keeping the peace. We do not believe you yourself condone the bombing of civilians. We do not know if you have any children but we do ask you to imagine how we feel at the cutting short of a happy, fun-loving life. Sadly many other parents of civilians and soldiers have suffered similarly during the troubles. People say that you are associated with the IRA. If you want to show that this is not true, please distance yourself from these IRA hardliners and call a ceasefire thereby marginalising these men of violence. By so doing, Sinn Féin would have a stronger case to be admitted to the peace talks.' We received a handwritten letter from Gerry Adams expressing his regret at Stephen's death, though at the same time outlining his political views as a republican.

But the violence did not stop. The general election on 1 May brought the Labour Party to power and hope of new impetus in the Northern Ireland situation. The new government had a huge majority unlike the outgoing Conservative government, which had been totally dependent on the support of unionist MPs in the last couple of years. There were now two Sinn Féin MPs, Gerry Adams and Martin McGuinness, but they maintained their party's policy of not taking their seats in the House of Commons. A new government, however, did not mean a totally different view of the future for Northern Ireland. The new prime minister, Tony Blair, said, 'None of us, even the youngest, is likely to see Northern Ireland as anything but part of the United Kingdom.' As expected, this comment was not to Sinn Féin's liking. However, at the same time, I remembered Margaret Thatcher's comment that she did not expect to see a British woman prime minister in her lifetime. Yet she became that first woman prime minister.

My next letter was written on 3 June when I sent a copy of the *World in Action* video 'When Mourning Comes' to Tony Blair, Mo Mowlam, David Trimble (the leader of the UUP), Ian Paisley (the leader of the DUP), John Hume (the leader of the SDLP) and Gerry Adams. On 14 July I wrote to them again, enclosing a copy of the *Sunday Times* Magazine article by Michael Bilton about Stephen's death. I said: 'I know Stephen is only one of many and being a soldier put him in the front line, but at the same time I do believe that if all parties had put more effort during the ceasefire into the peace talks instead of putting up impossible barriers then progress might have been made and Stephen might still be alive today. I continue to support the efforts of the Prime Minister and Mo Mowlam in trying to reach a settlement and I hope you will take note of my lone voice. Many people in England do not care what happens in Northern Ireland as long as the violence does not come over here. However, despite Stephen's murder, or perhaps because of it, I do care and want the people of Northern Ireland to live in peace.'

The prime minister said a genuine and unequivocal ceasefire would have to have been in place for six weeks before Sinn Féin could take a place at the multi-party negotiations due to start in September, whose target was agreement on Northern Ireland's future governance. President Clinton said the United States would work to nurture this 'moment of great possibility'. The USA provided the chairman of the talks, Senator George Mitchell, a bespectacled, mild-mannered senior politician. His personal aura of calm was to be sorely tried over the coming months. Participants in the talks would have to accept the Mitchell Principles of commitment to democratic and peaceful means to resolve political issues, a renunciation of violence and the threat of violence, and a willingness to abide by any final agreement. Whatever agreement was achieved would be ratified by a referendum and would be dependent upon total disarmament by participants within a set time and overseen by an independent commission.

Despite the problems at Drumcree, suddenly events seemed to be moving, and the rerouting or cancelling of contentious marches on 12 July seemed to help the process. Six days later, Gerry Adams hinted that a ceasefire was imminent, saying he had approached the IRA because of a commitment by the British and Irish governments to inclusive peace talks. The onus, he said, was on the two governments, and in particular on the British government, to demonstrate the political will necessary. The ceasefire would present a historic challenge to the unionist leaders because it would involve fundamental and thoroughgoing political and constitutional change – there would be no return to unionist domination. He added that as an Irish republican party, Sinn Féin would be guided by its aim of a united Ireland, would be seeking an end to British rule in Ireland, and would be asserting the constitutional rights of Irish nationalists. In any agreed political settlement, he added, the political allegiance of northern nationalists must be given expression and effect. Adams had earlier issued a joint statement with John Hume saying that the last ceasefire had been wasted and that their principal concern was that that dreadful mistake should not be repeated, a view I totally agreed with.

The fact was that a stalemate had been reached: the British army could not defeat the IRA without using means that would alienate the Catholic population, and the IRA was convinced that further violence in the near future would yield no political reward. The IRA announced that the restoration of the 1994 ceasefire would come into force at noon on Sunday, 20 July. Tony Blair spoke of 'a new mood of hope for peace and lasting political settlement in Northern Ireland', though Ken Maginnis, the UUP security spokesman, remained sceptical of the IRA's long-term intentions. So, the ceasefire that we had hoped to see by Easter finally came in July. During those few months, IRA gunmen had killed two policemen in Lurgan and had injured a policeman and a policewoman in separate incidents, though Stephen was the only British soldier killed in 1997.

Unionists, like the previous government, were still demanding that terrorist weapons must be surrendered before talks, whereas the Mitchell Principles stated that arms 'decommissioning' should occur *during* talks. The unionists saw another sell-out, claiming Blair had given concessions in return for a ceasefire that could again be broken. David Trimble said his party would not go along with the peace strategy if the government was not prepared to insist that IRA arms be surrendered as talks got under way. Ken Maginnis said the IRA had used the previous ceasefire to recruit and train personnel and buy weapons. Peter Robinson, deputy leader of the hardline DUP, accused Blair of caving in to the IRA and warned that another phoney ceasefire was on the cards. He added, 'No one in Northern Ireland should be fooled into believing this is a real ceasefire. ... It is a concession to violence.' Mitchel McLaughlin of Sinn Féin said the IRA would not give up any arms until the last day of the talks. He added, 'What will remove all weapons is a democratic political settlement arrived at by those with a mandate.'

Unionists remained sceptical of the new ceasefire. Many people thought the announcement did not mean that the IRA struggle for a united Ireland was over, merely that for the time being it was taking a different form. Everyone realised that Trimble was in a difficult situation. If he led his party into talks, he would be accused of negotiating with terrorists, but if he led his party away from talks and they collapsed, Sinn Féin and the IRA would say he had not given peace a chance. However, it seemed to me that not admitting Sinn Féin to the talks would defeat the very purpose for which the talks were intended. The DUP and the UKUP said they would not join in talks with Sinn Féin while it remained part of the IRA. The DUP questioned whether unionists would accept an agreement that included Sinn Féin but not those unionists loyal to Ian Paisley.

Talks between the main political parties in Northern Ireland were due to commence at Stormont on the outskirts of Belfast on 15 September 1997. I decided to be there to emphasise the personal aspect, the loss of life that had occurred over the years, and that more lives could be lost if a compromise agreement was not reached. I planned to hold a vigil outside the talks building.

I flew to Belfast on 11 September and was met at the airport by a member of a Belfast peace group at whose house I would be staying. The following day I went into Belfast to the Peace People's offices for a TV interview. This group arose from a family tragedy on 10 August 1976. Anne Maguire was walking with her four children in Andersonstown, a Catholic area of Belfast, when a car crashed into them. Its driver, a seventeen-year-old IRA gunman, Danny Lennon, had been shot dead by British soldiers pursuing him in army vehicles. Mrs Maguire was badly injured and three of her children were killed. In response, her sister Mairead Corrigan and Betty Williams founded the group and held peace marches in Belfast and Dublin, which Protestants also joined. Mairead and Betty became international figures and won the Nobel Peace Prize but the Peace People had become less influential by the end of 1977, although the group has continued its work for peace. Betty Williams left Northern Ireland but Mairead is still involved with the Peace People.

At the Peace People's offices I was interviewed by a TV crew about my visit to Northern Ireland and the fact that I would be attending a Youth for Peace rally the following day outside the main gates to Stormont. The crew also interviewed Lyndsey, the seventeen-year-old student organising the rally, who had invited me to attend it. After the interview, I was given a lift to the Glengall Street headquarters of the UUP where I had an appointment with David Trimble and Jeffrey Donaldson, the UUP MP for Lagan Valley. I had phoned a few days previously and they had agreed to see me. At this time, I didn't find this unusual – I expected politicians to agree to meet me – but looking back now I find it amazing. Perhaps some thought they could win me over to their point of view, realising that my views were sought by the media. (I sometimes doubt if I had any influence at all on people in Northern Ireland; yet I was driven by a need to become involved and as John F. Kennedy said, 'One man can make a difference but everyone should try.' If I only made them stop and think about the future they wanted for their children and grandchildren, my efforts were worth it.) Trimble, the bespectacled former law lecturer, outlined his party's position on the situation in general and on the talks. Now and then Donaldson would take over, and as he spoke, I couldn't help thinking how very young he looked, despite being in his thirties. The UUP had been in power continuously from the partition of Ireland until the imposition of direct rule. There was a huge sea of change to be faced in the future if any peace agreement was to be reached and made to work. I wondered if these politicians were willing to make those changes, to share power with nationalists. I couldn't help feeling that most of them hadn't suffered bereavement within their own immediate family as a result of the conflict. If they had, perhaps they would have tried harder to end the current situation, to acknowledge the injustices felt by the Catholics. Perhaps those were just the simple thoughts of an English mother. But even the Progressive Unionist Party (PUP) and the Ulster Democratic Party (UDP), with their links to working-class loyalist paramilitaries, felt they had done the fighting for better-off unionists, not benefiting themselves. They, like the IRA, felt they had reached a stalemate, that the violence could not continue and that they should try a different way – at least for the present. I felt rather despondent as I left the UUP redbrick headquarters with its closed-circuit cameras guarding the entrance. There seemed to be no leeway in their stance, and if the talks collapsed, the situation could return to the days when cameras would not be enough to protect them.

The following morning it rained heavily, dampening the spirits of the young organisers of the Youth for Peace rally, especially as very few young people joined them. Apathy is as strong in Northern Ireland as in England. Those with extreme views on both sides can mobilise their supporters, but it is very difficult to capture the interest of those with more moderate views. Never having been to Stormont before, I took this opportunity to check exactly where the talks building was and that I would be standing near the entrance. We drove quite a distance through the grounds, past the imposing white parliament building, where we met a police car which escorted us to the front of the talks building. Now I knew I would be close to the action on Monday, I returned to the centre of Belfast. As I wandered through the crowds on these shop-lined streets, it seemed strange to me that life was so normal. Many soldiers and policemen had paid a high price for this normality and I hoped people would remember that and not take it for granted.

Yet another TV interview was scheduled for Sunday morning. I spoke about my visit and what I hoped to achieve. I find interviews daunting. Although I know what I hope to achieve, I have great difficulty in putting it into words. I certainly wouldn't make a politician – they always seem to have a pat answer or are able to totally sidestep the question. We were filming in a park, and towards the end of the interview the crew wanted to film me looking at the children's playground. I watched two young boys being pushed on a tyre swing by their father and it brought back memories of Mark and Stephen when little. After getting the boys' father's agreement, the crew filmed me watching them and chatting to their father about his boys and mine. I hoped that by the time these young boys were adults Northern Ireland would be a happier, safer place, the bombs and shootings just something their father remembered.

That afternoon my friend took me on a tour of County Armagh. We drove first to Armagh city and visited the two cathedrals crowning two hills within the city. The Catholic one, built in the nineteenth century, is very ornate, while the Protestant one is older and more austere. From there we drove through Keady and Cullyhanna to Crossmaglen — a heartland of republican support. The initials IRA in wood decorated roadside poles, declaring the allegiance of this area. The square at the centre of Crossmaglen, overshadowed by the heavily fortified army/RUC base, seemed so normal with its flower borders. I had imagined this square, where so many British soldiers had been killed by the IRA, to be totally bare. I felt it should be a symbol of the coldness of heart of those men who had taken so many young lives and of the depths of sadness suffered by the families they left behind. It was an eerie feeling travelling through this countryside which was at once so beautiful with its green, rolling hills, and yet so threatening. I wondered what the locals would feel about my presence. Would I be welcomed like any other visitor, or would their feelings change if they discovered I was the mother of a British soldier, even a dead one? Would the women have compassion, seeing me as a mother who like some of them had lost a son in the conflict? Or would the inbuilt hatred of British rule prevent them seeing our common bond? Would that hatred be turned on me personally just as it had cost my son his life? With these thoughts weighing on my mind we drove on towards Newry and the road back to Belfast. So ended my tour of 'bandit country', where during the troubles soldiers travelled by helicopter, removing the opportunity for the IRA to blow up their vehicles with landmines buried beneath or beside the roads, and army foot patrols were always aware that IRA snipers operated in the area.

On the day of my vigil I awoke to the sound of a high wind buffeting nearby trees and rain lashing down: not the best weather to stand outside. So I wore jeans and Stephen's waterproof anorak. Inside this, with the hood up, I was totally dry, if unfashionable. I took up my position outside the fence surrounding the building and stood there for a while waiting for the politicians to arrive. Two newspaper reporters came over to interview me. The notepad of one was so wet that she couldn't write on it; the other couldn't get her pen to work. That's a good start, I thought. The TV interviewer of the previous day came over to take me to the press compound inside the fence to do a live interview. As I walked through the compound, suddenly all the other reporters surrounded me. They poked their microphones in my face and shouted over one another with their questions. The microphones and tape recorders kept obscuring the cameraman's view so instead of being live, the TV interview had to be recorded and edited later. From there I was taken to a radio car for a live interview on Radio 5. Events had worked in my favour. Because the Ulster Unionists refused to attend that day, the reporters had no one to interview after the other politicians had entered the building so they turned their attention to me.

After the interview I intended to take up my vigil again in the still-pouring rain. However, a press officer from the talks building invited me inside for a cup of tea. He could see I was soaked and probably realised I was feeling rather shattered after all the interviews. After a very refreshing cup of tea, totally to my surprise, he asked if I would like to meet some of those taking part in the talks. I was introduced to former Senator George Mitchell himself and to his two co-chairmen: Harri Holkeri, a former Finnish prime minister, and General John de Chastelain, the former chief of the Canadian Defence Forces. I showed them the photo of Stephen smiling broadly in his camouflage uniform. It was on the film in his camera when he died. The regiment developed the film and gave me this photo when we visited Bessbrook in March. It is the most beautiful picture of him, and it gave me strength in the dark days that followed his death. I always feel he is near me when I look at that photo.

Leaving Senator Mitchell's office, I was taken to the Secretary of State's office. I am a great admirer of Mo Mowlam, the first woman to hold this post. She is very natural, down-to-earth, and has the personal touch so often lacking in politicians. Many of her predecessors had seemed very formal and distant, not at all what is needed to reach out to the ordinary people of Northern Ireland. One of her characteristics is hugging people: one comedian joked that she'd dumbfounded the strait-laced unionist politicians as even their wives didn't hug them! Kicking her shoes off, she sat beside me and over coffee asked how I was coping with Stephen's death. She said she was hopeful about the talks but it was hard work trying to make all the parties agree. After I left Mo's office, I was shown the chamber where the talks would be held and then was introduced to representatives of the Alliance Party and the Women's Coalition. I was very impressed by the Women's Coalition and I believe that women should be more prominent in politics in Northern Ireland, not just at local council level but as members of parliament. Politics has in the past been very much a male preserve in Northern Ireland. While I was in the Women's Coalition office, John Hume, leader of the SDLP, walked in and we were introduced. I was delighted to meet the man who has worked so hard over the past thirty years for a peaceful solution to the Northern Ireland problem and who stood firm against the outcry over his talks with Gerry Adams through which he hoped to move Sinn Féin towards political discussion and away from violence.

The one party at the talks I had not met was Sinn Féin. The pain of Stephen's death was still too raw for me to meet men who were linked to the IRA. Also I might be seen as betraying Stephen and all the others who had died through IRA violence if I met Sinn Féin representatives. Coming down the staircase from the Women's Coalition office, I almost froze as I saw Martin McGuinness coming up the stairs towards me. There was no escape. As we passed, he said, 'Good morning, Mrs Restorick.' Automatically, I said, 'Good morning,' surprised that he knew my name, though looking back I realise Sinn Féin would have quickly learned that I was in the building.

When I took up my vigil again the rain had stopped and the sun had forced its way through the clouds. If any symbol was needed of what people hoped could be achieved through the talks, that ray of sunshine after the wind and rain provided it. Beside me was a group of Women Together members who were cutting out paper doves for people to write their hopes for the future on and hang on the fence around the building. Another group was campaigning for an independent investigation into Bloody Sunday, when thirteen unarmed Catholic men were killed by the British army during rioting after a banned nationalist civil rights march in Londonderry in January 1972. They introduced themselves and I told them I believed the army had made a mistake under pressure that day and there should be an inquiry. A little later, Gerry Adams came over to the group and spoke to them for a while. I was standing near them but fortunately he didn't approach me – I wouldn't have known what to say to him. I could have said that I was pleased his party was taking part in the talks and hoped they would be willing to find a compromise settlement as enough people had died for the Sinn Féin aim of a united Ireland. But I expect I'd have just frozen and mumbled something useless. He moved on to a family group campaigning on behalf of the man arrested for the murder of two policemen in Lurgan three months previously. This man was later released without charges being brought against him. Feeling I had done all I could that day to put my views across to the numerous reporters, I left about mid-afternoon. It really was up to the politicians now, and I hoped they would negotiate seriously and not waste time on matters of procedure. Unfortunately, the DUP, led by Ian Paisley, refused to have any involvement with the talks.

The following day my friend drove me to Enniskillen to meet Marie Wilson's mother, Joan. Marie was the twenty-year-old nurse killed in the town with ten other people by the IRA bomb on Remembrance Day 1987. Joan had written to me soon after Stephen's death, enclosing a copy of the book about Marie's death. It had helped me a lot to read how another family who had lost a very special person had coped with it. We met Joan at a hotel just outside Enniskillen and she took us to her home where we enjoyed her delicious home-made soup and cakes and talked of Marie and Stephen. Joan is a lovely person who shows no bitterness about the terrible tragedies that she has gone through. Marie's death led her father Gordon to become involved in the search for peace. In recognition he was nominated as a senator in southern Ireland, a great honour for a Protestant from the north. He met representatives of the IRA to ask them to call a ceasefire but was unsuccessful. This meeting led to personal attacks by some unionist politicians which Joan and he found very hurtful.

After lunch Joan drove us to the war memorial, showing us where Gordon and Marie had been standing when the bomb went off, burying them under the rubble of a collapsed wall. It was only now, ten years later, that the bombed buildings were to be cleared; for all that time Joan had had a daily reminder of that terrible event. She always points out, however, that they were not the only family to suffer bereavement and some are still suffering from their injuries – one man is still in a coma. From the war memorial we went to the cemetery, Joan showing us where Marie and Gordon rest together. Nearby is the grave of Peter, Joan and Gordon's son, who was killed in a car crash leaving a wife and young children. Joan drove us back to the hotel outside Enniskillen and said goodbye. I shall always be grateful for her reaching out to us after Stephen's death. My mind went back to the evening when John, Mark and I were travelling to the chapel of rest to see Stephen, and I thought of Marie and Colin Parry's son, Tim. To me they seemed to form a kind of trinity: a young woman from Northern Ireland, an English boy, and Stephen who was a young man but also a soldier. I had now met Joan and in the months ahead I was to meet Colin Parry.

After the long drive back to my friend's house, I busied myself packing my suitcase for the flight home. It had been a busy, long weekend and I was shattered. I thought of all the politicians I had met and hoped that Stephen and I would stay in their memories as they took part in the talks. I wanted us to be symbolic of all those who had lost their lives or been bereaved through the violence and a warning of what could happen again if the politicians didn't listen to each other's viewpoints and wouldn't compromise.

A few days later the UUP joined the talks. Because of the refusal of the DUP and UKUP to take part, the UUP needed the support within the talks of either the PUP, led by David Ervine, or the UDP, led by Gary McMichael. Although throughout the talks Trimble refused to talk directly to Sinn Féin representatives, saying he wouldn't talk to terrorists, he had no such reservations about PUP and UDP representatives, despite their links with loyalist paramilitaries, and in January 1998 he visited UVF and UDA prisoners in the Maze prison to discuss the talks process.

The talks continued with both the UDP and Sinn Féin expelled for short periods because of paramilitary involvement in a number of murders in January and February 1998. It seemed more than coincidental to me that Sinn Féin's expulsion should have taken place when the talks moved to Dublin for a week. By using a gun easily traceable to the Provisionals, it seemed to me, an IRA splinter group had manipulated events to cause embarrassment to Fianna Fáil, the party in government in the Republic. They were supposedly supportive of aspirations for a united Ireland, having been formed by Eamon de Valera. Perhaps with silent approval from the two governments, Sinn Féin started a legal action in the Dublin courts to delay their expulsion, which finally took place when the talks had returned to Belfast and lasted for a couple of weeks. The talks continued, week after week, with little sign of any progress. But at least they were still talking, and as long as they talked there was hope.

IO

CORRYMEELA

Corrymeela is people of all ages and Christian
traditions who, individually and together, are
committed to the healing of social, religious and
political divisions that exist in Northern Ireland
and throughout the world.

STEPPING FROM THE MINIBUS that had brought me from Belfast, I
read the above words on the sign at the entrance to the Corrymeela centre, near Ballycastle on the north Antrim coast. Those
few words outline the community's aims which have guided its work
over the past thirty years. I had come in early August 1997, shortly after
the IRA declared a new ceasefire, as a volunteer to see the work carried
out by one of the groups dedicated to peace and reconciliation in
Northern Ireland. I had first heard about Corrymeela from Gary Trew,
the teacher I had met on my visit to schools in Antrim. He told me of
the school groups he brings to Corrymeela as part of the Education for
Mutual Understanding programme in schools. Wanting to learn more,
I wrote to the community for some literature and the video about their
work. After watching the video, I noticed that the credits stated that it
was produced through a donation by the parents of Gunner Miles
Amos who was killed in Northern Ireland in 1989. I realised that as a

gunner he too was in the Royal Artillery. Wanting to know more about him, I phoned army headquarters in Northern Ireland. After checking the facts, a man at the other end said, 'He was killed when his vehicle went over a landmine just outside Londonderry. He was eighteen years old. Another soldier was killed with him, Lance-Bombardier Stephen Cummins.' When I heard those last two words a shiver went down my back, for his parents had written to us immediately after our Stephen's death saying their Stephen was a few months older than ours when he was killed. I discovered this connection with Corrymeela four months after Stephen's death, and I felt that someone was telling me I was dealing with my loss the right way, that others had travelled this path of grief before me, and they too had turned from hatred and bitterness.

The Corrymeela community was founded by Ray Davey in 1965. He had been a YMCA field worker during the Second World War and was captured by the Germans at Tobruk. (Immediately after our marriage in 1967, John and I lived in Tobruk for eighteen months when John was stationed at RAF El Adem, about twenty miles inland. Many of the bombed buildings still stood, and with the nearby war cemeteries they were a silent testimony to the horrors of war.) Ray's wartime experiences led him to seek new ways to deal with conflict situations and to develop new relationships between 'traditional enemies'. He became the first full-time Presbyterian chaplain at Queen's University in Belfast, and the forty founding members of Corrymeela were largely drawn from students, graduates and staff at the university. The vision of reconciliation has inspired Corrymeela's work. They have learned that when people feel accepted and safe, it is possible for them to tell their story and listen to others. In this way understanding can grow, trust can be established across the social, political and religious divides, and reconciliation becomes a possibility.

The community uses volunteers in addition to a small core of professional staff. This limits their running costs so they do not have to accept funding from trusts or government bodies which might have strings attached, and therefore enables them to keep independence of thought and action. Volunteers also bring with them new insights and ideas

125

which challenge the community to review its current practices. In addition to the short-term volunteers who stay for one or two weeks, there are a small number of year-long volunteers who come not only from Ireland and Great Britain but from around the world. My two weeks as a volunteer at Corrymeela would give me the opportunity to meet people without their labels of 'Protestant' and 'Catholic' and to see how they got on together when taken out of their divided communities. It would be a difficult time for me as it would be the first time since Stephen's death that I would be totally on my own with no husband to support me emotionally.

I caught a Ryanair flight to Dublin. Never having been to the Republic before, John and I intended to meet in Dublin after my two weeks at Corrymeela to spend a few days seeing the sights. But now a taxi sped me from the airport to the railway station in the centre of Dublin to catch the Belfast train. As the train approached the border near Newry in south Armagh, I saw the army security towers on the hilltops. Stephen had sometimes been based there, watching the countryside for movements of suspected terrorists. Some people in the area dislike this surveillance, feeling that all of them are being watched. But it is necessary as long as splinter groups continue the terrorist campaign. I am sure the majority of the people in the area would be only too pleased if the surveillance prevented the bombing of innocent people.

Arriving in Belfast, I took a taxi to the home of John and Shirley Morrow, who had kindly said that I could spend the night at their house before I travelled up to Corrymeela the next evening. John, a Presbyterian minister and lecturer, was one of the founder members of the Corrymeela community, and was leader of the community from 1980 to 1993. He and his wife Shirley, who is also very involved in the community, made me very welcome and introduced me to Neil Bole the community's financial director who happened to be there at the time, and who for some reason reminded me of Sean Connery. I think it was the moustache and soft accent. After we had all got to know one another, I made my apologies and went to bed. I was very tired after the flight and the train journey.

I awoke to the sound of army helicopters clattering overhead. After breakfast, Shirley took me to the Corrymeela office near their home and introduced me to some of the staff. Leaving my suitcase in their safekeeping and armed with a map, I ventured forth to explore the city centre as this was only my second visit. A very pleasant day was spent touring the shopping area, the site of many bombings in the past but peaceful now the IRA ceasefire was in force. Walking down a pedestrian precinct, I heard a voice call my name. I spun round, wondering who on earth in Belfast knew me. A man with a little girl was smiling at me. He asked what I was doing in Belfast. He was a reporter from one of the local papers and had interviewed me on the phone soon after Stephen's death. He said he had recognised me from the television news. He asked what I was doing there and I told him I was going to Corrymeela, but he wasn't to write that in his paper!

Late that afternoon, I made my way back to Corrymeela House to catch the minibus which takes volunteers to Ballycastle. We jumped in, piling our bags in the back, and off we went. The journey took about an hour and a half with a cigarette break on the way. I had already noticed that people in Northern Ireland seem to smoke far more than in England and was told this was because of the stress they had to live under because of the terrorist violence. We arrived at Corrymeela and had a light meal in Coventry, the annual volunteers' accommodation, so called because it was built with money given through Coventry Cathedral. After we and the annual volunteers had introduced ourselves, there was a short talk about the work of Corrymeela, what we would be doing as volunteers and how important it was to make everyone feel welcome and safe. Rooms were allocated: the single volunteers were to stay in a house called Cedar Haven, while I shared a three-bedroom chalet with another volunteer and her two sons. My room had bunk beds, but as I wasn't sharing I had the luxury of the bottom bunk. I was very tired after the journey and my walkabout in Belfast, so was soon fast asleep.

Next morning, stepping out of the chalet door, I saw the fantastic view across the bay to Rathlin Island. Immediately in front of me was a huge wooden cross round which curved a low wall which served as seating. Many a time I would sit there thinking, sometimes crying, while at other times I would just enjoy the view. One lovely starry night I lay on my back on the wall for ages just gazing up at all the stars.

As a Village helper, I would be looking after the family groups who come for a break during the school holidays. They stay in a large self-contained unit known as the Village, but my chalet-mate was in the Housekeeping group which meant lots of washing and cleaning for her, and so she asked me to keep an eye on her boys during the week. But I had time to look around the site until the families arrived at midday. Next to our row of chalets was another building containing the lounge, dining room and kitchen for the groups that normally stayed in the chalets. The old house, the community's original building, had recently been demolished, as it was considered a fire hazard. A new, specially designed house was rising in its place, and of course the build-ing work was an attraction to young children, despite the surrounding fence, and so was strictly out of bounds. A few yards across the lawn from the new house was a long, white one-storey building called Tara which during the building works housed Reception, the laundry, kitchen and 'the pub with no beer' which was the venue of the weekly 'Corry-o-ke' and disco for the children. The whole building had been built through the assistance of the TV series *Challenge Anneka*, in each programme of which the attractive blonde female presenter Anneka Rice would be given a challenge which she would have to complete within a set time. Of course local firms and craftsmen came forward to help her as it was good publicity for them.

The heart of Corrymeela is the Croi, which is Irish for heart. It is a circular building built into a low mound and contains a small, round chapel, a sitting area and a room in which concerts or talks can be held. In the sitting area is a small statue of Saint Francis and the doves, and on the wall behind it is the prayer of Saint Francis: 'Make Me a Channel of Your Peace'. The chapel is very simple, painted white, with chairs round the outside and large cushions in the centre for people to sit on, and a simple wooden table with a cross and the Bible. The only decora-tion is a small arched stained-glass window depicting Jesus in the manger with an angel above, and on one wall a brightly coloured, tex-tured panel of tapestry. The Croi is always open and always there when someone wants a few moments of contemplation. The short, simple services held each morning and evening are nondenominational and because of their informality appeal to both adults and children.

Just before lunchtime, the families arrived, mothers with children ranging from babies to teenagers. The Village helpers this week were two annual volunteers: Dinger (surname Bell) and Aislinn (from Dublin), and two weekly volunteers: Debbie (from England) and myself. We helped the new arrivals to carry their cases to their bedrooms, and then we all gathered in the lounge to introduce ourselves. So began a very tiring week: I have never washed so many dishes, laid so many tables and made so much toast in my life. I remember that neither mothers nor children liked the crusts, which they called heels, to be toasted whereas I love them. The children were very boisterous: coming from an inner-city area they were not accustomed to having so much space to run around in. I must admit that at first I had great difficulty understanding the Dublin accent. I remember one small boy asking me something four times and I still couldn't understand what he said. Fortunately Aislinn translated.

A programme of activities for the week had been planned in consultation with the group. There would be football and overnight camping for the older children, art and craft sessions for all ages, and a playroom full of toys for the younger children. There would be trips on the Corrymeela bus and some days, weather permitting, we would go to the nearby beach. We made a checklist of volunteers for each activity. I quite liked the idea of the river walk, imagining a nice stroll along a riverbank. However, when it was pointed out to me that it was a walk *in* the river and involved wearing wetsuits and clambering over rocks, I decided against it after all. One of the trips was to a farm. The children soon discovered a rabbit hutch containing mother rabbit and about five babies, which they found irresistible. Baby rabbits were lifted out, stroked and fussed over. The children kept disappearing with them to show their friends. So I spent quite a while rounding up individual children, making sure they put the baby rabbit back with its mother, only to see a couple of seconds later yet another child disappearing with one towards the swings, the café or wherever. To tire the children out we took them on a walk along a trail laid out through part of the farm. By the time we returned to the bus, they were shattered, and they sat on a jetty in the lake cooling their feet in the water. Another trip was to the swimming pool. This enabled me to have a quiet couple of hours as I sat at the side watching them while other helpers were actually in the water with them.

Thursday evening was children's fun time, with face painting, a barbecue and 'Corry-o-ke' in Tara. The children thoroughly enjoyed themselves. Later that evening there was a special meal for the mothers and Village helpers followed by a trip down to a pub in Ballycastle. At the pub there was a karaoke and one of the songs was 'Unbreak My Heart'. The words are about a girl being left by her boyfriend, but they seemed so relevant also to how I felt that I was soon in tears. Everyone understood because by now they all knew about Stephen.

It was during this week that there was a face-to-face interview on television between Ken Maginnis of the UUP and Martin McGuinness of Sinn Féin. There are no televisions at Corrymeela but I was invited by some of the staff to a nearby bungalow used for staff overnight accommodation, where I enjoyed a very pleasant meal before watching the interview. McGuinness put Sinn Féin's point of view with calm and reason. Ken Maginnis made many valid points but his presentation was often strident and confrontational. One of the people watching the programme with me was Brendan McAllister, a Corrymeela member who leads the Northern Ireland Mediation Network which, when friction arises between the two sections of the community, tries to bring them together to discuss and overcome the problem. A few days later I met Brendan's wife Elizabeth and I spoke to her about my grief and how being at Corrymeela was helping me. She later sent me a wonderful tape about bereavement, comparing how it was dealt with traditionally in Ireland with the present day and covering the various stages of grief. It was all spoken in a soft southern Irish accent and with little Irish turns of phrase.

I got on really well with the mum I was sharing the chalet with. Her younger son, about ten years old, was called Stephen which immediately attracted me to him, while her other son, John, was about four years older. They were both very well-behaved for boys of their age, and I often kept an eye on them during trips as she had to stay behind working. I had realised she was Catholic when she joined the group going to Mass in Ballycastle on the Sunday morning. I had had my suspicions the previous evening going into the Croi service when she had said quietly that she would probably be damned. Perhaps she was only joking, but it is sad when Christians cannot worship together, or have been taught that they should not. The day before she was due to go home I was sitting on the low wall around the cross in front of our chalet and she joined me. I said that I hadn't told her who I was as I hadn't wanted her to judge me immediately. I then told her all about Stephen being a soldier and about his death. She then showed me the compassion that so many women from both sides of the community in Northern Ireland have for one another, having suffered so much for so long. She told me they lived in a Catholic area of north Belfast but she had always tried to keep her boys open-minded. Then she gave me a little sculpture of two rabbits to thank me for keeping an eye on her boys. This is now a constant reminder of my time at Corrymeela and of the many rabbits that shared the grounds with us. I said goodbye to her and her boys at midday on Friday when they left on the bus back to Belfast with the Dublin group, an ordinary mother trying to bring up her sons in a way that hopefully would help them face a better future than she had known.

After my hectic week I had just a few hours to put my feet up and relax before the next group arrived that evening. The second week was not as busy as the first as there were far more volunteers helping in the Village. Many were couples and seemed to know other helpers from previous stays at Corrymeela. I was sharing the chalet with a family from Newcastle and sharing my room with another lady. I had gallantly offered to take the top bunk bed but soon regretted it as I had visions of rolling over in the night and landing with a thud on the floor. This week's group were from Northern Ireland so I had less difficulty with the accent, but I do recall a problem with one young mother. I thought she was asking me, 'Is the top here?' She had her baby's bottle beside her and I could see the top was next to it. However, what she was actually asking was 'Is there a tap here?' The two words sounded identical to me. There was yet another boy called Stephen; he was about eleven years old with fiery red hair.

I met some very special people this week. Firstly, I was privileged to meet the founder of Corrymeela, the Reverend Ray Davey, and his wife Kathleen. Corrymeela has developed into a powerful symbol of his vision for reconciliation. Ray and Kathleen took me to meet Hylda Armstrong. Her son Sean, a 31-year-old Protestant social worker with both communities, was killed at his Belfast home in 1973 by a Protestant gunman who presumed that with an Irish Christian name he must be Catholic. A similar tragic story was told by one of the volunteers who suddenly said to me one day that I had very sad eyes. I blurted out what had happened to Stephen. She told me that her husband, who was Catholic, had been killed by an IRA gunman who had come to shoot his Protestant workmate. She was left with a young family to raise on her own. I thought of the words Mother Teresa had said during her Corrymeela visit to a group of mothers whose husbands were in prison: 'You mothers are very privileged. You are able to share the pain of Our Lady. You have to watch your dearest ones suffer and can do nothing about it. And you must smile five times a day – it is good for the children.' Her words also apply to so many bereaved women in Northern Ireland who have to struggle on each day for the sake of their children.

Gary Trew, the Antrim teacher, came to see how I was getting on. I was surprised that although Gary had brought many school groups to Corrymeela he had never met Ray. He was thrilled to be able to do so at last and to discuss with him the community's work with schools.

One trip we made that week was to the indoor funfair at Portrush, which on a wet day turned out to be a good idea. Another day started out sunny, but after breakfast the sea fog rolled in. After lunch, however, the fog totally disappeared, giving a lovely sunny afternoon, so we went to the beach. Some of the adult helpers braved the freezing sea with the children, but not me. I built sandcastles with the little ones, making channels around them for the sea to run into. Many times I had done the same with Mark and Stephen; I have a lovely photo of

Stephen sitting on the sand, spade in hand, putting the finishing touches to his castle.

Another day we took the children on the Corrymeela bus to a leisure centre for a swim. As we pulled into the car park a song came on the radio and yet again the words upset me and I started to cry. It was as if there was a whole lake of tears inside me waiting to be released. Aislinn sat with me on the grass outside the leisure centre and we had a really good talk about the situation in Northern Ireland and about Stephen. She was only in her early twenties but despite our age difference at no time did she make me feel it was any trouble for her to listen. My emotions were still in turmoil. I was angry inside, angry with a God who if he existed had allowed my son to be taken from me. At Corrymeela I never went to any of the twice-daily services (there is no pressure to attend although it is a Christian community). During the evening services I stood instead looking at the beautiful sunsets over the narrow strait between Rathlin Island and Ballycastle. Those sunsets touched my soul when no man-made religious service could.

The week ended with the usual parties. The children's party was the same as the previous week, but the mothers' party was a beach barbecue in the lounge! The room had been decorated with coloured-paper fish and crabs, and there was a canoe across the middle of the floor. Two of the annual volunteers acted as waiters, dressed in bermuda shorts and bright Hawaiian-print shirts. Surfboards were used as food trays, which took a lot of balancing skill. The food was delicious, and although there was no alcohol as it's not allowed at Corrymeela, its absence didn't inhibit us. A great time was had by all. The next day we all said our goodbyes and went our different ways, taking with us many happy memories.

The community says that 'Corrymeela provides a safe and shared space where people can meet and trusting relationships can grow, providing hope of a new way of living together. For reconciliation to work, we need to know that new relationships between our divided communities are possible. We need to hear how people who were once "enemies" are now "friends", and we need to see how that change can take place. Healing is needed for victims of violence and prejudice;

many sense their suffering no longer matters to others so they need to meet those who are still willing to listen. Those who have contributed to violence need to build new lives. They need to find ways of contributing to peace.' My stay at Corrymeela enabled me to see how these words are put into action.

But I had seen only a small part of the Corrymeela community's work. Support is also given to families, whether they are coping with family breakdown, difficulties with children, the pressures of single parenthood, domestic violence, or the particular problems that arise when a family member is in prison. Parents and children are given the space they need and the opportunity to take part in a wide range of activities such as arts and crafts, drama and play. The families programme is extending to include work with women's groups, men's groups, and senior citizens who may need respite. The community is deeply involved in youth work and recognises that personal development is not only about gathering academic qualifications but also involves the shaping of our values and beliefs. It is important for young people growing up in a divided community that issues of politics, religion, culture and social environment are discussed and explored so that they can form a broader perspective. The schools programme actively encourages this work, and Corrymeela complements the statutory Education for Mutual Understanding programme which is part of the curriculum for all schools in Northern Ireland. Corrymeela provides the opportunity for young people to meet, share their experiences and listen to each other. (Lorraine McElroy told me that she was eleven years old before she met a Protestant girl, as she grew up in a republican area of Newry, a predominantly Catholic town.)

In addition to its youth work, Corrymeela also brings together groups from neighbouring churches of different denominations to build cross-community relationships, to deepen understanding of one another and to consider possible areas of partnership in their own districts. It also provides a number of programmes that allow people to explore the connection between Christian faith and contemporary issues, enabling them to grow in their understanding of different Christian traditions.

Through all these programmes one vision shines brightly like a candle in the darkness. It is the Corrymeela community's commitment to the healing of social, religious and political divisions that exist in Northern Ireland and throughout the world. Janet Shepperson, a Corrymeela member, wrote the following poem which speaks of the hope for peace in Northern Ireland. It is called 'I Offer You This Hope':

> I offer you this hope.
> It is so small
> the wind could blow it out.
> Its feeble flickering
> turns up in unexpected places
> and seems to annoy those
> with a big investment in dazzling light,
> or in measuring the strength of darkness.
> If this hope lives
> it will be like swallows' wings,
> erratic, unpredictable,
> always on the move.
> If this hope dies,
> it will be buried shallow
> like grass seed.

My time at Corrymeela left me with some wonderful memories of caring people committed to the Corrymeela community's work for peace and reconciliation, so necessary in that troubled land. I also have many photos to remind me of the fun enjoyed by the family groups and my fellow volunteers. But more than that, Corrymeela helped me personally by giving me the emotional support I needed, the space to express my emotions, and to come to terms with my feelings.

II

DUBLIN AND BESSBROOK

BEFORE I LEFT HOME FOR Corrymeela, I had phoned the office of the taoiseach, Bertie Ahern, to ask if he would meet us during our time in Dublin. He kindly agreed to see us, as did John Bruton who had been taoiseach when Stephen was killed. The other person we were going to meet was very special to me. Although we had spoken on the phone a number of times, I had yet to meet Lorraine McElroy, but now we were going to visit her home in Bessbrook on the following Tuesday.

I arrived in Dublin by train from Belfast about mid-afternoon on Saturday. John met me, having flown into Dublin that morning, and we took a taxi to our hotel, just off Grafton Street. After unpacking, we went for a walk along Grafton Street, one of the main shopping areas in Dublin. We saw a notice about a 'literary pub crawl' that evening. This sounded a very Irish combination to us but also interesting, so early that evening we went to the pub from which the tour starts. A very enjoyable evening was had visiting Trinity College, the old parliament building and various pubs, the literary connections of which were outlined by our two guides, both actors earning a little extra money. Of course, time was allowed for the participants to partake of a pint at the pubs we visited.

The next day we joined a bus tour along the coast south of Dublin and on through the Wicklow Mountains. The bus driver kept up a running commentary about the areas we were travelling through and interspersed this with jokes, none of which I can remember now but which at the time made us laugh. When we stopped for refreshments, I went up to him and thanked him for making me laugh, adding that I hadn't had much to laugh about over the past six months. When I told him why, like other Irish people we met he was full of apologies for what had happened. With hindsight, it was rather unfair of me to be so upfront about what had happened to Stephen, but I felt an overpowering urge to tell everyone and make them think about the situation in Northern Ireland.

Monday was the day of our appointments with the taoiseach and John Bruton. Looking back, it seems incredible that two such prominent politicians would spare time from their busy schedules to meet us; I doubted if British politicians would be as accessible. It made me realise even more that Stephen's death was regretted by many people in the Republic, and that they sympathised with us very much in our loss. Talking to people during our visit we had come across a number of viewpoints; these varied from a wish for a united Ireland but not supporting the means used by the IRA, to at the other extreme a total lack of interest in Northern Ireland and the fear that the violence would spread to the Republic. The Republic's economy was booming and they certainly didn't want the expense and political minefield of the north.

We took a taxi to Leinster House, a beautiful Georgian building, where we were shown into a small waiting room near the taoiseach's office. His private secretary greeted us, saying the taoiseach was just finishing a meeting with Ray Burke, the Foreign Minister, who had asked if he also could meet us. As he at that time had responsibility for matters relating to Northern Ireland, we were very pleased to be able to meet him. After a few minutes we were shown into the taoiseach's office. Bertie Ahern sat at a long, highly polished table with Ray Burke. They stood up to greet us and made us feel very welcome and at ease. After introductions we all sat at the top of the table. We spoke about Stephen, and I showed them some photos of him that I had brought with me. I said I hoped they would do all they could to find a solution to this problem. In turn they said that a united Ireland could not be brought about by IRA violence and wasn't what their government or the people of the Republic wanted. If and when a united Ireland came about it would have to be by consent, as agreed between the Irish and British governments. Some people might say this policy hasn't been reflected in action by the Irish government against the IRA in the past. However, I do feel that there is now far more co-operation with the British government. The government in the Republic cannot round up every suspected IRA sympathiser in Dundalk and Donegal and imprison them, for despite the hatred in the south for IRA violence, the government would be seen as betraying those who fought for the Republic itself as well as those still fighting for a united Ireland. They have to walk a tightrope. So when the British government has sought in the past the extradition from the Republic of IRA men believed to have committed terrorist acts, this has been refused. It seemed a little ironic to me that a country that gained its independence by fighting the British army claimed not to support those who were doing exactly the same in the north. However, times are different, and the Protestant majority of Northern Ireland make that particular situation very different from the one that led to the creation of the Republic in 1921.

From the taoiseach's office we went to meet John Bruton. I thanked him for sending the Irish ambassador to represent his government at Stephen's funeral and told him it had meant a lot to us. I also thanked him for the replies he had sent to various letters I had written to him about the Northern Ireland situation. I remember one in particular in which I said I had read in a newspaper that the sniper who killed Stephen was from Dundalk, where many IRA men lived, and asked him why he didn't round them up. He wrote back saying that the Garda Síochána and the RUC had investigated the allegation but it was purely speculation by the press. He said the gardaí would do everything in their power to bring Stephen's killer to justice. The man eventually charged came from the Republic but from Castleblayney, not Dundalk.

As in the UK, there had been a general election that spring in Ireland. In it, John Bruton's party, Fine Gael, had been defeated by Bertie Ahern's Fianna Fáil, a party that was seen as having somewhat more sympathy for the republican viewpoint. In the UK, the balance of power had changed from Conservative to Labour. It seemed that everything was falling into place after so many years. The governments of the UK, the Republic and the United States were all pulling together to help the people of Northern Ireland find a solution that would lead to peace. But much was being asked of the politicians in Northern Ireland. They had to put aside their confrontational attitudes and try to work together in order to agree the compromise that was needed.

The unionists had to give a little on their principle of not talking to Sinn Féin because of the latter's links with the IRA. I believe principles have to be flexible – only the Ten Commandments were set in stone. The one commandment that had been broken so often in Northern Ireland in the past was 'Thou shalt not kill.' In order for that commandment no longer to be broken, a way forward had to be agreed. Some strongly held principles had to be closely looked at and perhaps rejected as no longer useful to the present situation. There is a mountain of hurt within both communities: so many families have been touched by the troubles and the violence has been carried out not only by the IRA but by loyalists as well. Politicians should lead their people towards peace, a peace they so badly wanted but which would involve coming to terms with what had happened in the past and seeing that neither side was totally innocent or totally guilty in the events of those times.

That afternoon we joined a bus tour of the sights of Dublin city, visiting the Guinness brewery, St Patrick's Cathedral, O'Connell Street and the famous General Post Office, a key site of the 1916 Easter Rising. From there the bus crossed over the river to an area with lovely Georgian terrace houses. We left the bus here, going into the nearby park known as St Stephen's Green. As we were tired by now, we lay on the grass like many others in the lovely, warm sunshine – we had been very lucky with the weather considering this was Ireland! The meetings with Mr Ahern and Mr Bruton made me feel I was putting a personal face on not only the sufferings of those who had lost loved ones but also the hopes for peace of so many. Perhaps to these two men the meeting did not hold as much significance, but I shall always be grateful that they made the time to meet us.

The next day, we travelled by train from Dublin to Newry, then by taxi to Bessbrook, about three miles away, to visit Lorraine McElroy. As we drove into Bessbrook I suddenly realised that we were on Green Road and approaching the checkpoint where Stephen had been killed. Not only that, we were approaching it from the direction that the gunman had fired at him. I had never given any thought about which way we would come into Bessbrook. Suddenly, I felt John stiffen beside me as he too realised where we were. At the checkpoint a soldier stopped the taxi and asked our driver where he was taking us. It was a replay of what Stephen had done at that very spot only six months before – except that now an IRA ceasefire was in force. The driver said we were going to an address in Bessbrook. I explained we were expected at the Mill a little later and the soldier let us through.

The taxi driver dropped us off at Lorraine's house. At the station I purposely hadn't told him who we were visiting, only the address, but it is a small community and he immediately recognised it as Lorraine's address. I don't know if he recognised us – he didn't give any indication that he did. When we told Lorraine she wasn't worried, believing she knew who the driver was. She made us very welcome, and for a while we sat talking about both our families and how we were all coping. I showed her the photo album of Stephen that I had brought with us. We met Lorraine's two sons, Sean, a very mature thirteen-year-old, and David, who was going through the terrible twos. Lorraine used the Irish term 'very bold' to describe him, which I took to mean mischievous. I happened to look at the picture on the wall behind the settee on which John and I were sitting. I could not believe my eyes – I had exactly the same one in my hallway. It is a country scene, with a road winding towards a farm with some oast houses beside it and a team of horses ploughing in the nearby field. The picture had belonged to my next-door neighbours, who knowing how much I liked it gave it to me when they changed their colour scheme. It seemed such a coincidence because Lorraine also had been given the picture.

After about an hour we had to go on our way as we were due at Bessbrook Mill. We saw Stephen's memorial stone there and were pleased that the cherry tree we had planted was growing well. An escort of soldiers took us to the checkpoint where I tied a spray of silk poppies to the fence. I left a photo of Stephen for them to put on the fence if they wished to.

Our next meeting was with the RUC team who were compiling the case against the man charged with Stephen's murder. We met two of them at Corry Square police station in Newry. As they were introducing themselves, the young army officer came up to us who had been at the checkpoint when Stephen was killed. His artillery regiment had since taken over from 3 RHA, Stephen's regiment. It was lovely to meet him again. I thought how difficult it must be for him having witnessed Stephen's shooting to return soon after to the same area. A few weeks later I wrote asking him to tell me exactly what had happened that night and how much pain Stephen had been in, because as his mother I desperately needed to know all the details. In his reply he said he reached Stephen about twenty seconds after he was shot, when he was still conscious and groaning loudly. He told Stephen the ambulance was on its way and he would be all right. He said Stephen was already very pale and going into shock. Removing Stephen's clothing, he and the other young officer told Stephen to keep his eyes open and stay awake. He responded for a minute or two by opening his eyes, but by then he was making no noise and not speaking. By the time they had finished bandaging the wound Stephen was unconscious. The ambulance arrived a couple of minutes later. He added that never a day went by when he didn't think of him and what happened.

We went inside the police station with him to meet some of the soldiers based there, and we discovered that one of them came from Shropshire like me. They live a very confined life in Northern Ireland; when not on duty they stay in the barracks, and the short time off duty is usually spent eating and sleeping, any spare time being spent reading, watching videos or phoning home. From Corry Square the two RUC officers took us to another police station in Newry for the briefing. It still seemed in a way unreal that it was our son's murder we were discussing. Although soldiers were being killed in Northern Ireland, though far fewer now than in previous years, we never thought one of them would be our Stephen. There were so many soldiers in Northern

Ireland that the odds on it being him were huge. But the man who fired the gun was determined a British soldier would be shot and Stephen was 'in the wrong place at the wrong time and the bullet had his name on it', as soldiers say.

We were shown files about the murder including maps of the area showing the position where the shot was fired from. On the map I noticed that the surname of the man charged with the murder was written on a house near which the car had stopped for the shot to be fired. I was told that the family living there shared the same surname but there was no connection with them. The police told us that people in Bessbrook, unlike during previous investigations into murders of soldiers or policemen, hadn't shut the door when the police called making enquiries but had said how sorry they were about what had happened. However, information was still hard to come by, either because people did not know or because they feared IRA retribution.

We returned to Newry station for the train back to Dublin. It was almost half past five and we were both very tired, having packed so much into one day. As the train travelled southwards we left the watch-towers on the hills and the helicopters clattering overhead and returned to the normality of the Republic. We passed through such beautiful countryside, seen at its best on this sunny August day. But so much sadness had been caused over this divided land. Parts of it near the border were the haunt of IRA sympathisers and gunmen. There were arms dumps and training areas hidden amongst these beautiful green fields and hills. As the train headed towards Dublin, I began to think more deeply about the justification behind an armed struggle and the type of men who carry it out.

What is it that makes a person believe that killing another person can ever be justified? How can they believe that killing a British soldier will make the British government change their policy towards Northern Ireland? How much of the violence is a form of retaliation for the death or injury of a family member or a member of their community? How many paramilitaries are ideologically influenced, whether for a united Ireland or to remain in the Union, whilst others conveniently find their acts legitimised when in other societies they would be treated purely as criminal. Was natural male aggression given justification through terrorism instead of finding an outlet in football hooliganism or a Saturday-night punch-up with usually nonfatal results?

Living in a divided society such as Northern Ireland, it can be very easy for a young person to pick up the hatred that is caused by the violence and feeds on the distrust between the two communities. It is far more glamorous to be a 'hard man' in your area than a petty criminal. Terrorism legitimises criminal acts in the minds of those carrying them out and in the minds of those with the same political aims. Our friend Eamonn, who had told us how his younger brother became involved as a teenager in the IRA in Londonderry and imprisoned, had described his brother as an idealistic young man at an impressionable age who was motivated by the stories of Patrick Pearse and his fellow republicans in the 1916 Easter Rising.

Why is it mainly working-class young men who turn to violence? Is it due to the high unemployment in both the Protestant and Catholic working class now that the heavy engineering that used to provide a lot of male employment has declined? As the saying goes, 'The Devil makes work for idle hands.' Middle-class Protestant young men train for the professions, and in their homes in the leafy suburbs they are perhaps cocooned from the violence. Having attained their profession they can sit back and condemn the men of violence in their community, seeing no connection between the words of hardline unionist politicians and the actions of the working-class loyalist gunmen. If they have little understanding of the gunmen within their own community, they are unlikely to have any at all of those from the nationalist community.

Was Stephen any different? As a soldier he had to use that aggressive streak in most men. He knew he might have to kill a person who the British government considered a threat to his country, whether it be in Northern Ireland or anywhere else in the world. Through training, the army does its utmost to ensure a man does not see his opponent as another man like himself. For an army to be effective this has to happen: no soldier could be depended upon if his own personal feelings and beliefs were allowed to affect his actions. There are also differences in the ways individual regiments are trained to react to situations. For instance, the Paras are seen as the hard men of the army, the troops who go in first, hard and fast against the enemy. In my view, to use them during the banned civil rights march on 30 January 1972 in Londonderry was very unwise.

There is the question of how much we influence our children. Does giving a young boy a toy gun, an Action Man figure and a camouflage uniform, as we did with Stephen, encourage an aggressive streak and make him want to be a soldier? I do not believe so. Stephen was never aggressive, and had wanted to join the RAF not the army. It was unemployment in a time of economic depression that made him turn to the army, like so many young men in the past who do not have a family tradition of army service.

Looking at the broader picture, and having read about the background to partition, I find it very difficult to understand how the descendants of unionists, who in 1914 threatened to use guns bought from Germany to prevent their inclusion in Home Rule for Ireland, can eighty years later rail against men of the present day who try to achieve a united Ireland in the same way. It was politically expedient for the British government to agree to their six-county Ulster, but the Catholics in Ulster had no say whatsoever in that decision and had to live under what the unionists themselves called 'a Protestant Parliament and a Protestant State'. While there was the danger of war in Europe or with Russia this situation suited the British government as it meant that we had a foothold on the island in case the Republic did not remain neutral. Britain's fear through the ages has been that Ireland would be used as a stepping stone in the invasion of Britain. That threat no longer exists, and now Britain is taking a neutral stance on what the future will hold for Northern Ireland, so long as that future is agreed by consent of the majority.

Do we perhaps see things in black and white when it comes to people fighting against our presence in their country, for example Kenya and Cyprus? All that is seen then is the violence they use; we either do not look behind their actions to understand their reasons, or we do not accept their reasons as justified. I am not saying that violence is justified, but it is sometimes seen as the only way possible against the British establishment. We ourselves have stories about the fight by ancient Britons against their Roman rulers and by Saxons against the Normans. We see Boadicea and Hereward as folk heroes, but cannot see a similarity between them and other people who see us as an unwanted presence in their land. Is there a difference between killing sanctioned by the state and killing by a terrorist organisation that sees that state as an intruder into its country? Many would admit that any terrorist conflict is a dirty one, and the response to it sometimes questionable. There were allegations that the RUC had a 'shoot to kill' policy against the IRA; an investigation was held into this by the Greater Manchester deputy chief constable, John Stalker, and Colin Sampson, chief constable of West Yorkshire. One of the incidents that gave rise to the allegations was the killing in 1982 of three IRA men by RUC officers. The court case against the RUC officers was dismissed by the judge, Lord Justice Gibson, who commended them for sending the Provisionals 'to the final court of justice'. On 25 April 1987, the IRA killed the judge and his wife, as they crossed the border from the Republic, by means of a bomb placed under the road near Killeen, County Armagh. The Provisionals said they had sent the judge 'to the final court of justice'.

At times IRA members have complained of being beaten up either during capture or during interrogation, and indeed the man charged with Stephen's murder and those arrested with him made such claims, having received hospital treatment for cuts and bruising. Few terrorists surrender willingly, but information given under duress is not only unreliable, it is unacceptable in law. In England itself, the treatment of those arrested for the bombings in Guildford and Birmingham in 1974 was unacceptable. It led to false confessions and many years spent in prison before their convictions were found unsafe. However, the IRA's methods of dealing with their own men accused of informing are hardly kid-glove treatment. Terrorism allows no room for feelings of humanity for one's opponent. It is made even more difficult because this 'war' is not taking place in some distant part of the world but within the United Kingdom. Our own army is being attacked by people whose lives and surroundings are very like our own.

In Northern Ireland an entire generation has grown up with the violence. It was said when the IRA ceasefire came into force in 1994 that life would be able to return to normality, but for the people of Northern Ireland the violence is normality. It will take quite a while for them to learn to live together in peace. Perhaps in the future a Protestant man from the Shankill will be able to walk down the Catholic Falls Road, and a Catholic man down the Shankill Road, whereas in the past he would possibly have been targeted by paramilitaries and paid with his life. Even in the larger picture, some Catholics in the Republic share a common fear with some Protestants in Northern Ireland. Both told us that the reason they didn't visit the other part of the island was the fear that their car number plates would identify their origin and could lead to their car being vandalised and perhaps they themselves being attacked. So the two rarely meet, and the stereotypes continue.

Many people in England aren't interested in what happens in Northern Ireland, in the viewpoints of the different sides, or even what the final outcome is, so long as the bombings and killings happen there and not in England. Few know the background to the situation. Most people in England have not been touched personally by the violence in Northern Ireland, and this can lead to an inability to look at things in proportion. When the Grand National was cancelled in April 1997 because of an IRA bomb threat, at least one person said it was a tragedy – the horses were at their peak for the race and people had travelled long distances to enjoy the race. I wondered how he could call that a tragedy. Two months previously, my son had been killed serving his country in a part of that country that many English people would like to see cut adrift and floated out into the Atlantic for all the seemingly endless trouble it caused. That was a tragedy. All the thousands of people in Northern Ireland who had been killed in the conflict, that was a tragedy. All the people who had suffered terrible injuries in the many bombings, that was a tragedy. But not the cancellation of a horse race that despite the postponement was held two days later. The dead and injured could not be returned to normal two days later.

With these thoughts lying heavily on my mind, we returned to Dublin. Our first visit to the Republic had shown us the friendly, hospitable side of the Irish people, the majority of whom do not support the IRA and want nothing to do with them. Stephen's death in contrast showed another side of the Irish character, and the ruthless violence used by some in their fight for a united Ireland.

12
WOMAN OF COURAGE

'WE WERE ALL GIVEN HOPE and inspiration by your courage and ideal for peace transcending your tragedy.' These words come from a letter I received from Lady Lothian, founder president of the Women of the Year Lunch, telling me that I had been elected as a guest of honour to their lunch to be held in the autumn. Guests attend by nomination only and represent the widest possible cross-section of women, each one particularly distinguished in a special field of work. The lunch, held annually since 1955, raises money for the Greater London Fund for the Blind, and the theme this year was 'Making a Difference'.

To my surprise, I had been nominated a Champion of Courage. I was very reluctant to accept at first as I felt I had not really done anything courageous. I had only done what seemed natural to me at the time. However, my family said I should attend, so I finally accepted on the understanding that it was in recognition of Stephen's courage as much as any courage I had shown through what I had said or done. The invitation arose from our plea for no retaliation following Stephen's murder, though it was the same plea that has been made by most victims' families in Northern Ireland, who, like us, had not wanted others to go through the suffering they were experiencing. In the lunch brochure I wrote the following:

People seem surprised that after Stephen's murder we said his death should not be used as an excuse by Protestant paramilitaries. We knew that it would be innocent Catholics who would be killed, not IRA gunmen, and we did not want any more families to go through the terrible feelings of losing a loved one. Too many people have been murdered due to the problems in Northern Ireland and we want to make people see that violence is not the way forward. Talks between representatives of all political parties must decide a peaceful, lasting settlement, and members of both communities must respect each other's beliefs. Everything I do towards these aims I do in memory of Stephen, who so loved life and left a positive impression on many people – I have to try to make something good come from such a terrible act.

There were two other Champions of Courage: Doreen Lawrence and Lisa Potts. Doreen also had a son called Stephen. He was an eighteen-year-old black A level student, stabbed in an unprovoked racial attack by a group of youths on 22 April 1993 as he waited with a friend at a bus stop in Eltham, south London. He died at the scene. At the same time as news bulletins covered our Stephen's murder, the other main item was about the inquest on Stephen Lawrence and his parents' fight for justice. In a number of ways, I felt a link between Doreen and myself, not only because our sons shared the same name. Eltham was one of the areas south of the Thames we had passed through when visiting our Stephen during his initial army training at Woolwich in 1992. Perhaps we had even passed the bus stop where Stephen Lawrence was murdered a year later. Also I saw a parallel with the sectarianism of Northern Ireland. Doreen's son was murdered by white youths who saw only his colour. In Northern Ireland some people see others only as Catholic or Protestant, not as people very like themselves if they made the effort to get to know them. In some cases this led to sectarian murders there. Doreen's words about racism apply just as much to sectarianism in Northern Ireland: 'Children are our future, they need us to teach and guide them in the world and to show them right from wrong, especially when it comes to racism. Their acceptance of everyone seems to change as they grow older. Why is it that some children will have black friends at primary school but not at secondary school? When and why does colour become an issue in children's lives?'

Lisa Potts was the third Champion of Courage. She was a young nursery nurse in Wolverhampton in July 1996 when a crazed intruder with a machete started to attack the three- and four-year-olds who were enjoying a teddy bears' picnic in the school playground. Lisa was awarded the George Medal for bravery for protecting the children that day, though she herself says that what she did was instinctive and that most people would have done exactly the same thing in the circumstances.

The chairwoman of the lunch committee was Floella Benjamin, who I remembered from the days when she was a presenter of *Play School* and *Play Away*, two children's programmes I used to watch with Mark and Stephen when they were little. She phoned me a couple of times about arrangements, and her bubbly, friendly personality came across immediately.

A couple of months before the big day, I travelled to London to have my photo taken for the brochure. I hate having my photo taken, and I usually tear up any photos of myself. But this had to be done, there was no getting out of it, and it would be a top professional photographer taking the pictures so they should be OK. Doreen and Lisa were to be there as well so that a joint photo could be taken, but Lisa was ill that day so I didn't meet her until the day of the lunch. However, using the photographer's skills our photos were combined and I was amazed to see us on the front cover of the lunch brochure.

The day of the lunch arrived, Monday, 6 October. I wore the same blue jacket and patterned skirt I had worn to Stephen's funeral. I had decided that I would wear these clothes to any formal event in connection with Stephen to show that whatever I did was in his memory but I am sure some people must think I have a very limited wardrobe of clothes. Arriving at King's Cross, I took the underground to Embankment station then walked along the Embankment beside the Thames to the riverside entrance of the Savoy Hotel, the venue. In the foyer I met Pat Campbell of Women Together, a Northern Ireland peace group, who had also been invited. Together we went up the wide staircase to the reception room. The large room was crowded but the VIP guests, who included the Champions of Courage, were cordoned off at the top end from the other guests. I met Doreen Lawrence again and Lisa Potts for the first time. Doreen is slim and petite, but the strain of events since her son's death showed on her face, just as probably the same strain showed on mine. In contrast, Lisa was a pretty 22-year-old blonde. We had our photo taken with Queen Noor of Jordan, the royal guest of honour. She comes from a distinguished Arab–American family and is tall, blonde and beautiful, with a degree in architecture and urban planning. Her charm and lack of formality immediately put us at ease. A number of reporters interviewed Doreen and Lisa; when they questioned me, I told them I believed a true woman of courage was Lorraine McElroy. Because she was a Catholic mother living in a republican area, speaking out against the IRA took a lot of courage. I added that I hoped more women would enter politics in Northern Ireland for they would then be, as the theme of the lunch said, making a difference.

The five hundred guests ranged from Harriet Harman, the social security secretary and Minister for Women, to Caroline Hamilton, leader of the first all-woman expedition to the North Pole. They included female consultants, managing directors, lawyers, writers and politicians. A few names I recognised were Diana Rigg the actress, Helena Kennedy QC, and newsreaders Moira Stuart and Zeinab Badawi, though I didn't meet them. There were many other eminent women at the lunch but I didn't know most of them, though they were of course well known to their fellow professionals. I felt very much out of place in such a gathering, although Lady Lothian and Floella did their utmost to put me at ease. It was a pity that there was not enough time to speak to the other guests before the lunch; most left as soon as the lunch was over.

After a while we went into the ornate dining room. As guests of honour, our seats were in the centre of the top table. I sat between Harriet Harman and Doreen Lawrence. On Doreen's right were Lady Lothian,

Queen Noor, Floella Benjamin, and Lisa Potts. The top table stretched the whole length of the room and the problem was that it was only possible to talk to the people each side of me, so conversation was a bit limited. All the other tables were smaller and round which enabled the conversation to flow across the table.

After a minute's silence for Diana, Princess of Wales, killed in a car accident in Paris two months previously, we enjoyed a delicious light meal. We had a laugh when Floella ordered the waiters out of the room because they were collecting dishes and generally making a noise during her introduction to Queen Noor's speech. Queen Noor spoke about ordinary women in her country who had overcome adversity and started businesses in their own homes. She presented the Frink Award to the Director of Community Services at South Ayrshire Council. Blind for twenty years, she held the most senior position of any blind person in local government. Harriet Harman spoke next about the problems faced by single mothers and the government's intention to do something for them. Before the last speaker, Vivienne Westwood, could rise to her feet, a message came from the chef to say that the sorbet was melting so could they please serve dessert before the next speech. Floella gave her permission. Finally, Vivienne Westwood, one of our foremost fashion designers, spoke about eccentricity and the bullying children suffer for failing to fit in.

After the lunch, Pat and I went for a cup of tea at a little café near the Embankment. It was a chance for us to talk about our sons. Pat's son Philip, a chef, had a fish-and-chip van to make a little extra money. One night he was shot dead by gunmen in his van outside the town of Moira. He was Catholic, his killers were Protestant. Nobody was arrested for the murder, even though someone had been heard bragging in a bar about what they had done. I asked Pat why they hadn't gone to the police about it. She told me she feared for the safety of the rest of her family if they had. Another of their sons had narrowly escaped death when the hut at their workplace was riddled with bullets. We talked generally about the situation in Northern Ireland now that the IRA ceasefire was in force and the peace talks were taking place at Stormont. Then we said our goodbyes as I had to get to King's Cross station for

152

my train back to Peterborough.

I leaped onto the train standing in the platform, checking it was the one for Peterborough. I then settled back in my seat and thought back over the day. I had met such a wide cross-section of women, some of whom had achieved prominence in their chosen careers, whilst others like Doreen Lawrence, Lisa Potts and myself had achieved something through being thrust into a situation which we would never have imagined would happen to us but which we had faced and fought through. In the same way, the murder of her son had motivated Pat Campbell to continue her work in the peace movement in Northern Ireland and not to give up in despair.

Women can achieve many things – there is the saying that the hand that rocks the cradle rules the world. As Doreen Lawrence said, children are our future, they need us to teach and guide them in the world and to show them right from wrong. I believe that women in Northern Ireland could and should have more influence on the situation there. It is a very male-orientated society, dismissive of women in the political sphere. The presence of a female Secretary of State for Northern Ireland must have meant a great deal of adjustment for their male politicians. As I said earlier, the theme of the Women of the Year Lunch was 'Making a Difference'. I believe women can make a difference, women should make a difference and women must do all they can to make a difference in Northern Ireland. That is how I see it from England.

13
DOWNING STREET

I WAS STANDING OUTSIDE 10 Downing Street, the heart of British government, handing a Christmas card to Gerry Adams, the leader of Sinn Féin and the man who had said that our son's death was regrettable and need not have happened. No this wasn't yet another dream, this was really happening.

Early in December I had read in the newspaper that a Sinn Féin delegation led by Gerry Adams had been invited to meet the prime minister at 10 Downing Street. This was the first meeting there between an Irish republican leader and a British prime minister since Michael Collins met David Lloyd George in 1921. There were differing views in the press about whether Sinn Féin should have been invited. The newspapers asked whether the prime minister should be talking to people who had caused so much suffering, and who had not given up a single gun or ounce of Semtex. The prime minister had already met the leaders of the other main Northern Ireland political parties taking part in the Stormont talks. He was determined to hold this historic and symbolic meeting. Because Sinn Féin would be milking this meeting for all the publicity they could get, I decided I would put a little balance into the day. I was also going to be there to give a message to Gerry Adams. I was going to tell him that he had to be sincere about the Stormont talks – he couldn't just bask in all this publicity, it came at a cost. People did not want a return to violence, they hoped Sinn Féin was willing to

154

make the compromises necessary to reach an agreement, just as the other parties would have to.

But first I had to get permission to enter Downing Street as I knew security would be very tight that day. I knew the visit would be at 2 o'clock on 11 December, so the day before, I phoned the prime minister's private secretary's office asking permission to enter Downing Street and give Gerry Adams the same Christmas card and message that I had already sent to the prime minister. I was very doubtful whether I would get permission, but if you don't ask you don't get. I was delighted when a phone call came early that evening giving me permission.

Arriving at King's Cross station at about a quarter past eleven, I caught the tube to Westminster. Leaving the station I found myself looking up at Big Ben. It had been shrouded in scaffolding the last time I had seen it, but now it looked very impressive. The stonework had been cleaned and the gold paint shone in the sun. I had time to spare before I had to go to Downing Street so I walked over to Westminster Abbey. I wanted somewhere quiet to sit and think, and to gather up my courage. But before long it was time to leave this sanctuary of peace if I was to be at Downing Street twenty minutes before the delegation arrived.

As I walked up Whitehall towards Downing Street I could see about a hundred people on the other side of the road opposite its gates, some with the Union Jack and the flag of Ulster, some with the Irish tricolour. They were in two separate groups kept apart by the police. I walked up to the huge, black wrought-iron gates at the entrance to Downing Street, around which a small crowd had gathered, and told one of the many policemen my name and that I had permission to enter and hand a card to Gerry Adams. He had obviously been forewarned, for he opened a small side gate to let me through. I was met on the other side by another policeman who led me the short distance to Number 10, past a huge bank of reporters and photographers on my left. Ahead of me I saw a Christmas tree beside the most famous front door in the land. We went straight up to the door and into the entrance hall. I had never expected actually to go into Number 10, presuming I would wait on the street. I was introduced to some of the Press Office staff and to Paul Murphy, the Northern Ireland Minister, who arrived a few minutes later.

A message came that the Sinn Féin delegation was about to arrive so I was taken outside and waited with a member of the prime minister's staff on the pavement opposite the ranks of press and TV reporters, who did not seem to notice my presence. The members of the delegation were greeted with shouts, cheers and jeers from the flag-waving crowds on Whitehall as they walked through the gates and towards Number 10. I stepped in front of them and they formed a small group in front of me. I handed the card and message in a sealed envelope to Gerry Adams as Martin McGuinness and the other representatives looked on. I don't know whether Adams had been told I would be there but he seemed a little surprised. He recognised me and I said, 'I would like to give you this Christmas card and I hope Sinn Féin's approach to the talks is sincere and you are willing to make compromises to reach peace.'

The Christmas card, with its picture of a white dove, message and photo of Stephen with Mark, were the same as those I had sent to the leaders of all the political parties at the talks, the prime minister, the Secretary of State for Northern Ireland, the taoiseach, the Catholic and Protestant archbishops of Armagh, and the Moderator of the Presbyterian Church in Northern Ireland. My message was simple – that I hoped the talks would lead to a lasting peace and that no other young men would lose their lives while politicians seemed unwilling to listen to each other and compromise. I added that Christmas would be a very sad time for us, as it is for the families of all those killed in the violence that has blighted Northern Ireland since 1969. I asked if politicians could justify the possible collapse of the talks for the sake of principles on which compromise could be made without giving up those principles completely. Finally my message said there had been so many changes in the past decade throughout the world which we would not have thought possible. Surely an agreement leading to lasting peace in Northern Ireland was also possible. Adams thanked me for the card then stood with the rest of the delegation in front of the door of

Number 10 as photos of that momentous occasion were taken by the press.

As the Sinn Féin delegation disappeared behind the door, my thoughts turned to the parallels the press had drawn between today's meeting and that with Michael Collins in 1921. Like Adams, Collins led his delegation to 10 Downing Street seeking freedom from British rule. Like Adams he was a charismatic figure, though from accounts he was the more dashing and good-looking of the two. In the July before his visit, a truce had brought to an end the Anglo-Irish War. For two years Ireland had been the scene of bitter fighting between the IRA, led by Collins, and the notorious Black and Tans and Auxiliaries, former British soldiers whose savage reprisals led ordinary Irish people to support the IRA. The talks between Collins and Lloyd George culminated in a treaty, signed on 6 December, under which the Irish Free State came into being. In signing, the Irish representatives were agreeing to the existence of a separate Northern Ireland, as created under the 1920 Government of Ireland Act. Previously, that Act had been ignored in the south. Defending the treaty, Collins said it gave 'not the ultimate freedom ... but the freedom to achieve it'. Disagreement on partition and the inclusion of an oath of allegiance to the king led to two years of bitter civil war between Irishmen. Republicans split, supporting either Collins and the treaty or de Valera, who rejected it. On signing, Collins had said he was signing his own death warrant. His prophecy was fulfilled when he was assassinated on 22 August 1922.

The Free State government came down hard on the IRA, and in May the following year, de Valera ordered his men to dump arms. But he was to triumph in the end, taking his seat in the Dáil without taking the oath of allegiance. His party, Fianna Fáil, won the 1932 election. He became head of a government that dismantled the 1921 treaty, removing the oath of allegiance to the king and passing a new constitution by which in 1949 southern Ireland became an independent republic. Articles 2 and 3 of that constitution laid claim to the six northern counties. In 1936 de Valera had declared the IRA an illegal organisation as its members had sporadically challenged his government. They operated undercover, concentrating their fight against British rule in the north, a fight which culminated in the present thirty-year conflict. In 1970 the Provisional IRA, based in Northern Ireland, split from the Official IRA, which had been moving towards left-wing politics. Men such as Gerry Adams and Martin McGuinness, who had been part of the fight since the outbreak of the troubles, came to the forefront in Belfast and Derry respectively. From 1981 on, they had adopted the strategy of the 'Armalite and ballot box', leading republicans into politics in Northern Ireland through Sinn Féin. Slowly they were encouraged, by John Hume and the Irish taoiseach, Albert Reynolds, to accept the peace process, the use of democratic means to achieve their goal of a united Ireland.

This was the history connecting the visits of Michael Collins and Gerry Adams to 10 Downing Street. Would history repeat itself and Adams pay the same price as Collins? Everyone knew the end of partition was not on the bargaining table in the near future. Could he accept less and say as Collins had that it gave 'the freedom to achieve it'? Only time would tell. I walked over to the press ranks and asked if anyone would like to hear the day's events as seen from a different angle. Unfortunately, I happened to be standing in front of two reporters from papers known for their right-wing bias, and they gave me quite a grilling. 'Do you want revenge against the people who shot your son?' 'No,' I replied, 'Do you think that the people who support murder and who will not condemn it should be invited into the headquarters of British democracy?' I replied, 'If anything can help to stop the killing, to keep the talks going, to find a compromise, then it's worth it. If the Berlin Wall can come down and Nelson Mandela can be president of South Africa, surely they can sit down and talk here.' Next they asked if I was aware that Adams had been a senior IRA man. I simply answered 'Yes.' The questions went on. 'Do you realise that Sinn Féin are the mouthpiece for the IRA who killed your son?' I said that of course I realised this but that I had said all along that we have to talk to them as long as there is a ceasefire otherwise the gunmen will claim that the gun and the bomb are the only things we listen to. I was asked again if it was right for our prime minister to be talking to Sinn Féin. I replied that they had two MPs and as the prime minister had met the leaders of the other political parties it was right that he should also meet Sinn Féin.

I was getting nervous by now but I said, 'I am an ordinary mother. I don't have pat answers like politicians. Some people would think what I say is wrong while others might agree. But if someone had themselves lost a son, even if he was in the army, then they would want to do whatever they could to bring this situation to an end which has caused far too many deaths already. Terrorism polarises people and I hope that Mr Adams will prove the trust the government has given him is right.' I had brought with me an extract from the newspaper of one of the reporters, an extract listing all the IRA's victims over the past thirty years. Showing this to them, I said the list was very selective, ignoring the victims of loyalist violence during that time, many of them innocent Catholics. In the next half-hour I was interviewed by many other reporters for the press, TV and radio, but none were as difficult and antagonistic as the first two. In these interviews I covered the reasons I was there and said that through the talks process the prime minister was doing all he could to try to find a solution that would lead to peace. I told them of seeing Sinn Féin election posters on the Falls Road after the May general election saying 'Vote Sinn Féin, Vote for Peace' – now they had to deliver on that.

About an hour after the delegation had entered, the door opened and they came out. I saw Gerry Adams try to put the card into his overcoat pocket but then hand it to one of the women in the delegation. They stood in front of a row of microphones to answer a barrage of questions from the press. Adams said, 'The hurt and grief and division which has come from British involvement in Ireland must end. We must move on from the old, failed agenda, towards a new agenda.' However, it still seemed that this could only be achieved by doing what Sinn Féin and the republican movement wanted. I stood about twenty yards away watching them and making eye contact with Adams as often as I could when he looked in my direction, though I don't know if he was aware of this. A reporter from Northern Ireland asked Adams how he felt about my presence and if he had anything to say to me. He said that there were thousands of Mrs Restoricks in Northern Ireland, that I was not unique in my suffering. This rather hurt me as I had always stressed in interviews that I tried to represent the suffering of mothers in both communities and in the rest of Britain due to the conflict, that we suffered the same heartache. Because I am English I have felt able to speak out, whereas a mother in Northern Ireland might find it more difficult. However, I am very aware that opinions on what I say differ, some seeing me solely as a mother of a British soldier, one of those who they believe should not be in their country, while some unionists would not agree with my views that Sinn Féin should be included in the talks, and perhaps some victims' relatives would also not agree with my views. But they are my views and I always stress that I only speak for my own family and for our hopes for peace so that in years to come there is an end to the killing.

After the delegation had left, an American TV crew interviewed me. By this time it was beginning to get dark and a cold wind was blowing, I felt a few sharp spots of rain. I was feeling very cold so, with the interview over, I walked back down Whitehall to a pub for a whisky and ginger to warm me up. The pub was quite full, and as I stood at the bar I noticed that the group of men standing next to me included some with Irish accents. Perhaps one of my faults is that I am at ease talking to complete strangers, so I waded in saying that I noticed their accents and asked if they had been part of the flag-waving groups opposite Downing Street. They said they had been there watching, but not with the groups. I asked where they were from. One said he came from the Republic, another was from Northern Ireland, and the third was English. I asked them what their hopes were for the peace process and should Sinn Féin be at Number 10. The man from Northern Ireland definitely did not think Sinn Féin should be there, but the other two disagreed with him.

The man from Northern Ireland brought into the conversation a friend of his who had come over from Enniskillen for the day to take part in the unionist demonstration outside Downing Street. The discussion started to get rather heated as these two obviously had strong views in support of the Union and Ian Paisley. One of them said the Labour Party only won the election because of the votes in Northern Ireland. I found this totally incomprehensible given the huge Labour majority, and I said that it was the Conservative government who had depended on the unionist MPs to keep them in power and because of that the previous ceasefire had been wasted due to the insistence on decommissioning before talks began. One of the northerners said that you couldn't hold talks with people who had guns under the table. However, the man from the Republic agreed with me and said that the IRA would never hand over weapons before talks because that would be tantamount to surrender. The discussion was becoming heated, but fortunately somehow the conversation turned to the England–Ireland rugby match. I decided to make my exit before things got even more heated. I gave my apologies and said I had to catch my train, although they did ask me to stay for another drink.

So ended a very eventful day for me and a historic day for Sinn Féin. I hoped that my reason for being there was understood by most people, whether they supported my views or not. I was not there to gain publicity for myself but to show that behind this visit lay a very serious subject more important than publicity for political parties. That was the human cost if the peace talks were not given a chance and the parties involved were not willing to agree to some sort of compromise that could provide a basis to be built on in the future. I did not know what that compromise might be, the two sides at the time seemed so entrenched. But I believed there was hope as long as they were talking.

I arrived home at about 9 o'clock, but my hasty supper of fish and chips was repeatedly interrupted by phone calls from reporters. I still wondered if my actions would meet understanding and approval from others, especially the families of victims. Two phone calls showed that some people, at least, supported me. A man living in the south of England but originally from Northern Ireland and whose brother had been murdered there, said he supported what I had done. Later, Joan Wilson phoned from Enniskillen with her support. My mind felt a little more at ease, especially when the next day I read in the papers that Colin Parry, whose twelve-year-old son was killed in the IRA bomb in Warrington, had said Sinn Féin had to be in the peace talks if they were to have any meaning.

Next day the newspaper coverage of the Sinn Féin visit was extensive and included some of what I'd said and pictures of me holding the Christmas card. Apparently I was not the only person to make eye contact with Gerry Adams on that historic day. The papers said that the prime minister had looked Gerry Adams straight in the eye as he told him that a return to violence would waste 'the best possibility for peace for a generation'.

Just before Christmas, Gerry Adams sent me a copy of his book *An Irish Voice – The Quest for Peace*. This consisted of articles from his column in the New York newspaper the *Irish Voice*. In the article covering 19–25 February 1997 he said of Stephen's death:

> His death, like all the other deaths, diminishes all of us. Yes, he was a soldier. Yes, he was heavily armed and well-trained. But he did not need to die. Not in Ireland. Not at the age of twenty-three. Why did it happen? Stephen Restorick is the latest victim of the long war on this island. His death is an indictment of those who refuse to talk peace. It is tragic proof of the failure of our efforts to end the war here. Stephen Restorick paid with his life for the short-sightedness and stupidity of British policy. My heart goes out to the parents and family of Stephen Restorick. His death is a tragedy not just for them, though they are the bereaved, but for the rest of us also. It did not have to happen. The organisation behind the killing has, of course, to face up to its responsibilities. But so too have the rest of us.

Were his words sincere? Gerry Adams was born the same year as me, 1948, and his only child Gearóid was born in 1973, the same year as Stephen. In a way I feel a kind of parallel between us and can see that different circumstances may lead to different outcomes in people's lives. Adams's parents came from old republican families, and political events in his teens led him down the path he took. On the other hand I have never had to face the question of how I would react to what I considered political injustice. Would I try to achieve my aims through political channels, although as a minority having little effect? Or would I take up arms? Also, as a woman I have been conditioned to try to find a solution by talking and not using violence. This is not to deny though that women have taken part in IRA activity.

14
FOR WHOM THE BELL TOLLS

W E HAD HOPED THAT STEPHEN'S DEATH would be the last in the conflict in Northern Ireland. That was a naïve and futile hope. Each murder after February 1997 showed us how meaningless Stephen's death was to the situation in Northern Ireland. By then, over three thousand people had been killed, so what right had we to hope that his death would make any difference? In a way it was an insult to all those others who had died, to think that our Stephen was different, that his death should mean something. Yes, our son was special to us, but every other son and daughter killed over the past thirty years was special to their family. Other mothers had suffered the same terrible emotions. Other fathers had tried to cope with their own grief and be strong for their wives. Brothers and sisters had watched their parents' sorrow while trying to cope with their own equal but different sorrow. Now, in the months after Stephen's death, every subsequent murder was a blow, forcing me to accept that Stephen's death was as random and pointless as all the others. It was only significant to me – and because of that I tried to make it have meaning. Now I saw beyond the name of each new victim in the paper to what that person's family, and particularly his mother, was going through. Each death awakened memories of the terrible pain I'd suffered in those first dark days of my own journey through grief. So often, when we read of such tragedies, we think 'There but for the Grace of God . . .' But I could no longer say that. As the John Donne poem expresses it, 'No man is an island . . . therefore never send to know for whom the bell tolls, it tolls for thee'. What follows therefore is a year's journey through grief and sadness not only for the families concerned but for me too. This waste of young lives is an indictment of us all for allowing the violence in Northern Ireland to continue instead of all sides making the compromises necessary to end that situation.

The first murder after Stephen's death took place on 14 March 1997. Although the assertion cannot be proved, I believe it was in retaliation. The victim, 44-year-old Catholic John Slane, of west Belfast, like so many other victims was an easy target with no interest in politics. He was shot in his kitchen as he prepared the bottles for his 16-month-old twin girls. He left a 34-year-old wife, five other children aged from 6 to 14 years old, plus three older children from a previous marriage. Gerry Adams carried the coffin at his funeral on St Patrick's Day though there were no republican trappings. Adams sat impassively as the Bishop of Down and Connor said, 'The murder of John Slane was morally evil. The murder of Stephen Restorick was equally morally evil.'

There followed a spate of murders. On 27 April Robert Hamill, a 25-year-old father of three children, was savagely beaten by a thirty-strong loyalist gang in Portadown, County Armagh, a predominately Protestant town. He died twelve days later. Next came the murder of Constable Darren Bradshaw, aged twenty-four, shot in the back in a Belfast pub while off duty. The INLA claimed responsibility for what was believed to be a revenge attack for the murder of Robert Hamill. In retaliation Sean Brown, a Catholic father of six, was murdered in Bellaghy by the LVF. Off-duty RUC constable Gregory Taylor, a 41-year-old father of three, was murdered on 1 June, not by republican terrorists but by loyalists who kicked him to death outside a bar in Ballymoney, County Antrim. A fortnight earlier he'd been on duty at Dunloy when the RUC blocked an Apprentice Boys parade into the staunchly nationalist village. Officers were attacked with stones and bottles by loyalists, and after the parade dozens of police officers had their homes attacked.

On 11 June Robert Bates was gunned down in the Shankill area of

Belfast. He was a former UVF man and had been a leading member of a gang known as the 'Shankill Butchers' who had carried out several murders of Catholics in the early years of the troubles. He was convicted in 1979 of ten murders and was sentenced to fourteen life terms. Bates served twenty years in prison during which he 'found God'. Since his release the previous October he'd been working as a helper at a drop-in centre for ex-prisoners on the Shankill. Surprisingly, it was not the IRA who shot him but a fellow loyalist – in revenge for the killing of a UDA man twenty years previously. I have to admit that I did not shed any tears over his death, though I realise he was a product of the situation at that time.

Five days later, two RUC officers were killed in Lurgan, County Armagh; they were shot from behind by at least two gunmen as they patrolled their beat. Constable John Graham, thirty-four, was married with three young daughters, and Reserve Constable David Johnston, thirty, was the father of two young sons. The IRA admitted responsibility. British officials believed elements in the IRA who did not want to give up terrorism were behind the shootings, and that a battle could be under way between hardliners and those who wanted to engage in peace talks. There was great fear that this could be the act that pushed loyalists over the brink – that the outlawed UVF and UDA would return to full-scale violence. At the funeral of David Johnston, Dr Sam Hutchinson, the Presbyterian Moderator in Northern Ireland, voiced what many were thinking about the IRA and Sinn Féin. He told the mourners, 'The time has now come to pay more attention to ordinary decent people who never in their lives threw a stone in anger, let alone fired a shot. Many had doubted from the outset whether much would be achieved by talking to Sinn Féin but those involved were honourable people who were willing to try, lest any chance for peace be missed. The time has now come to face reality. There is a natural human reluctance to accept bad news. What further proof is needed now? You have spent time and effort trying to bring the extremists in from the cold, and some had hopes and dreams of what might be. In the cold light of this sad morning those dreams lie shattered.' At Constable Graham's funeral service Pastor Edward Betts said that Constable Graham was 'a good man, a decent man, a man who would not have one shred of sectarian hatred in his heart'.

On 15 July there was the shocking murder of an eighteen-year-old Catholic girl from Lurgan. Bernadette Martin was shot in the head four times as she lay asleep in the home of her Protestant boyfriend's family at Aghalee, a hardline loyalist village in County Antrim. She died twelve hours later in a Belfast hospital. Her father, Laurence Martin, said, 'She was special – we had the same temperament; she was part of me. We loved her so very much it is hard to believe she is gone. I just woke up this morning and it was still there – terrible, terrible pain.' Mr Martin, who has four sons and another daughter, said he bore no ill will towards the murderers. 'I forgive them and hope that God can forgive them too. I feel sorry for them but I feel no bitterness. I just hope they realise what they have done. If her death means it is the last death in this country, then maybe it is worth something and we can live in peace. We do not want any repercussions or people claiming reprisals.' Mr Martin said he had admired the late Gordon Wilson, who forgave the killers of his daughter Marie after the Enniskillen bombing in 1987. 'I often wondered how I would feel if it happened to me. Now I feel the same way that he did. I don't see the point of revenge and bitterness. If you always get somebody to pay for a death, where does it end? You're going to kill the whole human race.' He said of the political parties, 'They should talk until their throats are sore and when their throats are sore, they should still keep talking. What's the alternative – another thirty years of people dying? I want the name of Bernadette Martin to be the last on the list of the dead.' We had spoken very similar words following Stephen's death, and we too had hoped that Stephen's death might be the last. We knew all too well the terrible pain that the Martin family were going through.

Just as horrific was the murder of James Morgan, a sixteen-year-old Catholic boy from Castlewellan. He was kidnapped and tortured by loyalists, his body being found on 27 July in a pit full of dead animals. The local population were so shocked by what had happened that they came together to remove the flags and paint from the pavement edges which they felt made the village seem sectarian. However, someone wishing to cause fear in those trying to reach out to each other daubed the slogan 'We know who you are, paint removers'.

The IRA ceasefire began on 20 July. From October to early December there were three killings for which loyalists were thought to be responsible. Then on 27 December Billy Wright, the leader of the Protestant paramilitary group the LVF, was murdered in the Maze prison by republican prisoners belonging to the INLA. Neither group had declared a ceasefire, and neither approved of the peace talks. In response, the LVF murdered a number of Catholics, starting with Seamus Dillon, aged forty-five, a former republican prisoner, on the same night. On New Year's Eve, LVF gunmen fired into Belfast's Clifton Tavern, killing 31-year-old Eddie Treanor.

Also in response to Billy Wright's murder the UVF, who were represented at the talks by the UDP, were threatening to withdraw their support for the talks. On reading one of the death notices for Billy Wright I noticed that his second name was Stephen. This led me to write to the leaders of the LVF prisoners in the Maze enclosing a photo of Stephen. I told the prisoners about the link with the name Stephen and how my Stephen was killed by the IRA. As a mother I begged them to stop the retaliatory murders, so that no more innocent people lost their lives. I told them my heart had been broken by Stephen's murder but still I wanted the people of Northern Ireland to live in peace and do their utmost to find a solution to this dark period of their history. It would not be easy, but it could only be done by talking. The talks would surely collapse if the violence continued. I asked the LVF to encourage the unionists to stay in the talks to put forward their point of view. That would be a far harder thing to do than shooting Catholics. On a personal level, I told them a year had gone by since I last saw Stephen alive, and I just wished I could see him one more time. All mothers of both communities and in England had suffered this terrible loss through the violence. I said that on the day after Stephen's murder we had begged for no retaliation, and I questioned whether Billy Wright would truly want their actions to lead both communities back to the bloodshed that had started before my Stephen was born and had claimed the lives of forty-six others sharing his name, along with thousands of other innocent people. I ended the letter, 'I only want to see the people of Northern Ireland living in peace and ask you to bring back hope to this situation.'

I sent the letter to the governor of the prison asking him to confirm that he had passed my letter to the leaders of the LVF prisoners, which he did. But the killings continued. Ten days into the new year two LVF gunmen fired at doormen outside the Space nightclub in Belfast, killing Terry Enright, a 28-year-old Catholic married to Gerry Adams's niece. Enright was a community worker who fought for disadvantaged youngsters of whatever faith; one of his closest friends was a Shankill Road man, Billy Hutchinson of the PUP. Eight days later, LVF gunmen killed Fergal McCusker, aged twenty-eight, in Maghera, County Derry. The following day the INLA murdered senior UDA man Jim Guiney in Dunmurry. The murder of three more Catholics followed in Belfast: Larry Brennan, fifty-one, was gunned down by the LVF in his taxicab; then on 21 January a gunman killed Benedict Hughes as he left work in the loyalist Donegall Road area; two days later Liam Conway, thirty-nine, was murdered as he sat at the wheel of a mechanical digger. He was the sole breadwinner for his sister and two blind brothers. At his funeral, the Catholic priest said, 'The Conway family are not truly blind. The truly blind are those whose eyes are covered with the cataracts of bitterness and bigotry, hostility and hatred. You are the ones for whom we must pray today – because you are the ones who need the gift of true sight, who need the real vision.'

One particular murder stands out in my memory because it took place on my birthday, 24 January, and the victim had the same Christian name as my husband. He was John McColgan, a 33-year-old Catholic taxi driver with three young children. His wife's name was Lorraine and their elder son was called Sean. I immediately thought of Lorraine McElroy at Bessbrook whose elder son is also called Sean. With this in mind I wrote to Lorraine McColgan telling her that I was thinking of her and her children and I sent her a little heart brooch. A few days later I saw a photo of her with her daughter at a Belfast city centre rally against the murders and in support of the peace talks. I was so pleased when I saw she was wearing the brooch on her coat. I had not been able to go to the rally but I felt that in wearing the brooch she was linking my hopes with those attending and that the two of us had reached out in a small way across the divide.

On 26 January I wrote to Gerry Adams and to the leaders of the two loyalist parties, Gary McMichael and David Ervine, enclosing a copy of my letter to the leaders of the LVF prisoners. I said how saddened I was by the murders and that the killings had turned into an attempt to bring about the breakdown of the whole peace process and cause a return to all-out violence, despite the wishes of the majority of the people for peace and for the talks to continue. I sent Mo Mowlam a copy of that letter and of my letter to the LVF prisoners' leaders. I congratulated her on her brave action in meeting the loyalist prisoners in the Maze to persuade them to continue support of the talks, even though her actions were condemned by the press. Referring to the LVF and INLA, I ended by saying that those who do not take part in democracy should not be able to have an influence far in excess of their numbers. By sending these letters I felt that my views as the mother of a victim were being heard as well as the views of the prisoners, who seemed to be having perhaps too great an influence at that time. Some relatives were feeling angry that nobody was asking them for their views but politicians were all hurrying to the Maze to talk to the men of violence.

In early February 1998 two killings happened that were attributed to the IRA. Brendan Campbell was a well-known drug dealer and Robert Dougan was a leading loyalist. These murders led to Sinn Féin being expelled from the Stormont talks for a couple of weeks, just as the UDP had been expelled for a short while due to UFF co-operation in some of the LVF murders of Catholics.

A shooting that deeply shocked people happened on 3 March. On that day, two young men were murdered at a bar in the village of Poyntzpass, in County Armagh. They were Philip Allen, thirty-four, and his best friend, Damien Trainor, twenty-five, who had been friends since schooldays. That evening a loyalist gunman came into the Catholic-owned bar and ordered Philip and Damien to lie on the floor, presuming them both to be Catholic. He shot them both dead. Damien was Catholic but Philip was Protestant. Poyntzpass is a quiet little village, predominantly Catholic, where members of both communities get on well together. As the bar owner's son said, 'There are no republicans or loyalists here, and no one gets upset about parades on 17 March or 12 July. We never thought this would happen here. But we will make sure this horrendous incident draws us closer still.' In Prime Minister's Question Time at the House of Commons the following day, Tony Blair condemned the murders and said that the two men in their friendship showed the future, whereas the gunman showed only the past.

On the morning of Damien Trainor's funeral I went to my local Catholic church, which I had never visited before; in fact I hadn't been in any Catholic church in England, and I was a little unsure what to expect. It is a very modern building, very light inside, and the pictures behind the altar of Mary and Jesus reminded me of those John and I had seen on holiday in the Greek islands. I lit a candle for Damien and asked that he and Philip be remembered in prayers that day. Then I burst into tears because everything was being brought back to me about Stephen's death. The sisters made a cup of tea for me, and made me welcome. One of the nuns, originally from Ireland, had visited me a couple of times soon after Stephen's death. I returned to the church that afternoon for the service commemorating Women's World Day of Prayer, at which I joined both Catholic and Protestant women in a prayer for Damien, Philip and their families. My heart went out to their parents and families. But I truly felt I knew what Damien's mother in particular was going through. She too had lost one of her two sons.

15

DERRY

IN JANUARY 1998, WHEN SO MANY INNOCENT CATHOLICS were
being killed in response to Billy Wright's murder, I returned to
Northern Ireland. I had been invited by a famous US senator and
brother of a former president of the United States to take part in a lecture he was giving in Londonderry. (As this is a predominantly nationalist city I shall refer to it as they do by its original name of Derry.)

A few days after Christmas, Mark took a phone call from the office
of Senator Edward Kennedy asking if I could join him on Friday,
9 January, at the Guildhall in Derry. When the call came, John and I
were in Shropshire, but Mark gave Senator Kennedy's office our phone
number there. If Mark hadn't returned home ahead of us the Senator
would not have been able to contact us and we would have missed a
great opportunity to meet many influential people in Derry.

On our way to Birmingham airport the weather was atrocious. It
poured with rain and whenever we overtook a large lorry we could
not see a thing due to all the spray. I began to wonder if we would ever
reach the airport, let alone Derry. However, we did arrive safely and in
plenty of time. We flew to Belfast then transferred to a small propeller
plane. I was not looking forward to this flight as I had heard that smaller
planes are more affected by turbulence. But the weather was kind to us
and as we flew towards Derry we saw Rathlin Island off the north coast
of Antrim and snow on the tops of the Sperrin mountains. The

172

approach to Derry airport was hair-raising as it seemed for a moment as if we were going to land in nearby Lough Foyle but we were soon on the runway.

We were the first to arrive at the hotel, four miles outside Derry, so after a light lunch we went into Derry to see the sights. This was our first visit there, and the taxi dropped us off in the Diamond, the centre of the old city and within the city walls. From there we walked to the walls and along the top of them to the Guildhall. Here there are a number of cannons on the walls; they reminded me of a photo we have of Stephen when he was about five years old sitting beside a cannon in the fort at Almeria in Spain. From the Guildhall we walked around the outside of the walls up a short street in which every other door seemed to be the entrance to a bar. From there we made our way to St Columb's Cathedral, nestling just inside the walls, where we were shown a small museum about the siege of 1689 which began when a group of Protestant apprentice boys shut the city gates against the troops of their Catholic king, James II.

So much of the history of the present situation took place here in Derry. Catholics were in the majority in Derry, but after the siege of 1689 the town was regarded by Protestants as theirs. In the 1960s it was a hotbed of Catholic frustration. Not only was there gerrymandering in electoral wards – so that a city the majority of whose inhabitants were nationalist elected a unionist council – but there was also discrimination in housing and jobs. The first confrontation came on 5 October 1968 when a banned march, which included not only Sinn Féiners and left-wingers but also moderate nationalists like John Hume and three Westminster MPs, was blocked by a cordon of police who drew batons and charged the crowd without provocation. On 4 January 1969 a march from Belfast for Catholic civil rights was set upon by loyalists at Burntollet bridge just outside Derry. That night a number of policemen attacked the residents of the Catholic Bogside area; the residents erected barricades to protect their area and 'Free Derry' was born. The next flashpoint was triggered by the Apprentice Boys march on 12 August that year. Fierce rioting erupted between protesting Catholics and the police, leading to a three-day riot which became known as the

Battle of the Bogside. On 13 August, rioting spread to Belfast, Newry, Lurgan and other towns. The police lost control of the situation and on the following day army reinforcements from Britain were sent in. So the present troubles started. The first troops were welcomed with open arms by Catholics, who gave them cups of tea and sandwiches. But the problem was that the army was under the direction not of the government at Westminster but of the unionist government at Stormont. Gradually, Catholics lost confidence in the impartiality of the army, and the present-day seeds of mistrust were sown; a key event was the killing by paratroopers of thirteen unarmed Catholics during rioting following a banned march in Derry on 30 January 1972, now known as Bloody Sunday. This caused the greatest recruitment surge the IRA had ever known. Derry really was where it all began.

We returned to the hotel by taxi. I found the taxi drivers in Derry very unlike those in England as they hardly speak to you. Perhaps history has taught them not to get involved in conversations with strangers – so many taxi drivers have been the targets for sectarian murderers. Michael McGoldrick, a Catholic taxi driver in Lurgan, was shot in July 1996. It was around the time of the Drumcree march and the Portadown-based LVF claimed responsibility for the murder. Married with a young daughter (his wife gave birth to their son three months after Michael's death), McGoldrick had just completed a degree course at university as a mature student. He was yet another innocent person killed for being of a different religion. Now his father, also called Michael, like me had been invited by Senator Kennedy to speak at the Guildhall. He and his wife Bridie were at the hotel when we returned. They had written to us after Stephen's death and we felt a bond with them in their grief at the loss of a son, though Michael was their only child. Now we were able to meet them in person, to see the sadness etched in their faces and the pain in their hearts.

Eventually Senator Kennedy and his party arrived. He was a tall and imposing figure, whose girth had broadened with age. We all sat in the lounge in a large group comprising Senator Kennedy and his attractive young wife Vicky, his sister Jean Kennedy Smith, at that time the American ambassador in Dublin, Kathleen Stephens, the American consul in Belfast, John Hume, the leader of the SDLP and MP for Derry, his charming wife Pat, and ourselves. On the edge of the group were Kennedy's assistants. I had received a letter of condolence from Jean Kennedy Smith soon after Stephen's death, and I wondered whether this was because of the circumstances of his death or whether, also having a son named Stephen, his death touched her more. It was amazing how informal they were, which made us in turn feel relaxed. Kennedy asked how we pronounced our unusual surname, and we told him it came from the old Cornish language, a Celtic language like Gaelic. Although I had been introduced to John Hume at Stormont the previous September, this was the first time I had really spoken to him. He too is an imposing figure, very at ease with the Americans, having built close links over the years with many influential Americans. He told us that his grandfather, a stonemason, came from Scotland to Ireland in the nineteenth century to build station houses on the railway and had converted to the Catholic religion on his marriage to a Catholic girl.

The Kennedy party left us to go over arrangements for the next day, so John and I joined the McGoldricks for dinner. Mr McGoldrick told us of his charity work, taking lorryloads of donated goods to Romania, and also about the talks he gives to church groups about turning the evil of his son's murder to good. He also told us how they had heard on the radio about their son's murder and how his death had affected them.

The next day, after breakfast with Michael and Bridie, we were again joined by Senator Kennedy and he gave us a photo of himself with his brothers John and Bobby, signed by him and his sister Jean. Afterwards, we left with Michael and Bridie for the Guildhall. As we waited in the council chamber for the rest of the party to arrive, we were interviewed by some of the press covering the event. The reporters wanted to know how we felt about Mo Mowlam going to the Maze prison that day to talk to the loyalist prisoners trying to get them to support the peace talks. The prisoners were threatening to tell their political leaders, Gary McMichael and David Ervine, to withdraw as they felt that too many concessions were being made to the republicans. I said I wasn't prepared to discuss Mo's actions except to say that I fully supported anything she did to further the peace process. Yet again, the press were putting the

175

victims' families on the spot hoping they would come out with strong views against the peace process or politicians. Senator Kennedy's party arrived and we joined them in the Mayor's Parlour. We were introduced to a few of the many people there, including Cardinal Cahal Daly, the poet Seamus Heaney, and Mark Durkan, John Hume's right-hand man.

After a while we were taken upstairs to the reception room beside the hall where the lecture was to take place. Here I was introduced to the Reverend Roy Magee, a Presbyterian minister who has worked behind the scenes with loyalists in the peace process. Also in the room were a number of Derry Sinn Féin councillors, including Mitchel McLaughlin who was on their delegation at the peace talks. I knew they were Sinn Féin by the green ribbon on their lapels in support of the release of Irish political prisoners. Glancing at them for a few moments, I wondered whether I should go up to them or not. As the reporters of the Conservative-biased section of the press are always eager to emphasise, Sinn Féin represents the republican viewpoint of which the IRA is the other side of the coin. But how could I support Sinn Féin's inclusion in the talks and yet not be willing myself to talk to individual members? Only by talking can you reach out to another person and hopefully begin to see their point of view, irrespective of whether you agree with it or not. So I went up to them and shook hands. Perhaps I found it easier as the press were not in the room to take photos and sensationalise the handshakes.

As we were led into the hall where the lecture was to be given, on my right was a high stage with a wooden lectern while to my left I saw a sea of faces. Michael McGoldrick and I sat on either side of Senator Kennedy on the stage, with the other speakers to our left, while John and Bridie sat in the front row of the audience. Introductory speeches were made, then it was time for mine. I had never spoken in front of so many people before. I was nervous. Would the audience realise that I was not used to making speeches? Would the words I'd written down on the sheets in front of me come across as I intended or would they misinterpret them? Fortunately, once I started I forgot all those people and it seemed to flow.

I told them why Stephen had joined the army and how he was killed. I told them how after spending Christmas 1996 with us he had returned to Bessbrook on Saint Stephen's Day and that after his death I read in my bible that Saint Stephen had said to God, 'Don't blame them', as he was killed. I had felt that was how I should react to Stephen's murder. I should try to understand the background to what had happened to our small family and not show hatred or seek revenge, as I felt that our Stephen would have wanted us to understand why it had happened. Our attitude was influenced by Lorraine McElroy's words of humanity and compassion for our son. She saw beyond the soldier's uniform to a young man who had been smiling at her one moment and a few minutes later was dying in the ambulance beside her. I didn't believe that anyone who had not experienced it can imagine the heartache caused when a son or daughter is killed, but I knew that a lot of other people in Northern Ireland had felt the same heartache I was going through. The pain was as bad as that I felt when I gave birth to him. It wasn't only an emotional pain but a physical pain and as if I was crying tears that could only be released by a memory awakened by a tune or a word. I said there were still days when I would suddenly stop and think did he really die, or is he just away? This despite the fact that as he lay in his coffin I had stroked his hair as I said goodbye to him. I told them I would give anything in the world to feel him give me a hug and say ''Allo Mum' to me again as he walked in the door.

I told them I'd been amazed to learn there were forty-five others with the name Stephen killed in the troubles: British soldiers, Protestants and Catholics, RUC men, a British policeman and an Australian tourist in Holland. One of these, Stephen Cummins, was killed just outside Derry in 1989 by a landmine and had left the poem 'Do Not Stand at My Grave and Weep' for his parents. I read the poem to them and said we had used it at our Stephen's funeral as it echoed our feelings about his death. I ended by saying that since then I'd tried to be a focal point by bringing attention to Stephen's death, putting a personal face on the longing for peace that most people in Northern Ireland have, and trying to make politicians concentrate on the human cost if the peace process failed.

177

I sat down and was amazed when the whole audience stood up and clapped. I was struggling to hold back the tears and felt emotionally drained. Opening up my inner feelings to all those people had taken a lot out of me. I just hoped it had a lasting effect. Suddenly Senator Kennedy reached over and held my hand for a few moments, realising the emotions I was going through.

Michael McGoldrick spoke about his son and told us of his words of anger and pain when he learned of his death, crying out to God, 'Hanging on a cross is nothing to what I am going through.' John and I knew what he meant. But through his faith he had accepted what had happened and felt peace in his heart, which is where true peace starts. He spoke about his charity work and how the people of Northern Ireland could be so generous in their charitable donations to people in other countries and yet some wouldn't speak to others of a different religion two streets away. Again there was a standing ovation from the audience.

Senator Kennedy then gave the Tip O'Neill Lecture. He outlined the contributions of both Protestants and Catholics of Irish descent in the making of America. Now America wanted to help the people of Northern Ireland build peace and prosperity. He said the vast majority of Irish Catholics in America bore no ill will to Northern Ireland. He praised the many politicians in Northern Ireland who had taken great risks for peace, and Tony Blair, Bertie Ahern and Mo Mowlam for carrying the process forward. He added that George Mitchell was America's special gift to the peace process and proved America was scrupulously even-handed. But above all, he said, the people of Northern Ireland deserved credit for never giving up their dreams of peace and for constantly reminding political leaders of their responsibility to achieve it. While some tried to wreck the peace process, a new spirit of hope was gaining momentum. There must be no return to violence. Killing produces only more killing. Endless escalating cycles of death and devastation had brought unspeakable human tragedy, deeper divisions between and within the two traditions, and painful stagnation and failed prosperity for Northern Ireland. The peace process did not mean asking unionists or nationalists to change or discard their identity and aspirations – it meant using democratic methods, not bombs and bullets, to resolve the inevitable differences between them. The two communities in Northern Ireland must reach out and do what must be done – join hands across centuries and chasms of killing and pain.

Senator Kennedy ended the speech with an extract from a letter his father wrote after the deaths of his son Joe and daughter Kathleen when he was seeking to console a friend whose son had died. In the letter he said, 'When one of your children goes out of your life, you think of what he might have done with a few more years and you wonder what you are going to do with the rest of yours. Then one day, because there is a world to be lived in, you find yourself part of it again, trying to accomplish something, something that he did not have time enough to do.' Senator Kennedy said the lives of too many sons and daughters of Northern Ireland had been cut short, and we must dedicate ourselves to accomplish for them what many 'did not have time enough to do', a lasting peace for Northern Ireland.

After John Hume's short speech of thanks, we all left the stage and congregated in the corridor outside to meet some of the audience. I was suddenly met by a smiling face which I seemed in some way to recognise and realised that it was our friend Eamonn's brother Shane Paul, the Derry former IRA man who gives talks about his involvement in the IRA in the early seventies and his total rejection of violence since then. Two ladies from the group fighting for an independent inquiry into Bloody Sunday came up to me. We had met outside the talks building at Stormont, and now we embraced each other as women who had suffered the loss of a loved one. People who came up to me introduced themselves and said that my speech had been very moving. I was pleased that I had been able to touch so many hearts. I was also grateful that Senator Kennedy had taken the risk of asking the mother of a British soldier to talk to a mainly nationalist and republican audience in Derry.

16

THE PASSING OF A YEAR

WAS IT REALLY A YEAR since that terrible night when I had sat in disbelief as I was told that Stephen had been fatally shot? A whole year since my world was shattered? During that year my journey had taken me to both parts of Ireland, and through a sea of emotions. How were we going to face the first anniversary of the most terrible day of our lives? Should it be like any other day, or should we treat it as a special day? Should John and I be on our own with our sadness and memories, or should we share it with others?

We gave the last question a lot of thought and finally decided that we wanted to spend the anniversary in Bessbrook itself. As the date approached, I made numerous telephone calls to arrange flights, accommodation, and times of visits. As well as Daisy Hill Hospital in Newry, we would visit the checkpoint and the Mill, attend the dedication of a seat in Bessbrook, and the following day visit Corrymeela.

A week before our visit Gary Trew phoned saying he had nominated me for the BBC 'Making a Difference' programme at the Opera House in Belfast. From 6 o'clock on the evening of the 12th we had to be at a reception at the Europa hotel for those nominated and then join them for the show. So we would have to travel from Bessbrook that afternoon. I had also agreed to be filmed in Bessbrook for an edition of the BBC TV *Spotlight* programme about what had happened to us over the past year. It would certainly be a very hectic day.

Another phone call was from Women Together, a peace group based in Belfast, saying that STOP 96, the Dublin peace group, had called for a two-minute silence to be observed in workplaces across the whole island at 11 o'clock on 12 February. I phoned Paul Burton, the organiser, and told him it was the anniversary of Stephen's death and we would observe the silence at the checkpoint. He was delighted as he was having difficulty getting media publicity for the event in the north as a couple of weeks previously there had been rallies in Belfast and a number of other towns in the north against the recent murders and in support of the peace talks. So our observance of the silence in the north gave him another publicity angle.

On Wednesday, 11 February, we caught the flight to Belfast City Airport, arriving early in the afternoon. We were met by the producer and assistant producer of the *Spotlight* programme, who had kindly offered to drive us to Newry. On the way we stopped for a late lunch at the village of Hillsborough. It was at Hillsborough Castle that the Anglo-Irish Agreement was signed in 1985 by Margaret Thatcher and Garret FitzGerald, an event that some see as the first step of the peace process. This agreement gave the Republic a direct say in Northern Ireland's affairs, and was seen by unionists as the first step on the road to a united Ireland despite the fact that it recognised the principle that there could be no change in the status of Northern Ireland without the consent of the majority of the people of Northern Ireland. From Hillsborough we drove on to our little guesthouse in Newry. It had a fantastic view right across the valley in which Newry and Bessbrook nestle to the hills beyond. Our hosts could not have been kinder to us, though I had checked that our being the parents of a British soldier would not be a problem for them in this strongly nationalist area.

This Wednesday seemed to us more like the anniversary of Stephen's death than the true anniversary the next day. I was very aware between 6 o'clock and 7 o'clock of what had happened to Stephen on that Wednesday night a year before. As I looked at my watch I thought, now he was in the guard post at the checkpoint, now he was going out onto the road and Lorraine was arriving at the checkpoint in her car. Now he was checking her licence and smiling at her as he handed it back. And now the sniper fired and Stephen fell to the ground. Now he was telling the other soldiers to see to Lorraine as she had been shot. Now he and Lorraine were in the ambulance. Now he would be at Daisy Hill Hospital and they were declaring him dead. He became a 'legitimate' target and someone celebrated having killed a British soldier. The killer did not see that soldier as a young man, he certainly did not know his name, he did not know what regiment he belonged to – perhaps he thought he was shooting a Para, as they too were in Bessbrook. He did not know that he was my Stephen who I loved so much and who brought so much laughter into our lives. He only knew that he had killed a figure of hate, someone he believed should not be in his country. As he pulled the trigger did he think of friends of his who had been killed? Was he seeking revenge as well as a united Ireland? Or just revenge? Stephen would have been happy to sit in a little pub in that beautiful country with lads of his own age, a pint in his hand enjoying the crack. He wouldn't have cared whether they were Catholics or Protestants or nonbelievers. But he was unable to mix socially with the local people in Northern Ireland because he belonged to the British army. Like them, he was trapped in the web of history that caused the situation in the north.

We had arranged to meet Lorraine and her husband Tony later that evening at the Mourne Country Club on the outskirts of Newry. There was no one else, apart from close family, we would have wanted to spend that special evening with. A few minutes after arriving, Lorraine and I did interviews for the TV. Lorraine mostly spoke about how ordinary people should come together and work together to heal their differences. She also mentioned that every time she passed through the checkpoints it reminded her of that terrible night so they were planning to leave Bessbrook. (When the edited interview was broadcast it seemed as if she wanted to leave Bessbrook just because of the checkpoints, ignoring her point that they were a constant reminder.)

After the interviews we were able to relax. We chatted, had a few drinks and a few more. I have told Lorraine more than once that to me she is a very special person. It was her words that showed me that not all Catholics support the IRA. Her words of compassion for Stephen, and also for his family, guided my reaction to Stephen's murder. They led me to find out more about the situation and become involved in any way I could to help the peace process. We felt like we were with old friends – although we had only met Lorraine once before in the previous August. She is very open and warm-hearted, and her husband is a fine man too. But the hour was getting late and we had a long day ahead of us the next day so we said our goodbyes, arranging to meet Lorraine at the dedication of the seat the following afternoon.

12 February dawned. It was my younger brother's birthday, but now it had a sadder significance for me. As soon as we woke we switched on the TV for the 7 o'clock news. Lorraine's interview came on, and my mind went back to her interview a year ago. My attention snapped back as I heard the newsreader say that there would be a memorial service for Stephen at 2 o'clock that afternoon in Bessbrook. I said to John, 'Can't they ever get it right?' I hurriedly phoned the news studio and asked them to correct the item to say that a seat was being dedicated to all the victims of violence in the Bessbrook area. I knew some people would not attend if they thought it was to be a memorial service. There had already been one dark cloud over the dedication. Inviting church leaders in Bessbrook and councillors of Newry and Mourne District Council to attend the dedication, I had very carefully pointed out that there would be no military presence, realising this might cause a problem for some of the local community and their representatives. But one SDLP councillor said he did not feel able to attend as there was a continual military presence through the army being based in Bessbrook Mill. He made his views known to the local newspapers and before long they contacted me for my opinion on his views. It seemed to me that nothing could take place without controversy arising from one side or the other. It was so disheartening when I was trying to say that we had all suffered. I said that I respected his views but I also pointed out that south Armagh had seen a great deal of terrorist activity in the past and that the army presence was in response to that situation. They had not been there prior to the violence starting, just as the army was not on the streets of Scotland or Wales, nor did most of the soldiers want to come to Northern Ireland, and the British public in general

would prefer them not to be there. I also said that Bessbrook Mill had been built by a Quaker but was now occupied by the army and this was a sad reflection of the situation in that area. The councillor's objection was made more poignant to me as his name was Stephen and, though not related, his surname was the same as that of the man charged with Stephen's murder.

Despite these dark clouds, the weather forecast for the day itself was good with no threat of rain. After breakfast we went to the Daisy Hill Hospital where we met some of the staff on duty in the Accident and Emergency department the night Stephen was shot. The young lady doctor who had treated Stephen said he had suffered a traumatic injury which had caused severe internal injuries to the organs in his abdomen. There had never been any hope of saving him despite their efforts. As we talked over coffee with other members of staff, I passed round two photos of Stephen. I wanted them to see his lovely smile, to see him as he was, not as they'd seen him. They said things had seemed so much quieter at the time it happened and they'd hoped the violence was over. Because of the troubles, they'd gained wide experience in treating severe injuries; their worst day was in August 1979 when eighteen soldiers were killed by two IRA bombs at Warrenpoint a few miles away.

From the hospital we went to the checkpoint on Green Road in Bessbrook where we were met by two of the senior officers from the regiment based at the Mill. With 11 o'clock approaching, we were joined by Michael and Bridie McGoldrick who I had invited to observe the two-minute silence with us. To us it was very symbolic that these Catholic parents were willing to stand with the parents of a British soldier to remember those who had died in the troubles and express their hopes for peace. The senior army officer laid a wreath of yellow and white flowers by the fence on which was a photo of Stephen and some flowers. This was followed by the two-minute silence. The whole army was observing the silence in south Armagh so there were no helicopters clattering overhead and all traffic was stopped through the checkpoint. The silence was complete. I became very aware of the trickling of the little stream on the other side of the fence and thought how peaceful it all seemed. As I thought of the events of the past year, a song came into my mind that was popular when I was in the first few weeks of expecting Stephen. It was 'Vincent' by Don McLean and the words seemed very apt: 'They did not listen, they did not know how, perhaps they'll listen now.' Over the past months I had spoken to the press, trying to reach the people of Northern Ireland with my views on the situation. I so wanted the people to listen, to realise that they must not let the possibility for peace slip away, that they must not let things drift back to the violence of previous years. They had not listened to such calls in the past. But now I believed there was this underlying hope for peace, people were weary of the fighting. Perhaps they'd listen now.

The silence ended with a short prayer for peace by the army padre and I tied a little posy of red silk poppies to the fence in remembrance. After a few minutes we said goodbye to Michael and Bridie, who had made us very aware of the personal sadness caused to both sides of the community in Northern Ireland. I was reminded once again that with three thousand people killed in the troubles, each individual person is soon forgotten by all but those who are left to grieve for them and to ask why him or why her.

As I got into the car that was to take us to the Mill, I was momentarily startled when a lady leaned in and put something in my hand. It was a book of poems, given to her by the author of a poem about Stephen's murder. I noticed later that the book was printed in Peterborough. Arriving at the Mill, we went to Stephen's memorial stone and placed a wreath of red and white flowers at its base. Unlike a year ago, the helicopters were grounded during the short ceremony. As I stood there looking at the stone I thought how far we had come, over the past twelve months, from those first days of grief. I had left work and dedicated myself to reaching out to politicians and both sides of the community to voice the hopes of ordinary mothers for peace and for an end to the killing of sons and daughters they loved as much as I loved Stephen. Two of the memorial stones nearby were to soldiers also killed by IRA snipers in this area. I placed a red carnation from Stephen's wreath on each memorial stone in memory of these young men whose lives had been so tragically cut short.

We went into the Mill to the new study library, named the Restorick

Library in memory of Stephen. This room provides a quiet study area well stocked with books, a language laboratory and computers. There were a number of soldiers in the room, including some female ones. Stephen certainly hadn't mentioned any female personnel there during his time, and I am sure he would have if there had been any! I asked them about the type of work they did, whether they had to do duty at the checkpoints or go out on cross-country patrols. Then we stood with the commanding officer below a plaque and framed photo of Stephen on one of the walls as he gave a short speech of dedication. Afterwards we went to meet some of the other soldiers. But they seemed ill at ease, perhaps because they were in a different regiment to Stephen's. Or perhaps our presence made them more aware of their own vulnerability and the dangers they faced.

After a light lunch in the officers' mess, we walked up the road to College Square for the dedication of the seat. Newry and Mourne Council had given permission for it to be located on a grassy area overlooking a children's playground, the perfect location. The plaque in the centre of the backrest read 'In memory of the victims of violence in the Bessbrook area.' We were delighted that many local people had come, but were not so pleased to see the huge number of reporters. Finding Lorraine amongst the crowd gathered round the seat, we greeted and hugged each other. Councillor Smyth, the SDLP chairman of the council, was there, as were two unionist councillors, though we were not surprised to learn that the Sinn Féin councillors had decided not to attend. Archdeacon Hoey and Father Bradley, the two local ministers, introduced themselves to us. There too were Pat and Margaret, my two friends from Women Together for Peace.

My few words of dedication were that we had wanted to give something in memory not only of Stephen but of all the people who had been killed in the area and that we hoped people would make full use of the seat as they watched the children playing or looked at the lovely view. Archdeacon Hoey stepped forward and said a few prayers, including the Lord's Prayer and 'Blessed are the Peacemakers', and then Father Bradley said the prayer of Saint Francis: 'Make Me a Channel of Your Peace'. I told him afterwards it was the one prayer I'd hoped would be used in the dedication. After the dedication, Lorraine and I sat on the seat and faced numerous photographers and reporters. Lorraine told one interviewer that she would always have memories of that night and that pain. In fact she felt worse now than at the time because the situation had not changed. She said no matter what went on in Stormont, Dublin or London, it was down to ordinary people to have a change of heart to bring about change. During a short break when Lorraine was being interviewed, I went over to meet a group of children from St Paul's High School in Bessbrook and Father Benedict Fee their teacher. Some children and teachers from Bessbrook Primary School and St Joseph's Primary School also attended. Everyone was so kind to us, but because of the sheer number of reporters we were not able to meet as many local people as we'd hoped. We did however meet some of the relatives of the ten Protestant men killed in the Kingsmills massacre in south Armagh in January 1976, machine-gunned by the Provisional IRA as they were returning home from work in a minibus.

It was now just after 3 o'clock, the short dedication ceremony having stretched to an hour. We had been invited to the primary school for a cup of tea but were running late. I was exhausted and didn't want to keep the people at the school waiting any longer. But a radio reporter wanted the interview I'd promised him when we'd arrived. I told him I had to go and didn't listen to his pleas. This was the first time I refused an interview and I was sorry to let him down. I know reporters have a job to do and we have usually found them reasonably considerate. But I don't think they realise how exhausting it is being interviewed by one reporter after another when you are not used to it and have no prepared statement that can be trotted out over and over again.

So we escaped by car to the school and were greeted by the headmaster. They had really put on a wonderful spread for us, but most welcome of all after so much talking was a lovely cup of tea.

All too soon, however, we had to leave to do some filming. The TV crew from the *Spotlight* programme took Lorraine, John and I to a small park nearby for the interview. Looking back on the filming it was quite amusing, though it didn't seem so at the time. We knew we had to work quickly as the light was fading, but everything seemed to work against us. As Lorraine and I were being filmed deep in conversation walking along the side of the small lake, a duck came noisily squawking towards us across the water. Then as we sat talking, helicopters were taking off, a bus rumbled past, and two dogs started fighting. I wouldn't have believed how difficult outside filming can be. But we eventually completed it and said goodbye to the camera crew and to Lorraine. It was now about quarter past four and we had to be at the Europa hotel in Belfast for just after 6 o'clock. We still had to return to Newry to collect our suitcase, make the one-hour journey to Belfast, check into our guesthouse, freshen up and change! Our driver did us proud with his safe, fast driving and we arrived in Belfast with time to spare.

Fresh as daisies, we set off for the reception at the Europa, the main hotel in the centre of Belfast, bombed many times. During the troubles, most of the press stayed at the Europa and it was jokingly said that the IRA brought the bombs to them. Now it was fully refurbished and very plush. The foyer was packed with people. We had arranged to meet Gary Trew and Seamus McNeill there but couldn't see Gary anywhere. Fortunately Seamus, who we had not met before, recognised us. But where was Gary with the tickets? He was late. What were we going to do? I went up to one of the security men at the entrance to the ballroom, where the pre-show drinks reception was being held, and asked him if we could go in although our friend hadn't arrived yet with the tickets. Recognising me, he let us in. So we had a glass of wine and talked to Seamus while we waited for Gary. We did not know anyone else there. They were just ordinary people like us who had been nominated for making a difference to someone else's life. Finally, Gary arrived and managed to find us but was soon whisked away to be interviewed by the *Spotlight* TV crew, who had travelled up from Bessbrook to film us again. He returned, saying he would not be staying for the show as he had to go to the finals of a competition he had entered but Seamus would look after us.

A little after 7 o'clock we were all shepherded across the road to the Grand Opera House for the 'Making a Difference' show. It is a very impressive building with its painted ceiling and plush boxes, but unfortunately our seats were in what was termed the Gallery but I would call the 'gods', being so far up it was not far from heaven! Not only were we right at the top but there were banks of TV lights giving off a terrific amount of heat, all of which rose to where we were seated. To add to our misery, right next to us was the control centre for the lights and microphones. The controller wore headphones and a microphone so he could speak to the director. But because of the headphones he didn't realise how loudly he was talking. Every so often members of the audience in our area would make 'shushing' noises, none of which, of course, he could hear. Despite this, the show was very enjoyable being a mixture of comedy, dance and music interspersed with short stories about how various people in the audience had made a difference. In the second half, Mo Mowlam joined the audience, to much applause from us all. At the end of the show she told the audience that tonight had shown what the real people of Northern Ireland were like. This was answered by huge applause from the audience.

After the show we all trooped back to the Europa and enjoyed the complimentary drinks. A few people recognised me and came over. But the events of that busy day were beginning to catch up with me. At about midnight John and I returned to the guesthouse; we were both really tired and fell asleep as soon as our heads hit the pillow.

The following day we had arranged to visit the Corrymeela centre near Ballycastle. Having spent two weeks there the previous August, now I wanted John to see Corrymeela. We took the train from Belfast to Ballymoney. The weather was dry and alternated between sunshine and clouds as we travelled through the beautiful scenery. At Ballymoney we were met by Alistair, one of the Corrymeela staff, who drove us to Corrymeela itself. Our visit began with a guided tour of the new house. Stepping over trailing cables and cans of paint, we went from room to room trying not to disturb the workmen who were still carrying out the finishing touches before the carpets were laid and the furniture was installed. The dining room, lounge and some of the bedrooms had fantastic views across the water to Rathlin Island. Outside would be a children's play area with swings and slides, and an area for barbecues or campfires, weather permitting. From the new house

Alistair took us on a tour of the other buildings in the complex. At lunchtime we joined other members of staff for a simple but filling meal, which included wheaten bread, a delicious Irish bread made with buttermilk.

After lunch, as it was sunny and warm, John and I walked down to the beach, with its rocks and little rock pools, then along the narrow coast road towards Fair Head's towering cliff. After the hectic day before, it was lovely to be on our own in such peaceful surroundings. A skylark was singing its heart out, and it felt as if spring was just a moment away. About mid-afternoon we returned to Corrymeela and went to the house known as Coventry, home to the year-long volunteers. A few of them were in the lounge, relaxing and listening to music on this free afternoon before the next group of children arrived. We talked for a while – they knew about Stephen because I had written a few months previously to one of the volunteers who comes from Bessbrook. Others were from New Zealand, Canada, the USA and England. I know from those I met the previous year that being a year-long volunteer is hard work – many were feeling exhausted by August – but it is also very rewarding work and I am sure none of them would regret the time they spent at Corrymeela.

It was now nearly 5 o'clock, and Alistair had offered to give us a lift in his car to Belfast with the bus driver who would bring the next group of children up to Corrymeela the following morning. We all piled into his car and set off again through the beautiful countryside, but we were both very tired and before long John was asleep. Eventually we arrived at our guesthouse in Belfast. I was so tired after all the fresh air but John decided he was hungry so we went into town for a meal. On our return we both tumbled into bed and slept like logs until the next morning. In fact we overslept and had to eat a hasty breakfast as I had arranged to be at the Europa to meet Alf McCreary, the journalist and author, just after 9 o'clock. I had written to him about his column in the *News Letter*, a local newspaper. It seemed to me to be a few columns of sense and balance in a paper that mainly covered the unionist viewpoint. I believe journalists like him, writing in newspapers aimed at one section of the community, could put forward other points of view and counteract the drum beaters and mob orators. He had written back saying how deeply he regretted Stephen's murder because he came from Bessbrook and played football as a young lad on the field right next to where the checkpoint now stood. He had sent me a book about his childhood there, and though he was a little older than me, it reminded me of my own carefree childhood in Shropshire in the mid-fifties and early sixties. Now, at the hotel, we chatted for a while. Then, as he left, Maura Kiely joined us for coffee. I had wanted to meet Maura after hearing from the people at Corrymeela about the Cross Group which she had formed as a support group for bereaved parents in Northern Ireland in the early 1970s. In 1975, when her only son, Gerard, became a student at Queen's University in Belfast, she had told him to make sure he still attended Mass on Sunday now he was away from home. One Sunday, loyalist gunmen fired on a congregation as they left Mass – Gerard was killed. After her son's murder, Maura had felt a need to meet other mothers who had lost a son or daughter in similar circumstances. She trawled through the local newspaper death notices for the previous year and compiled a list of names. She visited their families, and from this initiative the Cross Group was formed. In meeting her own needs, Maura provided support for other bereaved parents at a time when there was no such thing as counselling and no self-help groups. She knew that in sharing our grief we help one another. This quiet-spoken, grey-haired mother had lived through her own grief and the grief of so many other mothers since the outbreak of the violence. It was not until the summer of 1998 that the needs of victims were recognised by the British government following Sir Kenneth Bloomfield's report which recommended measures to help them.

After Maura left, we had time to spare until our flight home so we took a walk through the shopping area looking for a bread shop – I wanted some wheaten bread to take home. Now and then people who recognised us from the television the previous day stopped to ask what we were doing in Belfast and said how sorry they were about Stephen. It was strange being recognised like this, whereas in Peterborough nobody would stop us in the street and speak about Stephen – perhaps that is the result of British reserve.

We arrived home in the early evening. Both of us were tired, but we were also pleased that we had returned to Northern Ireland at such a meaningful time for us. We had met a lot of people, all of whom had shown us nothing but kindness. It is sad that we had never visited Ireland, north or south, before Stephen's murder. One man's hatred had caused us to visit Northern Ireland but the majority of people we had met, whether Catholic or Protestant, had shown us the best side of the Irish character.

17

AGREEMENT AND REFERENDUM

THE STORMONT TALKS WHICH BEGAN ON 15 September were dragging on and on with apparently no possibility of reaching any sort of compromise. Therefore, on 26 March, Senator George Mitchell, the chairman of the talks, set a deadline of Thursday, 9 April, for the parties to reach an agreement.

During the last few weeks of the talks there were bombings in Moira and Portadown. These towns were obviously chosen to cause maximum embarrassment to their political representatives at the talks, Portadown being in David Trimble's constituency and Moira in that of his colleague, Jeffrey Donaldson. There were also finds of bomb-making equipment in the Republic. Opinion was that responsibility lay with the INLA or the Continuity IRA who were not on ceasefire and did not support the talks.

Tuesday, 7 April, was a grim day for me personally. The UUP claimed the draft agreement drawn up by Mitchell was unacceptable, as did the UDP. John Taylor, deputy leader of the UUP, said he would not touch it with a forty-foot bargepole. The document had been intended as a basis for the parties to finalise agreement on, but the UUP felt it was biased towards Sinn Féin. It seemed as if the past seven months had been a total waste of time and the parties were as far apart as ever. The rejection led to a flurry of activity. Tony Blair flew to Belfast that night and had a two-hour meeting with David Trimble. He also had meetings with leaders of the Alliance Party and the PUP, and a telephone conversation with John Hume. Finally, having sounded out these representatives, he met with Mo Mowlam and Senator Mitchell. It seemed as if everything was collapsing and they never would reach an agreement. I was very emotional about it all but John wasn't there to share my feelings as he was in Nottingham working. So I had a good cry in Stephen's room, feeling so close to him there. I was angry with the politicians that they did not seem willing to make compromises. 'No surrender' and 'Not an inch' still seemed to be the slogan on both sides. How much longer did these people expect British soldiers to be pig in the middle between them, allowing them to put off decisions that would enable them to live together in peace. To me, these politicians seemed more concerned about loss of power or forcing a united Ireland than stopping bloodshed in the future.

Early the following morning Bertie Ahern, the taoiseach, arrived at Hillsborough Castle for talks with the prime minister, followed by talks with Sinn Féin and the SDLP. Tony Blair again held talks with the parties while Bertie Ahern left for his mother's funeral in Dublin, returning to Belfast that evening for more talks. They were going over the draft document point by point to get an agreement. Ian Paisley, leader of the anti-talks unionists, held a press conference outside Stormont and claimed no agreement would lead to peace.

On 9 April, I phoned Senator Mitchell's office and asked for a message to be given to all the parties. The message was: 'I hope the politicians will meet the challenge of today and provide the forward-looking leadership needed to reach an agreement and to encourage the people of Northern Ireland to accept that agreement with hope and trust and not, as in the past, give in to those who live in the past.' The person I spoke to remembered my visit in September and said that the message would be given to the talks participants. As I put the phone down it was as if I could hear Stephen saying, 'Good on you, Mum, you tell them!'

Easter was only a couple of days away. Now I sent my first ever Easter card and it was a very special one. It was to the man held in the Maze prison awaiting trial for Stephen's murder. The Easter message of reconciliation and forgiveness led me to contact him. Jesus' words on the cross – 'Forgive them for they know not what they do' – could be repeated to terrorists on both sides by parents bereaved in the troubles. One quick terrorist act would lead to years of grief and unfulfilled dreams. In the card I wrote, 'We were all guilty for what has been done in the past and we should all ask for forgiveness.' I hope he understood what I was trying to tell him. As I walked back from the post box I met Eamonn's son Bernard who was on holiday from university. Bernard said his father was glued to the radio listening to what was happening at the talks. It seemed a fitting moment to meet this young man who had been one of Stephen's friends when they were both in the Air Cadets. His father's brother had belonged to the IRA in his youth, and his arrest had caused Eamonn to leave Derry though he still returned there with his family to visit relatives. Would Bernard have been tempted to join the IRA if he had been born there instead of in England? Would he have felt that the English should not be in his country and have hated British soldiers?

The talks dragged on through Thursday night without a break. Ian Paisley and a group of his followers arrived at the gates of Stormont. He was allowed into the press Portakabin but was heckled by supporters of the loyalist parties in the talks. He blustered that he had a right to be there as he had been part of the talks 'until gunmen were included' – a reference not only to Sinn Féin but also to the PUP and the UDP, parties that are linked with loyalist paramilitaries. But the interview showed that Paisley no longer had the huge support he once had from loyalists, though he was still a force in Ulster politics.

At just after 5 o'clock on the afternoon of 10 April, all the parties at last reached an agreement, though the UUP and Sinn Féin had to get their members' approval. The UUP claimed it strengthened the Union with Britain, whilst Sinn Féin saw it as transitional and a basis from which to advance. Many saw it as symbolic that 10 April was also Good Friday; in our own small family it was significant as it was Stephen's grandfather's eighty-eighth birthday and on the same day the previous year, a man had been arrested for Stephen's murder.

The following morning, I went again to the local Catholic church. Lent had ended, the church could be decorated again, and some ladies were doing flower arrangements beside the altar. Just as the church was coming out of a period of death to one of new life so I hoped was Northern Ireland. It was on the first day of Lent, Ash Wednesday, the previous year that Stephen was killed. Some would say that he too now had a new life, I just wished I could believe it. I sat quietly and suddenly the tears began. I looked up at the picture of the stations of the Cross showing Mary holding Jesus' body and I thought to myself I know what she felt, and the tears flooded out. It was a release of the tension that had built up through that week. One moment everything had seemed lost then finally agreement was reached. As I cried, I said to myself that every tear for Stephen in future would be a silent prayer for peace in Northern Ireland.

On Easter Sunday we travelled to Market Drayton and spent a few quiet moments at Stephen's grave. Our feelings were of sadness at our loss and also that Stephen couldn't see how much had been achieved. For us this new dawn had come too late, yet we felt hope for the future. It was early days: the green shoots of peace would need much tender care and there were many who would try to destroy them. There was much hurt and distrust between Catholics and Protestants which would take a long time and much work among those communities to heal. Yet the majority of people did want peace, they did not want their children to grow up with the violence as they themselves had done. I just hoped they were willing to accept the compromises needed to make the agreement work.

On 15 April I wrote to Tony Blair, Bertie Ahern, Mo Mowlam, and the leaders of all the parties involved in the talks, thanking them for the hard work they had put in to reach the agreement and saying that I hoped it would be rewarded by a Yes vote in the referendum to be held on it in Northern Ireland and the Republic. I added that I hoped the voters would be allowed to give the agreement a chance to work and would not be misled by visions of a sell-out that opponents to the agreement would be all too ready to provide. I told them Stephen was born in 1973, the year of the Sunningdale agreement, and I couldn't help but wonder how different things might have been in Northern Ireland if that had been given a chance by the unionists. We could only hope and pray that the people of Northern Ireland would rise to the occasion and take the first step on the long road that lies ahead of them in working together and healing the division and hurt that the years of violence have caused. I also hoped that politicians would provide the leadership this required by looking to the future positively, not living in the past. And I believed it important that the smaller parties in the talks should be included in the Assembly. I hoped Good Friday really was a time of forgiveness and rebirth for the people of Northern Ireland. We had all been guilty, even those like the English public who shut their eyes and ears to the situation and allowed it to continue for so long. I ended the letter saying that I, myself, hoped true peace could be established before the end of the millennium.

An agreement had been reached, but the people of Northern Ireland had to vote for or against it in the referendum to be held on 22 May. A booklet setting out clearly the main points was sent to every household in Northern Ireland, and an Irish-language version was also available on request. Also on 22 May, a referendum would be held in the Republic on whether articles 2 and 3 of their constitution, which laid claim to the whole of the island of Ireland, should be replaced by new articles expressing a wish for a united Ireland with the consent of the people of the north.

The prime minister could not dispel Orange Order concerns about RUC reform, early release of prisoners and decommissioning, so the Grand Lodge of the Orange Order decided not to support the agreement. They said, however, that their members should vote according to their consciences. This was rather worrying, as many male unionist voters belonged to the Orange Order.

On Saturday, 18 April, at their annual meeting in Dublin, Sinn Féin deferred their decision about the agreement to a special meeting on 10 May. It seemed to me they were waiting to see what the UUP did, hoping they would tear themselves apart over the agreement and reject it, thereby saving Sinn Féin members from making difficult decisions. At a meeting in Belfast that same day, members of the UUP gave Trimble the 72 per cent majority needed for acceptance of the agreement. However, six of the party's ten MPs voted against and joined the

No campaign led by Ian Paisley of the DUP and Robert McCartney of the UKUP, both unionist hardliners. On hearing of the majority vote, Gerry Adams in his speech at the Sinn Féin meeting said, 'Well done, David.' Of course, this message could be taken either way, as a genuine message of congratulations or as meaning that in accepting the agreement the Ulster Unionists were playing to Sinn Féin's agenda.

Reporting on IRA splinter groups, the *Guardian* ran an article on 13 April with the headline 'Terror risk to peace deal' and a picture of an IRA sniper road sign changed from 'at work' to 'job seeking'. Below it was a sign pointing to Bessbrook Community Centre. A few days later the paper printed my letter, saying the picture was especially poignant to me as Stephen was killed by an IRA sniper in Bessbrook. I said the first soldier killed in Northern Ireland was Gunner Robert Curtis of the Royal Artillery, and I hoped that my son, who also served in the Royal Artillery, would be the last. I added that I hoped for a Yes vote in the referendum. Two Northern Ireland newspapers, the *News Letter* (Protestant/unionist) and the *Irish News* (Catholic/nationalist) printed a letter from me. I felt compelled to let people of both communities in Northern Ireland know how strongly I felt about what had happened in the past and my hopes for the future after the agreement. I said that Stephen was born in 1973, the year of the Sunningdale agreement, defeated by the Ulster Workers' Council strike, leading to twenty-four years of inertia by unionists. The 'not an inch' and 'no surrender' hardliners had as much to answer for as those who used violence. I thought that if the majority of unionist politicians did not support the agreement in the run-up to the referendum, our government should consider how much longer they could support them both financially and militarily. Huge amounts of British and EC money had been pumped into Northern Ireland through peace and reconciliation funding, for very little result, it would seem, when these politicians hold forth. I mentioned my visit to the local church and my vow that every tear I shed for Stephen would be a silent prayer for peace for the people of Northern Ireland. None of us was without guilt, even those who never turned to violence but through their unwillingness to make changes allowed the violence to continue. Easter was a time of forgiveness and rebirth. What more appropriate day than Good Friday for the talks finally to reach an agreement. I ended by saying it was time for the people of Northern Ireland to show the world they are able to work together despite the suffering over the past years and can meet the challenges of the future together.

In the period of just over a month between reaching the agreement and the referendum, local politicians appeared on TV and radio and at public meetings, and wrote newspaper articles putting their interpretation of the agreement across to their supporters and those still undecided. Needless to say, there was a huge difference between these interpretations. Trimble's unionists saw the agreement as strengthening the Union through the consent of the people of Northern Ireland. Paisley's unionists saw the agreement as a sell-out on the road to joining the Irish Republic. Sinn Féin too saw the agreement as transitional to a united Ireland, whilst the SDLP stressed the coming together of the two communities in power sharing.

A great deal of literature was produced for and against the agreement, and not only by political parties. Some was sent to me anonymously from Northern Ireland. One leaflet was entitled 'The Wright View, the True Ulster Loyalist View' and was dedicated to Billy Wright, the LVF leader murdered in the Maze prison. The headline read, 'Reject the terms of Surrender. Stormont "Peace Deal" will lead to a united Ireland . . . in your lifetime!' Denouncing the agreement, it said, 'the Ulster people have no right to national self-determination' (this despite the fact that any change to the status of Northern Ireland was dependent on consent). It attacked the PUP and UDP for being pro-agreement and ended with the words 'If you want a united Ireland vote "Yes", if you want Ulster to remain British and within the UK vote "No". Keep Ulster British: No surrender to the IRA. On 22nd May vote No.'

Along similar lines, a double-page advertisement in the *News Letter* on 17 April placed by the 'Silent Majority' gave '20 reasons why it's suicide to vote Yes'. A few of these were: 'Pan-Nationalist Rule, Democracy Overturned, Unionists – the Permanent Minority, the Consent Delusion, the Economic Ruin of Unionist Areas, Inbuilt Discrimination Against Unionists, and Undermining the Police.'

Referring to the last point, the advert said the independent commission that was examining the future of the RUC, with international representation, was 'code for do-gooders soft on terrorism, and would ensure the castration of the RUC', and 'encouraging community involvement' was a euphemism for putting paramilitary thugs into uniform. I wondered whether the paper's unionist readership would believe these claims and not bother to read the actual agreement document which set out clearly the checks and balances and the principle of consent.

Another angle came from Christians Against the Agreement based in Larne, a staunch Free Presbyterian and unionist area. Claiming to be 'A Christian Perspective', their pamphlet gave numerous reasons based on biblical texts 'Why Christians Should Vote Against the Agreement'. The introduction stated that 'The political situation in Northern Ireland is a mess. The reason for this is that, although there is much of the show of religion here, there is little practical and relevant Christianity.' I had to agree to a certain extent with that statement. However, I found great difficulty accepting the rest of the document. For instance, the answer to the objection 'There is no perfect solution' was 'There is a perfect solution – biblical standards. The problem in Northern Ireland is not about land or history or culture – it is about justice. And because the law of God is perfect ... we are presented with a perfect solution, if only people would heed it.' That to me seemed rather wishful thinking, and to ignore the fact that not all players in this arena were practising Christians. Also both sections of the community did see the problem as being about land, history, culture and justice.

In a similar vein, to the question 'What alternative is there?' the response was 'The Law of God. Since the problems in Northern Ireland arise out of accusation and examples of sectarianism, and all proposed solutions involve identical allegations, a true alternative must be sought in a source beyond any allegation of prejudice. The only alternative is God.' I wondered how the law of God related to such issues as the right of the Orange Order to march down the Garvaghy Road, and whether the Catholic residents and the Protestant Orangemen would accept a decision that required the judgement of Solomon.

I did agree, however, with the answer to the objection 'No point in voting at all' that 'Every vote counts in this referendum. For the sake of the cause of God and truth, make sure yours is used.' I doubted, however, if everyone would interpret the 'cause of God and truth' in the same way as the author of this pamphlet. The tract concluded with the instruction 'Vote No!', giving biblical texts to support this call. To me the whole of this pamphlet illustrated a type of thinking that only exists in parts of Northern Ireland, and nowhere else in the UK.

Meanwhile, Sinn Féin members met on Sunday, 10 May, in Dublin to vote on whether to support the party leadership's motion to campaign for a Yes vote in the referendum. Trimble's unionists had accepted the agreement. What would Sinn Féin do? At the meeting it soon became obvious that the groundwork had already been carried out behind the scenes to gain acceptance. Martin McGuinness, a Sinn Féin MP, told those present, 'This is an historic day. The whole world is watching, they are watching you to see whether or not you're going to go back or whether we are going to move forward on behalf of the people who are depending so much on us. I am calling on every one of you here today to move forward.' Gerry Adams, Sinn Féin president, said they should vote in support of the motions but vote in the referenda 'as your own conscience tells you'. Another vote was on whether Sinn Féin should take their seats in the Assembly. If they did, it would mean a change in their constitution and it would amount to recognising partition, something they had always refused to do. They had eventually overcome the same problem a number of years previously over taking up seats in the Irish parliament. However, that was at a time when articles 2 and 3 of the Republic's constitution laid claim to the whole of the island of Ireland. It would be a huge change of policy for Sinn Féin to accept their seats at Stormont after articles 2 and 3 had been dropped. Overwhelmingly the members voted in support of both the motions.

This result was no doubt helped by the appearance at the meeting of twenty-seven IRA prisoners given day release to voice the prisoners' support for the proposals. These included the so-called Balcombe Street Four, recently transferred to the Republic having served twenty-three years in English prisons for their part in the 1970s bombing campaign.

The *Irish News* quoted Gerry Adams's words to the delegates after the vote: 'We go into this next phase of the struggle and only with whatever mandate we receive, armed only with our political ideas and our vision of the future. Today is an important day for us, but it is not as important as tomorrow, or the next day or the day after that with all of the challenges that they bring. Today we cleared the way for the future, tomorrow we start to build the future. The future, my friends, is freedom. Together let us build a bridge to freedom.' There had been no split in Sinn Féin as many had feared. Sinn Féin seemed to have turned from the Armalite to the ballot box, but there was no mistaking the fact that although ready to enter the political arena, Sinn Féin's aim of a united Ireland had not changed.

It was at this point that John and I made another visit to Dublin. We had been invited by STOP 96, the Dublin-based peace group, to speak at a press conference in the Mansion House in support of the Yes vote in the Republic. It was only later that I realised how symbolic the venue was. It was in the Mansion House on 21 January 1919 that the first Dáil (parliament) met and declared an independent Irish republic. In the election the previous year, Sinn Féin had gained most of the votes. Refusing to take up their seats at Westminster, they met instead at the Mansion House, appointing de Valera as their leader. That same day the first shots rang out in the Anglo-Irish War, and in August 1919 the existing Volunteers were renamed the Irish Republican Army (IRA).

It was at the Sinn Féin ard fheis here in 1981, following the hunger striker Bobby Sands's election success, that Danny Morrison spoke of republicans taking power 'with an Armalite in one hand and a ballot paper in the other'. This twin strategy between the IRA and Sinn Féin existed from then until their ceasefire in 1997. Also here in 1986 Sinn Féin split over taking up seats in the Dáil. Those opposed formed Republican Sinn Féin; its armed wing, known as the Continuity IRA, attracted those disillusioned with the Provisionals.

Now, in 1998, people in the Republic were about to vote on replacing articles 2 and 3 of de Valera's 1937 constitution with more accommodating words recognising consent of people in the north as the basis for reunification. As I waited my turn to speak, I was very aware that the people beside me on the platform had been working far longer than me for an end to the troubles in the north. I was annoyed when the photographers kept taking photos of me while others on the platform were speaking. I felt very guilty that I was getting more attention. Anyway, my speech here, like my RTÉ radio interview earlier that morning, would probably be superfluous as polls suggested a massive vote in support of amending articles 2 and 3. After my speech I was interviewed for a Cork newspaper, a staunchly republican area. I wondered how IRA supporters there would take my words. They'd probably think my support of the Yes vote was proof that the agreement was in the unionists' favour, offering nothing to republicans, who had to recognise partition in accepting it. This was unacceptable to the sort of republicans who killed Michael Collins in 1922 for accepting less than a united Ireland.

That evening we travelled up to Banbridge, a predominantly unionist town in Northern Ireland. As we walked into the main street we could see the No campaign was in town. A couple of hundred people were listening to some anti-agreement unionist politicians giving their interpretation of the document. To me this interpretation bore no relation to what I had read in the actual document – it seemed to be pure scaremongering and misinformation. It all made me feel very disheartened and I wondered how many of the people who listened to these politicians as they travelled around towns in the north would just believe what they heard.

We had been invited to a 'peace praxis' at an integrated (mixed-religion) primary school in Banbridge. Our audience were pupils from the top year of this school and its linked school in the Republic, and some of their parents. To me, separate schooling along religious lines in Northern Ireland seems to continue the segregation that already exists in housing. Catholic and Protestant children don't have the opportunity to meet one another and become friends. Integrated schools seem the way forward but there are still very few of them, and often the pupils come from families who already mix with the other community. Among the speakers was a lady from Dublin whose sister, brother-in-law and their two very young children were killed with twenty-two other people by a bomb that exploded there in May 1974. At the time the Republic's government was debating stronger measures against the IRA and assumed it was responsible for the bombing. So they passed the measures, only to discover later that loyalists from Northern Ireland were responsible. At the school's request I spoke about Stephen's childhood and my hopes for peace. Mo Mowlam was guest of honour. It was lovely to meet her again – she had worked so hard to get the parties in the talks to reach an agreement, and she really has that personal touch with people. She asked me what I was doing on the day of the referendum and invited me to join her with Colin and Wendy Parry in Warrington.

The day of the referendum came at last. It was Friday, 22 May, and many hoped it would prove to be another 'good Friday' with a majority vote for the agreement. It was already known that the majority of the Catholic population, nationalist and republican, would vote Yes – except for a few hardline republicans. What was not known, however, despite the many opinion polls conducted in the run-up to the vote, was how many unionists would vote Yes. In this democracy it was no longer sufficient for a majority of the overall population to vote Yes; a sizeable proportion of each community, unionist and nationalist, had to show their support for the agreement to be workable.

I joined Colin and Wendy Parry's launch of their fundraising for a peace centre in Warrington. It would be a place where Protestant and Catholic children from the north and south of Ireland could stay and break down the barriers between them. Mo Mowlam was guest of honour and joined us at the proposed site after we'd seen a short introductory video at the town hall. Colin and Wendy's twelve-year-old son Tim had been critically injured by an IRA bomb in Warrington five years previously and died a few days later. Three-year-old Johnathan Ball was killed instantly. The peace centre would be in memory of these two boys, innocent victims, like so many others in Northern Ireland, of the inability to find a way forward. A few weeks after this launch, John and I joined Colin and Wendy for a fundraising dinner. The following morning, they took us into the centre of Warrington and showed us the plaque on the wall near where their son had been standing when the bomb went off. Tim's smiling face and Johnathan's looked back at us from the plaque, a touching indictment of man's use of violence to achieve political aims.

The results of the referendum were expected on Saturday afternoon. The parties supporting the No campaign had demanded that as well as the normal election seals on the ballot boxes they should be allowed to put on their own seal to ensure that they did not already contain Yes votes. They got their way as it ensured there could be no argument about the votes. The TV coverage of the count showed there were more bundles of votes on the Yes table, but were there enough?

Finally, the result was declared: 71.2 per cent in favour and 28.8 per cent against. Trimble had got the majority he needed. The people in the hall were ecstatic, except for Ian Paisley who claimed a majority of unionist votes, a claim that was hotly disputed by everyone else. He left the hall to chants of 'cheerio, cheerio, cheerio' from some, as he had earlier said he would resign if he didn't get a majority. Trimble's unionists had bravely voted for what they hoped would be a better future for their children and grandchildren. Only time would tell whether they were right. The important point behind this referendum and the one in the Republic was that for the first time since 1918 people in both the north and south of Ireland were given the opportunity to vote on which way forward they wanted to go. As expected, people in the Republic voted overwhelmingly to replace articles 2 and 3. It was up to the Northern Ireland politicians now to come together in the Assembly to make the intentions of the agreement fact. However, a section led by Ian Paisley would stand for election to the Assembly and do their utmost to prevent the agreement being implemented.

That evening I lit the large candle sent to me from Warrington at Christmas. I had put it away, saying I would light it when the future looked more hopeful. Every night since Christmas I had lit a white candle for peace in Northern Ireland. Now it was time to light the Warrington candle, to join with them in our hopes for the future in that troubled land. I knew people in Northern Ireland had only taken the first step on a long and difficult road, but they had shown themselves able to look forward in hope and not keep looking back to the past. They did not want that past to be repeated for years to come.

Commenting on the results, the prime minister said once again that he did not expect to see a united Ireland in his lifetime. Gerry Adams said that he hoped he lived a long life to see a united Ireland. No one knows what the future holds. Perhaps in time the Protestant/unionists in the north will not see joining the Republic as a threat to their identity and power. Perhaps the people of Northern Ireland will choose some other form of political status linked primarily to neither the Republic nor Britain but to both within the European Community. The important thing is that people move forward together and work to heal the divisions that have torn Northern Ireland's people apart and caused so much tragedy to so many families there and in the rest of the UK.

The referendum was followed in June by campaigning for elections to the Assembly. The UUP decided that apart from David Trimble and John Taylor, his deputy, none of its MPs could stand for election. This bar included Jeffrey Donaldson, who had come out against the agreement on the last day of the talks. The election was held on 25 June, but because of the intricacies of the transferable voting system the result was not clear until the evening of the 27th. The unionist vote was split because some opposed the agreement, so the SDLP returned the highest party vote. The final result was UUP 28 seats, the SDLP 24, Paisley's DUP 20, with the like-minded UKUP 5, and Sinn Féin 18. Smaller parties brought up the rear. There were even thirteen women elected.

At the first meeting of the Assembly, on 1 July, David Trimble was voted First Minister with Seamus Mallon of the SDLP as deputy First Minister (John Hume had decided his workload was already large enough with his work as MP and MEP). Seamus Mallon had told us that he was in Bessbrook the night Stephen was killed. What a long way events had come since then, and how symbolic that now he should be the deputy leader of the Assembly. David Trimble also seemed to have come a long way from that September day in Belfast when he outlined his party's views to me. I had come away very disheartened, but now it seemed that he might be looking to the future and trying to work with the SDLP. Two questions were uppermost in my mind. Could they keep Sinn Féin on board, and could the agreement be made to work despite the Paisley-led unionist politicians determined to see that it did not?

Although the Provisional IRA seemed to be indicating that the conflict was over, the INLA and Continuity IRA, both republican splinter groups, were willing to continue it. Only the previous week a group had appeared calling itself the Real IRA, said to be led by a former Provisional IRA quartermaster-general with several former high-ranking Provisionals. Many considered the 32-County Sovereignty Committee to be its political arm, though they denied this. This last group included Bernadette Sands McKevitt, sister of Bobby Sands. Would these groups cause as much bloodshed in the future as the Provisionals? My worry was that although the Provisionals themselves now seemed to indicate the war was over, other IRA groups would take their place.

On Saturday, 15 August 1998, a huge bomb blasted apart the centre of Omagh in County Tyrone. It was the worst atrocity in Northern Ireland. Twenty-nine people, mainly women and children, were killed, and nearly three hundred were injured. Three of the children were pupils at a school in Buncrana, County Donegal. With them died a schoolboy and a teacher from a Spanish school group on an exchange visit with the Buncrana school. Indicating how times had changed, Gerry Adams and Martin McGuinness denounced the horror, which was presumed to be the work of the Real IRA. Now, surely, the taoiseach had the support of the people in the Republic, if he had doubted it before, to move against these dissident groups.

The leader of the 1916 Easter Rising in Dublin, Patrick Pearse, believed a blood sacrifice was needed to motivate the Irish people to fight for their freedom from the British. Was this sacrifice achieved when he and many of his fellow fighters were executed by the British? Or did it continue through the Anglo-Irish War and the Civil War? How would he have felt about the blood that had flowed in Northern Ireland for the past thirty years? I wondered if he would have thought that the people there had paid enough of a sacrifice, that the fighting was counterproductive, turning Protestant against Catholic instead of bringing them together? I believe he would have seen that people would have to be coaxed towards healing their divisions and working together on their future political status.

18
TO TALK OR NOT TO TALK?

URING THE PERIOD BETWEEN Stephen's death and the Assembly elections, media attention on our family fluctuated. From the intense interest on 13 February 1997, it diminished to phone calls from reporters whenever a news item on Northern Ireland had some significance. Some would see this as press intrusion, but I wanted to talk about my hopes and fears for Northern Ireland. In spring 1998, this willingness to talk led me to discuss the situation in Northern Ireland with an Irishman on St Patrick's Day in Manchester and, on a later date, with two former IRA men, one of them from Newry, where Stephen had died. This happened through my taking part in two television programmes. The first, on 16 March, was about Colin and Wendy Parry's fundraising for a peace centre in Warrington. This was the first time I met Colin, though I had spoken to him a few times on the phone.

I travelled by train to Manchester where the programme was to be filmed. The train route was beautiful, with hills and valleys dotted with stone farmhouses on both sides of the railway. All around was the gentle, pale olive green of the countryside before the first flush of spring bursts it into life. But this gave way to the red-brick, nineteenth-century buildings of Manchester itself.

Having checked into the Palace hotel, freshened up and changed, I was ready to go to the BBC TV studio in the building next to the hotel.

I had to be there for half past five, in time for a rehearsal before the actual programme. In the greenroom where guests wait before going into the studio, I was introduced to Eilish O'Reilly whose brother Larry Brennan, a Belfast taxi driver, had been killed in January by loyalist gunmen. It must have been a difficult time for her, being only two months since his death. Also there were a UUP councillor from the hardline loyalist Sandy Row area of Belfast, and an SDLP councillor from the equally hardline republican/nationalist Falls Road. Like myself, they had been invited to be part of the audience and put a question to the Parrys.

At 6 o'clock we went into the studio for the rehearsal. It was a black, cavernous room with seating in tiers in a semicircle, opposite which was a wall where two videos would be shown. In the middle of the studio floor were three chairs for Colin, Wendy and the interviewer. The first video outlined Colin and Wendy's aims, the other was of Tim and showed his happy nature and ready smile. During the rehearsal two studio staff took the parts of Colin and Wendy, answering questions from us and other studio staff. In the row behind me sat the two councillors from Belfast. The UUP councillor asked what Colin and Wendy hoped to achieve through the peace centre as the situation in Northern Ireland required a political solution. I immediately thought this was a very narrow way of looking at the problem – a lot of work also had to be done at grassroots level amongst the two communities to help bridge the division that had grown up in many areas over the past thirty years. The peace centre could play a valuable part in bringing children of the two communities together.

Three topics were squeezed into this thirty-minute programme, so the item on Colin and Wendy had barely ten minutes for the video, interview and questions from the audience. The rehearsal went smoothly and we returned to the greenroom until about twenty past seven, when we returned to the studio. The members of the audience were now in their seats and a man was telling them about the topics and asking them to suggest some questions about the peace centre. Then we were on air, and Juliet, the presenter, came onto the floor to introduce the programme. Colin and Wendy took their seats beside Juliet, the first video was shown, and the short interview went smoothly. Then it was questions from the audience. Eilish and I were introduced and asked to put our questions. My question, suggested by the producer, was how Colin and Wendy thought they could get the wider English population interested and involved in their aims. Unfortunately, the other questions from the audience were not really relevant to the proposed peace centre, one asking if communism was a solution to the problem in Northern Ireland. The presenter even forgot to ask the two Belfast councillors to put their questions so they were none too pleased! When the item ended and the next video was being shown, they left the audience. After the programme Eilish and I were introduced to Colin and Wendy and a group of their friends from Warrington. We all adjourned to the Palace hotel where the conversation continued until almost midnight, when they had to drive back to Warrington.

The next day, after some sightseeing, I still had two hours to spare until the train home. It was St Patrick's Day and a good proportion of Manchester's Irish population were cramming the bars in celebration of their saint. Many wore green-and-white hats and, of course, a bunch of shamrock. I went to O'Shea's Bar, within staggering distance of Piccadilly Railway Station. The place was, as they say, heaving. There were so many people crammed inside there was no way I could get to the bar. A band was playing traditional Irish songs, and after a while I managed to perch on a seat at the edge of a group of revellers. The Irish couple nearest to me said they'd lived in Manchester for many years. As a man left the pub I heard the husband say to him in Irish the republican slogan meaning 'our day will come'. His wife, referring to the man who'd just left, said he was a 'chuckie', meaning a republican. I asked her husband if he agreed with the means being used to make 'our day' come, especially bearing in mind the June 1996 bombing of the Arndale Shopping Centre in Manchester itself. (By coincidence, the lorry in which the bomb was concealed had been bought in Peterborough.) He said, 'Who are you, Special Branch?' I said no, just interested in the situation. His reply was that the British should leave Ireland. I said I agreed with him personally but what would happen if we did and the loyalists took up arms? There would be civil war and many innocent people would be killed. He didn't answer that but said he recognised me from the television programme the previous night, which surprised me. We talked for a while about the situation in Northern Ireland and he discussed the matter without getting irate, perhaps because I was a woman. He even bought me a pint of Guinness when I said I couldn't get near the bar.

Eventually, as the Guinness began to have an effect, I told him about Stephen and why he'd joined the army instead of the RAF. He replied that it was ordinary working-class lads who joined the army and were facing the danger. I showed him a photo of Stephen. He looked at it and suddenly said, 'It's so unfair.' That was it. When he said that word 'unfair' it hit a raw nerve within me and I just burst into tears, sobbing my heart out. By this time I think his wife was getting a little annoyed at her husband talking for so long to this unknown woman who was now crying on his shoulder! She'd been unable to hear most of our conversation due to the noise in the pub. Anyway, she decided she wanted a drink so they went to the bar. Feeling emotional, partly due to our conversation and partly due to the Guinness, I decided it was time to leave, asking another man in the group to say goodbye for me. I made my way to Piccadilly station but missed the train I'd intended to catch. I had to wait half an hour for the next one, which stopped at almost every town on the route between Manchester and Peterborough. It had been a very full two days but I was pleased I had finally met Colin, Wendy and Eilish. It was the first time I had taken part in a live television programme, something I had felt very nervous about but which in fact had not been so bad. Colin agreed with me that the programme should have dealt with just the one subject rather than three, but at least he and Wendy got a lot of publicity for their proposed peace centre.

During the run-up to the referendum there was a lot of controversy about one part of the Good Friday Agreement – that providing for the early release of terrorist prisoners. I had received a number of phone calls from reporters asking my views on this. I told them all that we ourselves would be affected because if the man charged with Stephen's murder was found guilty, he too would be released by July 2000. I said that we would have preferred the release of prisoners not to be part of the agreement but it had been included in order to get the support of parties representing paramilitaries, without which no agreement could have been reached. We therefore accepted it. Nothing could bring Stephen back – therefore if the agreement helped bring peace to Northern Ireland it was a price we were willing to pay. Also, the prisoners were released on licence not by amnesty, so if they became involved in terrorism again they would be returned to prison.

Amongst these phone calls came an invitation to take part in a programme about the early release of prisoners on Central TV's *Wednesday Night Live*. I was told that the other guests would be Colin Parry, a former loyalist paramilitary and two former IRA men, Eamon Collins and Vincent McKenna. McKenna renounced all his associations with terrorist activity and has played a prominent role both in Families Against Intimidation and Terror and the Northern Ireland Human Rights Bureau. John and I travelled to Nottingham for the programme which was broadcast live at just after half past ten. In the greenroom I met Colin again and also the parents of a special constable who had been killed in Yorkshire by an IRA man on the run. His parents are very bitter about their son's death, as they have every right to be, and do not agree at all with his killer being released early. There were also two ladies from Northern Ireland, both relatives of victims.

There were no rehearsals this time: it was straight into the studio and a countdown of the seconds until the programme went out live. Again the seats were in tiers, but here they were in a complete circle with the presenter standing in the middle. Views were asked of a blind man, who the presenter said was a former soldier injured in Northern Ireland, and an Asian lady, the wife of a man badly injured in the Docklands bombing that had ended the IRA ceasefire in February 1996. They, a Conservative MP and the two ladies from Northern Ireland said the prisoners should not be released early. Colin Parry held the same opinion as us – that we would have preferred this provision not to be part of the agreement but it was and we accepted it, especially if it helped bring about peace.

Eamon Collins was asked why he joined the IRA. He said that in his teens a soldier put a rifle barrel in his mouth and threatened to pull the trigger. Whether this is true or not I don't know, but I accept that in the heat of the moment things are done that should not be done. Unfortunately, what could have been an interesting programme deteriorated into a head-to-head dispute between Eamon Collins and a reporter from the Conservative press, the reporter insisting the prisoners were murderers, while Collins said they were political prisoners. This was the same reporter who had given me such a grilling outside 10 Downing Street the previous December so it did not surprise me. He had obviously been invited for his confrontational manner and strong point of view. Our part of the programme was almost up and I thought the presenter had forgotten me. Suddenly he came over to me, quickly introduced me, and pushing the mike in front of me said, 'What message do you have for the people of Northern Ireland today?' The question took me totally by surprise as it was not related specifically to the prisoners and was not the sort of question I had been expecting. I replied that I believed the agreement was fair and balanced although we would have preferred it not to include the early releases and I hoped people would vote Yes in the referendum. With that our half of the programme ended.

Back in the greenroom, John and I talked to the two former IRA men, who were also talking to the former loyalist paramilitary. As in the Stormont talks, they had a common bond. I had bought Collins's book *Killing Rage* the previous August at a second-hand book shop in Belfast. It is a chilling account of his time in the IRA; he left a number of years ago. Collins said my letters to the *Irish News* had an effect in Newry, his home town, as I could see both sides of the situation. I thought to myself, perhaps some republicans believed they had a British soldier's mother on their side but if they actually read my letters carefully they would see I didn't support either side but just called on both to find a peaceful way forward. Collins told me that the Docklands bombing and Stephen's murder resulted from a power struggle between Gerry Adams and a hardline faction of republicans who wanted to continue the armed struggle. It seemed that Adams had won that battle. Interviewed on the BBC programme *Newsnight* on 25 February 1998, Collins said Adams and McGuinness had the support of their areas but the Continuity IRA, which had only about forty to fifty men, were still living in the 1950s. Pictures were shown of the sniper signs in south Armagh: 'Sniper at Work'. The sign below one said 'I have waited two years'. I wondered if it referred to the time between the 1994 ceasefire and Stephen's murder, actually two and a half years. Collins had made many enemies in republican circles, especially after the publication of his book in which he spoke of the incompetence of some IRA members. He experienced months of intimidation which he blamed on republicans, including the burning of the family farmhouse in Newry and threats painted on walls near his home. In January of the following year, 1999, Eamon Collins was found stabbed to death in Newry.

In the greenroom the blind former soldier was standing near me. I introduced myself and asked, 'Would Stephen think it wrong that I was talking to ex-IRA men? Would he feel I was betraying him?' I felt in a way that I needed this soldier's approval as my conscience was in a turmoil about whether I should be talking to them. To be truthful I cannot remember his exact words, but he didn't make me feel that I shouldn't be talking to them.

After the programme so many things were going through my mind. Like Colin Parry, I felt the programme had been a total waste of time, merely becoming a slanging match. My mind was still in turmoil about talking to former IRA men but I hoped Stephen would say that people should talk rather than fight. I'd had to make so many difficult decisions since Stephen's death which had really made me look at my values and beliefs.

19

THE TRIAL

ALMOST TWO YEARS AFTER Stephen's murder, the trial began in Belfast Crown Court of the five men arrested by the SAS on 10 April 1997 at Cregganduff Road, Crossmaglen. One of them, Bernard McGinn, was charged with killing Stephen and two other killings fifteen years apart in Keady: 23-year-old Lance-Bombardier Paul Andrew Garrett in December 1993 and Gilbert Johnston, a 25-year-old former UDR soldier, in 1978. Another, James McArdle, had been found guilty in 1998 of the bombing of the Canary Wharf office complex in February 1996.

The trial was not the first time we had come face to face with the accused. At the end of August 1998 we attended an arraignment at Belfast Crown Court. After waiting at the court for over an hour, we were told the defendants had refused to leave the IRA compound in the Maze prison. We were told they were not happy about the type of vehicle they were to travel in and demanded an armour-plated one, but all were in use for a visit to Belfast by President Clinton. The judge, although clearly annoyed, could do nothing but adjourn the court for a week. It had been a wasted trip but it had enabled us to meet Lance-Bombardier Paul Garrett's father, Gladstone. Joe, as he prefers to be known, is a quiet, dignified man who came to England from his native Guyana to serve in the army, had married and had a family here. He was very close to Paul, his elder son, and after his murder he

215

returned to Guyana with his family trying to rebuild their shattered lives. For the past six months Joe had been living in England waiting for the trial to begin.

We returned to court the following week, but yet again there was a problem. The judge said he had not been told he was to hear the case that day; fortunately he was in the court buildings hearing another case, but he had not yet read the papers so could not rule on the application by Michael Kearns – the owner of the property where the accused were arrested – to have his lesser case heard separately. So again the hearing was adjourned without any plea of guilty or not guilty being made. At the next arraignment the defendants all pleaded not guilty.

The trial was due to begin on Monday, 8 February, and the case was being heard by the Lord Chief Justice of Northern Ireland, Sir Robert Carswell. However, I had a problem on my hands and a big decision to make. My fifteen-year-old black-and-white cat Tigger was in poor health, hardly eating and getting thinner by the day. The vet said he had kidney failure, and despite expensive tests and treatment there had been no improvement in his health. But Tigger had seen me through so much during the years. He had joined our family as a kitten shortly after the death of my mother. It had been a great comfort to me then to have a small kitten to fuss with. He saw me through the death of my father, and then through Stephen's death. As he got older he always seemed to sense when I was upset or feeling depressed and would jump up onto my knee, purr deeply as I stroked him, and look at me quizzically as if to say 'What's wrong?' The problem was that his poor health meant we felt unable either to ask a neighbour to look after him while we were attending the trial or to cause him the distress of a cattery – as he had never stayed in one before. So I had a talk with the vet. The young man was doing all he could to help Tigger, but we decided that regrettably the final decision had to be made. John, Mark and I discussed it overnight and agreed that it would be kinder to put Tigger to sleep than force him to struggle on. So the next day I took him back to the vet and held him close as the injection was put into his leg. As it took effect I was left alone with Tigger for a few minutes. I cried and cried as his life ebbed away. I cried for the time I had not been with my mother and father when they died, and I cried for not being there when Stephen died. I cried at the irony of this young Irish vet doing all he could to help my old cat, yet one of his countrymen was charged with the murder of my healthy young son. Perhaps I was also crying because events in Northern Ireland had forced this decision on me. But at least now I would not be worrying about Tigger while we were at the trial.

John, Mark and I flew to Belfast International Airport on the Sunday evening and for security reasons stayed at RAF Aldergrove where we again met Paul Garrett's father. The next morning we left together for the Crown Court in Belfast city centre. The radio was on in the car and suddenly the tune 'Search for the Hero' came on. Played at Stephen's funeral, the tune now had a special meaning for us and often came on the radio at times like this. John, Mark and I looked at each other in surprise and I said, 'Steve is with us.'

We attended the court from Monday to Thursday, and on Friday, 12 February, the second anniversary of Stephen's death, we returned to Bessbrook and visited the position on Green Road where the checkpoint had been. Everything had been removed since the Good Friday Agreement, and now there was no indication that it had ever been there. As I placed a bunch of flowers on the fence I wondered if anyone in years to come would remember the young life lost there. The little brook trickled beside the road as I read aloud a poem written by Ann Holloway, another mother who had lost a son:

> There must be a reason 'Why?'
> But no answer can I find.
> Why an end to your lovely young life?
> Why the loss of your gentle young mind?
>
> Only silence answers my questions,
> So I must live with the sorrow and pain
> And trust in God and believe in my heart
> That we shall meet again.

From the checkpoint we went to Bessbrook Mill and Stephen's memorial there and the study library named after him, returning late that afternoon to Belfast International Airport for our flight home. During the flight I suddenly became aware that the young man sitting two rows in front of us looked exactly like Stephen from the back, even the way he turned his head. John also saw the similarity when I pointed it out to him. For almost an hour this young man sat in front of me, looking so like Stephen that I wanted to hold him though I knew it couldn't be him. I was in floods of tears when I got off the plane.

The trial continued for another month though there was hardly any coverage by the national press or TV. John and I and Joe Garrett were back in court on Friday, 19 March, to hear the judge's summing-up and verdict. Inside the court the public benches were full as the QCs and their assistants took their seats in the well of the court in front of us. One of them, however, was missing. I had recognised the blonde solicitor on the defence team when we had attended the court previously. She had a high profile in Northern Ireland and often represented defendants in such cases. However, unlike some people in Northern Ireland I had no problem with this. Legal representation in court is a basic human right, no matter what the charge. If a lawyer represents a person on a murder charge it does not mean that they agree with murder. The lawyer is there to make sure the defendant's case is put before the court in relation to evidence from the prosecution. The absent solicitor was Rosemary Nelson. She had been killed the previous Monday by a bomb placed under her car by loyalist terrorists calling themselves the Red Hand Defenders. It was believed that the reason for her death was her representation of the Garvaghy Road Residents' Coalition in Portadown over the Drumcree stand-off.

Four of the defendants, Michael Caraher, James McArdle, Bernard McGinn and Martin Mines, were found guilty by Lord Chief Justice Carswell of the charges against them, and Michael Kearns was found not guilty. As this book goes to press, the convictions are under appeal and a decision is pending. I have not, therefore, repeated here all the evidence given at the trial – although it was widely reported at the time – as it is only appropriate in the circumstances that I refrain from comment.

As we left the court precincts through a turnstile in the railings, we met a barrage of TV cameras, photographers and reporters. When asked about his feelings, Joe Garrett said, 'If the process towards peace works I'll think Paul has made a little contribution. This war is all about bitterness. If I hang on to that bitterness it means I'm no better than these people [the paramilitaries]. If it doesn't work then Paul's death will have been in vain. The suffering is an eternity, it goes and comes, goes and comes, you never know when it will hit you.' I knew only too well how Joe felt, the way the feelings of loss and sadness build up inside and tears flood out uncontrollably when you are walking in the countryside on a sunny day or when you hear a special tune in the shopping arcade, or when something about a young man walking further down the street suddenly reminds you of the son you will never see again. I had been aware often of how dignified but alone in his suffering Joe was, with his family left behind in Guyana for the last six months. John and I had each other, and we tried to reach out to Joe but often we wished we could do more for him on the few days we were together. We were driven quickly away from the court back to Aldergrove airport where we said goodbye to Joe.

That evening we went to our local pub for a pint but it was a mistake. We had moved from Peterborough the previous September to be nearer John's work. It was hard to leave our home in Peterborough with its memories of Stephen but at least there would no longer be that empty bedroom which had been his 'tip'. We now lived in a village in north Nottinghamshire surrounded by beautiful, hilly countryside with fields and trees, a total contrast to the flatness of Peterborough. But it takes time to make friends, especially as in my case I could not make friends through work or taking children to school. So, as we sat in our village pub I felt so isolated and detached, as if I lived in a different world to all these people. Only a few hours ago I had been in court looking at the four men charged with my son's murder. I felt as if I was in a totally different world to these people who were enjoying their night out. So we finished our drinks and returned home. The following day we travelled to Shropshire to celebrate my brother Ray's sixtieth birthday and my brother Neil's fiftieth birthday. We had not met together on the actual date of Neil's birthday, 12 February, as that was the date of Stephen's death and anyway we were in Northern Ireland. We went for a meal at a village pub, but as I sat with my brothers and their wives and sons, I suddenly became aware of the empty chair at the table, caused by a late cancellation. I tried as hard as I could but thoughts of who should be in that empty chair would not leave my mind. Stephen should have been there with us, having a joke with his cousins and enjoying a pint or two. I could feel the tears welling in my eyes as I rushed from the room, not wanting to spoil the celebration for the others. John and I made our apologies and left early: it was too soon after the trial to be able to return to normality. Fortunately everyone understood the turmoil I was going through.

20

THE DAWN OF A
PEACEFUL FUTURE?

T HE EARLY RELEASE OF PARAMILITARY PRISONERS was one of the
provisions of the Good Friday Agreement which caused disagreement among people in Northern Ireland and on the mainland, especially those who had suffered personally over the past thirty
years. The victims were, however, remembered in the agreement's
Declaration of Support:

> The tragedies of the past have left a deep and pro-
> foundly regrettable legacy of suffering. We must
> never forget those who have died or been injured,
> and their families. But we can best honour them
> through a fresh start, in which we firmly dedicate our-
> selves to the achievement of reconciliation, tolerance,
> and mutual trust, and to the protection and vindica-
> tion of the human rights of all.

The means of achieving these aims were covered within the agreement,
partly in the three strands: Strand 1, democratic institutions in Northern
Ireland; Strand 2, the North/South Ministerial Council; and Strand 3,
the British/Irish Council. They were also covered in the sections on
Rights, Safeguards and Equality of Opportunity; Decommissioning;
Security; Policing and Justice; and Validation, Implementation and

Review Procedures following Implementation. In addition, the Good Friday Agreement contained a section on Reconciliation and Victims of Violence. This covered in Northern Ireland the support and funding for community-based initiatives for young people, the promotion of tolerance, initiatives to help integrated education and mixed housing, and services for the needs of victims throughout the United Kingdom. A commission had been set up, under Sir Kenneth Bloomfield, by the government the previous October 'to look at possible ways to recognise the pain and suffering felt by victims of violence arising from the troubles of the last 30 years, including those who have died or been injured in the service of the community'.

Launching their report *We Will Remember Them* on 13 May 1998, Mo Mowlam said, 'The tragedies of the past have left a deep legacy of suffering and we cannot forget these people but can honour them with a fresh start.' As suggested in the report, a Minister for Victims was appointed to oversee the implementation of its recommendations, among which were training for counsellors and extra NHS provision to deal with pain and trauma and the possible establishment of a trauma centre, plus educational funding for children of victims. There were also more long-term suggestions of a memorial to the victims, a reconciliation day and a possible truth and reconciliation commission, similar to that in South Africa. The Victims Liaison Unit was established to identify and prioritise a package of measures to help victims, their families, and victim support groups. However, it is apparent that most of the support groups are based in Northern Ireland; the Victims Liaison Unit has had great difficulty reaching the more widely spread victims in the rest of the UK.

One of the report's recommendations was a review of the effectiveness of the Northern Ireland system of compensation for criminal injuries in serving the needs of victims. Sir Kenneth Bloomfield was appointed to undertake this review, and it was published on 2 July 1999. The recommendation on bereavement awards was the point which was closest to our hearts. Under the system in effect at the time, the parents of a minor received a bereavement award of £7,500 but if the son or daughter was over the age of eighteen the parents did not receive a penny in compensation unless they were financially dependent on their child. There was not even compensation for a parent who suffered depression due to the murder of their child if the parent was not present when the crime was committed. Sir Kenneth sought the views of many organisations in Northern Ireland, and a few in Great Britain and the views of individuals like ourselves who had gone through the compensation system within the past two years. My submission was that there should be an element to cover emotional distress caused to parents through the loss of a child over eighteen years old, if the parents are the next of kin, irrespective of any financial dependency on the deceased. I believed that many parents would want to put this money, which need only be a reasonable token amount, towards ways of remembering their child such as commemorative seats, donations to charities et cetera, so the money would ultimately be used for the benefit of the general public. I also stated that there should be no difference in the compensation system between Northern Ireland and the rest of the UK as we had been told that if Stephen had been killed by the IRA in England we would have received some compensation (I still do not know if this is true). My final point, like that of many victims' relatives, was that the review should have taken place years ago. Among the many recommendations of the report was one that would benefit parents like us in the future. Whilst recognising that 'no amount of money could ever be said to "compensate" for the loss of a loved one', it recommended there should be a bereavement support payment (instead of the existing term 'bereavement award') which would acknowledge the grief and sorrow of the relative caused by the deceased's death, and the loss of 'such non-pecuniary benefits as the relative might have been expected to derive from the deceased's care, guidance and society if the deceased had not died'. Also, parents and cohabitants should receive the payment, as well as a spouse and child. The sum recommended in the case of parents was £5,000 each. Unfortunately, the report's recommendations were not retrospective, so none of the existing parents would benefit from them.

As for progress on the implementation of the Good Friday Agreement, or the Belfast Agreement as some now called it, despite the best efforts of Tony Blair and Bertie Ahern, decommissioning again became the stumbling block, as it had prior to the collapse of the previous cease-fire in February 1996. The UUP would not accept Sinn Féin's entry into the Assembly without at least a token decommissioning or a statement from the IRA that the war was over. They asked what other democratic state would allow into government a party connected with armed para-militaries. Sinn Féin correctly stated that decommissioning prior to sit-ting in the Assembly was not part of the agreement. The wording of the agreement had been vague in parts in order to get all the parties to agree to its terms, but now this was causing a problem. The wording in para-graph 3 of the section on decommissioning stated, 'All participants ac-cordingly reaffirm their commitment to the total disarmament of all paramilitary organisations. They also confirm their intention to con-tinue to work constructively and in good faith with the Independent Commission, and to use any influence they may have, to achieve the decommissioning of all paramilitary arms within two years following endorsement in referendums north and south of the agreement and in the context of the implementation of the overall settlement.' May 2000 has been set as the deadline for decommissioning to be completed.

The UUP worried that if allowed into government Sinn Féin could say they had 'used any influence they might have' to ask the IRA to de-commission but if the IRA would not, then Sinn Féin would still be in government. Sinn Féin also claimed repeatedly that they were not the political wing of the IRA, perhaps hoping that if something is stated often enough people will believe it. Unfortunately, people have long memories and did not doubt the connection. Sinn Féin insisted they had a right to their seats through the votes gained in the Assembly elections.

Deadlines passed without agreement, culminating in Mo Mowlam calling the Assembly to meet on 15 July to appoint ministers. The result was a fiasco. The UUP did not attend, leaving Ian Paisley's uncompro-mising rhetoric to represent the face of unionism to television viewers around the world. More reasoned speeches were made by Monica McWilliams of the Women's Coalition and David Ervine of the PUP. In exasperation and frustration at events, Seamus Mallon resigned as deputy First Minister designate. I felt despair, like so many people who had felt such hope on Good Friday the year before. The politicians knew what the people wanted. Their votes in the referendum and in the Assembly elections had shown that the majority of the population supported the agreement. Disagreement on decommissioning should not be allowed to bring an end to everything again, including the cease-fire. Mo Mowlam announced that the agreement would go into review under the chairmanship of Senator George Mitchell. But all wondered if the hardliners in the IRA would lose patience and take up the gun and bomb again. Newspapers reported that some republicans were leaving the Provisional IRA and joining dissidents in the Real IRA and Continu-ity IRA. Although the Real IRA had announced a ceasefire after the Omagh bombing, for which they were believed to be responsible, the Continuity IRA had never been on ceasefire. Extreme loyalist paramili-taries under the name of the Red Hand Defenders and Orange Volun-teers were trying to cause IRA retaliation by throwing pipe bombs at Catholic homes in some mainly Protestant areas. Following a number of IRA murders and 'punishment beatings', there were even challenges as to whether their ceasefire was still intact. However, Mo Mowlam ruled that it was, for the government wanted to keep Sinn Féin in the review process which was adjourned through August.

A reminder of what could happen if the agreement did not work had been given the previous August when republican hardliners had bombed the centre of Omagh, killing twenty-nine people. On that ter-rible day, following a phone call that the bomb was outside the court-house, the police had shepherded people to the other end of the main street, where, unknown to them, the car bomb was parked. A year later, I was honoured to receive an invitation to take part in a commemora-tion on the first anniversary of this atrocity. The ceremony took place on a Sunday morning on the steps of Omagh courthouse. Taking part were representatives from Omagh, Buncrana and Spain, and clergy of various denominations. I participated in a symbolic pouring of water to represent the tears that had been shed over the past thirty years. Among the other symbolic pourers were Noreen Hill, whose husband Ronnie was still in a coma twelve years after the IRA Remembrance Day bomb at Enniskillen, and two mothers who I had written to following their bereavement: Marion Radford, whose son Alan was killed in the Omagh bomb, and Ann Trainor, whose son Damian was killed by loyalist gunmen at Poyntzpass. As I went through the courthouse door onto the steps and held my bowl of water up to the crowd, I looked down at a sea of people stretching the length of Market Street to the white hoarding at the opposite end which surrounded the bomb-shattered buildings. Holding the bowl to collect my water was Margaret McKinney from Belfast, whose son had been murdered by the IRA in 1978 but whose body had only recently been found near the border in the Republic following information from the IRA on the whereabouts of 'disappeared' victims. She was awaiting the release of his body by the authorities in the Republic so that she could finally lay him to rest after all those years. The denial for so many years of the right of the relatives of the 'disappeared' to bury their loved ones seemed to many people the ultimate in cruelty and callousness.

Taking part in a reading was a young schoolboy named Stephen Coyle. He had suffered a serious shoulder wound in the Omagh explosion and his life had been in the balance for a while. I had written to his parents, also injured in the bombing, saying that I hoped he would make a full recovery and would soon be smiling like my own Stephen in the photo I sent. Before the service I was introduced to Stephen and his family. I was so pleased to meet them and see that he was making a good recovery.

Attending the anniversary ceremony, and especially the short service the previous day at the Garden of Remembrance, awakened painful memories of how I had felt on the first anniversary of Stephen's death. Two and a half years after his death, I felt I was coping and I hoped that those I spoke to who had lost loved ones in the bombing could see that it did get better. The pain would ease. And yet I also had a feeling of guilt. Guilt that I was not in tears. That weekend marked thirty years since the start of the troubles and sadly yet again there was violence and rioting following the Apprentice Boys march in Londonderry – the original flashpoint. Would things ever change?

September saw Senator George Mitchell return to Belfast to conduct the review which was to concentrate solely on the decommissioning impasse. The situation on the streets was helped by the fact that the Orange Order marches in Belfast and at Drumcree had passed peacefully despite the latter again not being allowed down the Garvaghy Road, though rising tension prior to the Drumcree march had led to the loyalist murder of the wife of a Catholic in Portadown, killed in her home by a pipe bomb thrown through her window – she was a Protestant.

On 9 September there was some disquiet amongst unionists when the findings were published of the review, led by Chris Patten, of the RUC. Unionists saw the RUC as the front line against republican terrorism and saw the report as a betrayal of RUC officers killed in the conflict. The report suggested that the name should be changed to the Northern Ireland Police Service, that there should be a new badge and symbols 'free from any association with the British or Irish states' and an end to the flying of the Union flag over police stations. Much was also made of the suggestion that the size of the force should be reduced by half over ten years, though this would be dependent on the security situation. The RUC was currently 92 per cent Protestant, and to remedy this the report suggested recruitment should be on a fifty–fifty basis, Catholics-to-Protestants, to increase the Catholic representation to 30 per cent in ten years. Individual police officers would be required to register membership of organisations such as the Orange Order or the Masons. Sinn Féin had called for the disbandment of the RUC, and even moderate Catholics had reservations about them, so unionists saw these findings as a capitulation to republican demands, though more moderate unionists accepted that some changes were necessary.

Yet again, I was struck with the similarity between claims of sectarianism within the RUC and the findings of 'institutional racism' in London's Metropolitan Police by the inquiry into their investigation of the murder of Stephen Lawrence. We had met only kindness and helpfulness from the RUC, but I accepted that some Catholic families had grievances against them due to anti-IRA actions which affected many innocent Catholics. There was also ongoing republican and nationalist bitterness over the actions of the RUC's B Specials at the start of the

227

troubles and the alleged 'shoot to kill' policy of the RUC in the 1980s which was investigated by John Stalker and John Stevens. Some hardline unionists at Drumcree in 1998 also complained about their treatment by the RUC when they experienced how tough any police force can be in handling people breaking the law and using violence against them.

Under Mitchell's calm chairmanship, the UUP and Sinn Féin began to bridge the chasm that had opened between them over the summer. In the weeks that followed I experienced a rollercoaster ride of hope and despair over the talks. The situation was not helped by interviews the participants gave to the press, always playing to their own supporters and giving little to help the other side. Eventually, there was a press embargo for a week when the talks moved to Winfield House, the American ambassador's residence in London. This was yet another co-incidence for me, as Winfield is my mother-in-law's maiden name. On 12 October Tony Blair replaced Mo Mowlam with Peter Mandelson. It was known that Mo Mowlam was not popular with unionists, who saw her as pro-nationalist, and Trimble had called for her removal earlier in the summer. However, Blair had not replaced her then as he had not wanted to be seen as dancing to Trimble's tune. Unlike her Conservative predecessors in the Northern Ireland Office she managed to reach out to the Catholic/nationalist population with her down-to-earth character, and I believe that being a woman helped when meeting the people on the streets. She would chat, she would show compassion, she would even hug. Could Mandelson, who seemed more aloof, win the hearts of the ordinary people as well as the minds of the male politicians?

Suddenly, in mid-November, the parties reached an accommodation and a series of choreographed moves were made. The first came on 15 November with Senator Mitchell's statement that 'The pro-agreement parties and the governments share the view that devolution should occur and the institutions should be established at the earliest possible date. It is also common ground that decommissioning should occur as quickly as possible and that the Independent International Commission on Decommissioning should play the central role in achieving this, under the terms of the agreement.' On the same day the review of the Independent International Commission on Decommissioning was made public. It reminded all pro-agreement parties of their commitment to use their influence to achieve decommissioning by May 2000 and their 'total commitment to exclusively democratic and peaceful means of resolving differences on political issues, and opposition to any use or threat of force by others for any political purpose, whether in regard to this agreement or otherwise'. It emphasised that decommissioning was a voluntary act, it could not be imposed, and to bring it about the commission would need 'the co-operation and support of the political parties, using all the influence they have, together with the wholehearted commitment of paramilitary organisations'. It called on paramilitary organisations to respond positively by appointing authorised representatives; as soon as possible afterwards a date would be set for meeting with each of them, and a report would be issued within days of those meetings.

The day after Mitchell's statement all parties involved in the talks made individual statements on their positions, all in support of the review's findings. The UUP statement said, 'The UUP recognises and accepts that it is legitimate for nationalists to pursue their political objective of a united Ireland by consent through exclusively peaceful and democratic methods.' It added, 'Both of our traditions have suffered as a result of our conflict and division. This is a matter of deep regret and makes it all the more important that we now put the past behind us. The establishment of inclusive political institutions and the commencement of the process of decommissioning are the first steps in this process.' The statement concluded, 'Unionist, loyalist, nationalist, and republican must take these steps together to secure a new era of cooperation, reconciliation and mutual respect.' In their statement, Sinn Féin accepted that 'decommissioning is an essential part of the peace process. We believe that the issue of arms will be finally and satisfactorily settled under the aegis of the de Chastelain commission as set out in the agreement.' Concerning the IRA it said, 'IRA guns are silent and the Sinn Féin leadership is confident that the IRA remains committed to the objective of a permanent peace. By providing an effective political alternative we can remove the potential for conflict.' It added, 'All sections of our people have suffered profoundly in this conflict. That suffering is a matter of deep regret but makes the difficult process of removing conflict all the more imperative. Sinn Féin wishes to work with, not against, the unionists . . .' The statement concluded, 'We reiterate our total commitment to doing everything in our power to maintain the peace process and to removing the gun forever from the politics of our country.'

On 17 November the IRA issued its statement: 'The IRA is committed unequivocally to the search for freedom, justice and peace in Ireland. In our view the Good Friday Agreement is a significant development and we believe its full implementation will contribute to the achievement of lasting peace. We acknowledge the leadership given by Sinn Féin throughout this process. The IRA is willing to further enhance the peace process and consequently, following the establishment of the institutions agreed on Good Friday last year, the IRA leadership will appoint a representative to enter into discussions with General John de Chastelain and the Independent Commission on Decommissioning.'

The following day, in his final report on the review, Senator Mitchell said, 'I believe that a basis now exists for devolution to occur, for the institutions to be established, and for decommissioning to take place as soon as possible.' He added, 'Devolution should take effect, then the executive should meet, and then the paramilitary groups should appoint their authorised representatives *all on the same day in that order*.' He said he shared the conclusions of the Independent International Commission on Decommissioning that 'Decommissioning is by definition a voluntary act and cannot be imposed. To bring decommissioning about, the commission will need the co-operation and support of the political parties, using all the influence they have, together with the wholehearted commitment of paramilitary organisations.' He concluded, 'Neither side will get all it wanted and both will endure severe political pain. But there is no other way forward.' As he left for the USA he said, 'I say to you with my heart and soul: this is the best opportunity in many years to put the bitterness of the past behind you and to move on to a better, brighter future, to a society of peace and prosperity, justice and opportunity, and I hope you seize it.' To those, like five of the Ulster Unionist

MPs and the anti-agreement unionist parties, who felt that there was still no guarantee of IRA decommissioning and that Sinn Féin was being allowed into government before the IRA handed over their guns he said, 'There has been a lot of talk about guarantees. There is one. It's that if this process fails, there will be no chance whatsoever of decommissioning.' Trimble took the proposals to the Ulster Unionist Council on 27 November where he got a 58 per cent majority, having signed a pre-dated letter of resignation if decommissioning had not commenced by the following February and assured those present that another meeting would be held then to review progress on decommissioning. I just hoped that General de Chastelain's review due before that date would show enough progress to satisfy the UUP. Peter Mandelson, the new Northern Ireland Secretary, had also given guarantees about what steps he would take if decommissioning did not take place.

The timetable set out by Senator Mitchell now began. On Monday, 29 November, the Assembly met to appoint ministers under the d'Hondt system whereby each party chose in sequence and according to their political strength in the Assembly which ministers it wanted. The UUP and SDLP had three ministers each while the DUP and Sinn Féin had two each. The only surprise was when Sinn Féin chose Martin McGuinness to be Minister of Education. This caused some consternation amongst the anti-agreement members who felt that this former IRA figure should not be in charge of their children's education. Perhaps they also feared a rewriting of the history books and compulsory Irish-language lessons. However, within each ministry there was a counter-balance as the chairman of the committee below the minister belonged to a party from the opposite community to the minister and the committee itself was balanced. Northern Ireland politics was still, however, mainly a male preserve. Of the ten ministers appointed, only two were women: Sinn Féin's Bairbre de Brún and the SDLP's Bríd Rodgers. Yet for me the most important part of the meeting was the reappointment of Seamus Mallon as deputy First Minister. It was his resignation in July that had ensured a review of the decommissioning section of the Good Friday Agreement would take place, leading to this second attempt at setting up the Assembly.

On Tuesday, 30 November, the House of Commons voted in favour of the devolution Bill with only ten against, the No votes being counted by Willie Thompson, the hardline UUP MP, and Ian Paisley. Thompson had said he would resign from the UUP and stand as an independent if devolution took place. The next day the Queen signed her consent and at midnight power passed from Westminster to Belfast. On Thursday morning the British–Irish agreement was signed by Peter Mandelson and David Andrews, the Irish Foreign Minister. This set up the North–South Ministerial Council, the six cross-border bodies, and the British–Irish Council as in the Good Friday Agreement. Shortly afterwards the taoiseach, Bertie Ahern, signed the amendment removing articles 2 and 3 of de Valera's 1937 constitution which had laid territorial claim to the six counties of Northern Ireland, replacing them with articles that spoke of an aspiration for a united Ireland but with the consent of the majority in the six counties. To symbolise the events of the day, Mary McAleese, the Irish president, who herself came from Northern Ireland, had lunch with the Queen at Buckingham Palace. That afternoon saw the first meeting of the executive at Stormont. Ministers from the UUP, the SDLP and Sinn Féin sat round the table together, smiling and making small talk. However, two chairs were empty: the DUP ministers, Peter Robinson and Nigel Dodds, stayed away, refusing to sit with Sinn Féin, though many commentators pointed out that the DUP sits on councils with Sinn Féin in local government. Instead of the executive meeting they attended their leader's press conference in which he denounced the whole process. Just before 9 o'clock that evening, it was announced that the IRA had given General de Chastelain the name of its representative, though the name was not made public. So ended a momentous whirl of events delayed for nearly eighteen months by the unionists' stance on decommissioning.

The first step had been taken on what would no doubt be a difficult road ahead. Many doubts lingered. Would decommissioning take place? Would politicians who had previously been enemies be able to work together? Would the unionist politicians who did not support the Good Friday Agreement wreck the Assembly or use delaying tactics at every opportunity? Would dissident republicans carry out a bombing or shooting that would set both communities and their politicians against each other, destroying the trust that was slowly being built up? I had spent most of the day watching Sky TV's news coverage of the events. It included a montage of some of the killings over the past thirty years accompanied by the song 'Belfast Child'. As I watched, tears sprang to my eyes at this connection between such a momentous day, the atrocities of the past and the tune that we had chosen to be played at Stephen's funeral. I could only hope that this day was the dawn of a new future for the people of Northern Ireland. Dawn comes not instantaneously but slowly and almost imperceptibly at first, light gradually overcoming the darkness. I hoped the darkness of the past thirty years in Northern Ireland was a thing of the past. When looking at the compromises that have to be made, both sides have a tendency to look back at their dead in the conflict and question what they died for. I would say that we should instead look back in shame at the waste of those lives, the heartache caused to their families, the physical and mental scars of the injured, and do our utmost to prevent that conflict ever starting again. The best memorial to the dead would be peace, so that children can grow up without the daily fear of bombs and bullets, and young people are not led to take up the gun in what they are told is a just cause.

On that historic Thursday for Northern Ireland, President Clinton said, 'Democratic government by and for all the people of Northern Ireland is now replacing suspicion, fear and violence. It is now possible to believe the day of the gun and bomb are over.' The political situation in Northern Ireland had been transformed since the early hours of that Sunday morning, four days after Stephen's death, when I wrote to President Clinton begging him to 'do all you can to bring all sides together round the table to start talking, and keep them there'. And it was the patient involvement of his emissary, former senator George Mitchell, as chairman of the peace talks, that enabled the transformation. He was supported throughout by Tony Blair and Mo Mowlam, who continued the work of the previous prime minister, John Major, and by taoiseach Bertie Ahern. John Hume too was instrumental in persuading Gerry Adams that politics not armed struggle was the way forward – a view, I believe, Adams was halfway to accepting. David

Trimble has amazed me with his courage and leadership, though he, like Gerry Adams, made me despair at times. Credit is also due to the loyalist politicians, some of whom as prisoners saw similarities between themselves and republican prisoners despite their political differences, a development which eventually led to the loyalist ceasefire and their involvement in the peace process. Since the late 1980s many church leaders have also been working behind the scenes to bring paramilitaries into the peace process, most notably Father Alex Reid of Clonard Monastery with Sinn Féin and the Reverend Roy Magee with loyalist paramilitaries. Now it is up to the people of Northern Ireland to support their politicians in this political process and, perhaps even more difficult, to reach out to someone of the opposite community and begin to heal the wounds of the past thirty years. In the segregated areas within both communities, this will be the hardest part.

EPILOGUE

So MUCH HAS HAPPENED since that terrible night when I heard the words every mother dreads. I was an ordinary mother watching TV when my world fell apart. Only those who have suffered the death of a son or daughter fully know the pain and despair that follow. My family tried to help but it took a long time before I began to pick up the pieces again. Yes, I could be strong when I visited Northern Ireland and met people there. But people did not see me at home on the days when I did not want to get out of bed to face another day or when the tears streamed down my face as I longed for Stephen to be here again. Yet I was determined to make people look at my pain and loss and see in it the suffering of so many mothers before me who had lost sons and daughters in the conflict. I wanted to be the voice of all mothers who wanted an end to the waste of so many young lives. And I would keep on speaking out even if some people thought, 'What does she know about it, she doesn't have to live in Northern Ireland like we do?' Gerry Adams was thinking along these lines on that historic December day after his first meeting with the prime minister when he responded to a journalist's question outside 10 Downing Street with 'There are thousands of Mrs Restoricks in Ireland'. I was hurt by his remark because he had totally misrepresented or misinterpreted my point. I know there are thousands like me and my loss was no different to theirs. I was saying there should be no more, whether in Ireland, in England, Scotland or

Stephen at seventeen

Wales. Another way has to be found to settle this problem. Violence only drives people further apart; it creates hatred and mistrust and can never unite them.

Though I never would have believed it in the early days after Stephen's death, the pain is easing. As it says on Stephen's headstone, I feel I can begin to 'turn again to life and smile'. The tears still flow but less frequently now. Seeing a blond-haired little boy or a good-looking young man in his early twenties can awaken the memories of what was and open the floodgates. Or a piece of music may remind me of Stephen – an unexpected song on the background music tape can send me running from a shop in tears. It has been a long, hard journey, not only for me and my husband. Many people recognise the parents' loss but forget the surviving brothers and sisters. Stephen's death affected his brother Mark very deeply and we as parents were sometimes too overcome with our own pain to give him the support he needed. It is hard to live in the shadow of a dead brother and suddenly to become an only child. John's elderly parents too have had the sunshine taken out of their lives. My brothers Raymond and Neil and our friends Sue and Mike have given us much support during this difficult time without which we would not have coped. Yet deep inside me there is a terrible scream of 'No!' It is the scream I was not able to give voice to when I was told of his death. A scream that is buried so deep and is yet so powerful that if I ever let it out it would be deafening. It is the scream of all mothers who have lost a son they loved with all their heart and soul. Stephen was part of my flesh and bone, I cared for him through childhood, and saw him grow into an independent young man only to be snatched away in an instance without the chance for me to say goodbye.

This book has mainly shown my impression of Stephen, and perhaps a mother is a little biased, but I was very moved by the view of Stephen given a couple of months after his death by two of his army comrades to a journalist. I wish they had been able to say the same to me, but I was never with them long enough and perhaps they were too embarrassed. His staff sergeant spoke of his close friendship with Stephen despite their difference in rank. He told of a punishment march across Otterburn ranges on the bombardier leadership course: 'Many dropped out but

Steve kept on going and going with a big smile from ear to ear. He just had this optimistic view of the world, he was quite unique, nothing got him down. From his example other people learned to laugh off their problems.' He said there had never been any disciplinary problems with Steve. 'He had a quiet and tactful approach, he didn't believe in shouting for the sake of shouting. I thought it was good for young gunners who came after him to see Stephen's approach to life and see they could get on, because he was a very young lance-bombardier and would have been a young bombardier. Kids like that make your life easy – a very bright lad who would have gone on and done well for himself, would have made sergeant and perhaps beyond.'

Steve's best friend Robin spoke about hair-raising mountain-bike rides down Sutton Bank near Thirsk, about nights out together involving beer and girls, and about Stephen's continued friendship after Robin married Jane. He said, 'The things I remember about him most are his personality, his smile and his attitude towards life which was to enjoy it. He went at everything to the best of his ability and made sure he enjoyed it. His best features were his smile, his sense of humour and his ability to drink vast quantities of beer.' Speaking of Steve's death, he said he hadn't been able to cry although he had wanted to at the funeral but he added, 'I don't think he would want people to be upset, he would want them to carry on, enjoy themselves and remember him as he was.'

Robin summed up Stephen's and his comrades' feelings about Northern Ireland: 'Steve was there doing his job, trying to make the time he was there as enjoyable as possible. He would try and make friends with people, say hello to them. People saw him on the checkpoint and recognised his smile. He was always happy and always treated people well. He would take the time to talk to them and it was part of his character. They are human beings, you are a human being. It is only five per cent of the population who would try and hurt you – most are happy with peace and want peace. There is no reason why you cannot be normal with people. We are doing a policing job there. I think we saw ourselves creating the security within which ordinary people could live peaceful lives. I think he felt that it wasn't their fault – what was going on, that he was actually trying to protect them and get it across to them that he didn't hold it against them that he was there. He was just doing his job.'

I had last seen Stephen alive on Boxing Day 1996. Two years later on that exact day, Stephen came to me in a dream. Earlier that day I had been to the cemetery on my own and placed a little gold Christmas bell with a red ribbon on his grave. In the dream I was sitting on a dining chair on the pavement of one of the roads I had walked along on my way to the cemetery. Suddenly I saw Stephen walking towards me. He looked exactly as he was on that last Boxing Day. He was smiling at me and was going to go past but I reached out my hand, caught his wrist and gently pulled him round behind me. He bent over me with both arms around my shoulders, his face brushing mine and gave me a big hug. Suddenly I woke up, not in tears this time but with a wonderful warm feeling of love and comfort. I can feel that hug still, and I will carry that picture of Stephen with me until, I hope, we meet again when I make that final journey he has travelled before me.